Graham Howard

A FAN

for all seasons

Memories of Irish Football

Graham Howard has been watching
League of Ireland football for twenty-
five years. He currently lives in Dublin
with his wife and daughter.
This is his first book.

This edition published 2017 by Carrowmore

ISBN: 978-1-9998171-0-7

Carrowmore Publishing
50 City Quay
Dublin 2
www.carrowmore.ie
info@carrowmore.ie
@Carrowmore101

Design and Layout
Dennison Design
Rock Street, Kenmare, Co Kerry
www.dennisondesign.ie
hello@dennisondesign.ie

Graham
Howard

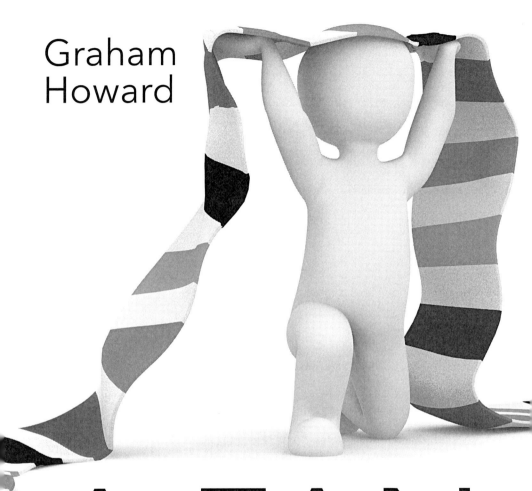

A FAN
for all seasons

Memories of Irish Football

Contents

Introduction

My first memories of football are a hazy collection of images from when I was about six years old. It was a grey Friday evening in Dalymount Park and my Uncle Pat had brought me along to watch my dad play in a junior cup final. We sat in the old wooden stand which was such a feature of Dalymount, and I remember the novelty of being out so late and of being taken to such a weird and wonderful venue. I'm sure the only thing my uncle remembers is me pestering him for the full ninety minutes, asking him to point out where my dad was on the pitch.

It wasn't until a number of years later that my interest in the League of Ireland began. It came about by chance one Sunday afternoon when I was ten or eleven. I was walking to my grandparents' house in Crumlin with my dad and we were chatting away. I was probably telling him about the newest Lego set I had seen and how well it would look in my room.

While we were walking through Crumlin village, I noticed another boy of around the same age as myself wearing a football shirt. What stood out, aside from the fact that the shirt was too big for him, was the eye-catching design from which I just could not turn away. The shirt was bright red with flashes and shafts of white everywhere, like strawberry sauce over crushed ice. It was shocking. I was amazed that a team could have a jersey that was so bizarre and such an assault on the senses. I wanted to know which team could wear such a kit and I asked my dad whether he knew. Surely he would have the answer; all dads do.

He told me that a team called Shelbourne played in this melted ice-cream-style shirt and that they were playing in the Cup Final that very day. I had never heard of the team. When we played football in our schoolyard, we pretended to be playing for Liverpool, Leeds United or Manchester United. This strange shirt and the unusually named team that wore it intrigued me. I was intent on finding out more about the league the team played in and their daring team kits.

A Fan For All Seasons

I pestered my dad for weeks to bring me to a League of Ireland match which must have been a bit of a shock to him as I had never really been that interested in going to a game before. Much to my disappointment, and his relief, the season was over but he told me that if I still wanted to go to one next season, then he would bring me. Unfortunately for my dad, I didn't forget over the course of the summer and I eventually browbeat him into taking me to a game for my birthday.

I'm not sure what I had in mind as we set out to Inchicore to watch an FAI Cup tie between St Patrick's Athletic and St James's Gate in Richmond Park. Having seen a few matches on television, I imagined all football grounds to be like Wembley, Anfield, or Highbury. I assumed that similarly sized crowds would turn out to watch the game in Inchicore.

As I entered through the stiles at Richmond Park, two things struck me: firstly, I wanted to know where the rest of the stadium was and, secondly, my nostrils were filled with the overpowering smell of Deep Heat. As no one else seemed concerned about the missing stands, I decided that it was okay and nothing to worry about. As the stand at the time had space for probably as few as fourteen people, my dad and I went to the terrace. Much to my surprise, the terraces consisted of a bank of dirt and gravel, which conveniently prevented the Camac River from flooding the grounds. I was ushered towards the railing that ran around the perimeter of the pitch and, after jumping up on the lowest bar of the railing, I settled in for my long-anticipated first taste of League of Ireland football.

A 5-0 win for Pats got me hooked. For the next twenty years, whenever we returned to Richmond Park, that same spot on the Camac side of the ground served as our vantage point. Old habits die hard.

This look back through the differing eras is not to catalogue the league and its records, that has been well noted elsewhere. My journey back in time is an attempt to capture the sense of excitement, joy and incident that has accompanied the league since its inception in 1921. As a nation with a rich sporting culture, I think it's important to uncover a side of sporting life in Ireland which has, for too long, sadly remained overlooked.

I hope to shed a new light on what makes the League of Ireland unique: the great teams of Cork United, Shamrock Rovers, Waterford, Dundalk, Derry City and Shelbourne, who played to packed houses on Sunday afternoons, and players like

Bob Fullam, Sean McCarthy, Frank O'Neill, Liam Tuohy, Johnny Fullam, Peter Thomas and Liam Coyle, who excited crowds from Kilcohan Park to Brandywell Stadium. I will look back at the early days, when the crowds flocked to games, through to the golden period of the mid-fifties and the clubs' progression towards embracing European football. I will recall clubs who are no longer with us and consider times when financial folly put clubs at risk, but also brought great achievements tantalisingly close.

As fans, we have shared nail-biting moments, watching our team hold on to a slender lead to win a title or avoid relegation; we have raged at referees' vision and their timekeeping, often at the same time; we have been both disappointed and elated at cup finals and on European nights. Like all football fans around the world, we have been on an emotional rollercoaster with our chosen team since the first day we passed through the turnstiles at our home ground. And for ninety minutes, plus whatever the referee adds on, we love it.

I hope this collection of League of Ireland memories will bring you as much enjoyment as I have experienced putting them together in this volume.

Graham Howard

**Early Days
1921 to 1940**

Bohemian FC was the first Dublin-based team to join the Irish League in 1902, leaving the Leinster Senior League. The Irish League had been in existence since 1890 and was historically the football league for all clubs in Ireland. All of the Irish League's original members were from present-day Northern Ireland, seven of the original eight from Belfast, with Milford FC representing Armagh. Shelbourne decided to join in 1904 giving their fellow Dubliners some company. By this time Linfield had already won seven titles and were well on their way to becoming the second most-decorated, league title-winning club in the world. The northeast had dominated the league since its inception, with the Dublin clubs making almost no impression.

Bohs resigned from the league in 1911, but were back again for the 1912 season, with another Dublin club, Tritonville. This brought the Dublin representation up to three; however, Tritonville lasted just one season before resigning their membership.

While the league did not offer much success for the Dublin clubs, with Shelbourne's runner-up place in 1907 being the closest any of them came to victory, they did have some success in the Irish Cup competition. Shelbourne won the trophy on three occasions, in 1906, 1911 and 1920. The 1920 Irish Cup was awarded to Shels after they beat Glenavon in the semi-final.

The other Irish Cup semi-final that year was declared void by the Irish Football Association (IFA) after both Belfast Celtic and Glentoran were thrown out of the competition. Bohemian FC also won the trophy once in 1908. Of the three winning finals for Dublin clubs, all would take place at Dalymount, which cemented the grounds' place as Dublin's home of football.

In 1920, both Bohemian FC and Shelbourne withdrew from the Irish League at the end of the season, with the result that there were no longer any Dublin clubs in the league. The 1920-21 season would see Bohemian and Shelbourne take part in the Leinster Senior League again in place of their reserve sides, which had competed while the clubs' first teams were playing in the Irish League.

According to the history of the Football Association of Ireland (FAI), an '… *historic meeting in Molesworth Hall on 1st June 1921 quickly led to the formation of a League of Ireland competition'*. This was hot on the heels of the formation of the FAI itself, which had recently come into being after a split between the Irish Football Association in Belfast and both the Leinster Football Association and Munster Football Association.

The first season of the Football League of Ireland – or Division A, as it was known – was somewhat misleadingly named, given that all of the original eight member clubs were based in Dublin. In fact, all of the original members had played in the Leinster Senior League the season before.

The 'Magic Eight' were: St James's Gate, Bohemian FC, Shelbourne, Olympia, Jacobs, Frankfort, Dublin United and YMCA. Of these, Bohemian FC is the only club who has been continually active in the league and has remained in the top tier of football competition throughout. It was, however, St James's Gate that emerged as champions and cup winners in the first season, proving that the double was not to be as mythical an accomplishment as elsewhere.

St James's Gate FC had been formed in 1902, as a football team made up of workers from the Guinness brewery of the same name. Dr Sir John Lumsden, who was a medical officer at Guinness at the time, was a driving force behind the formation of the sports club for Guinness employees. Dr Lumsden had been concerned by the high levels of tuberculosis among Guinness employees and undertook a review of their living conditions with approval from the Guinness board. As a result of his recommendations, the sports club was set up and redesigned housing was provided for the employees.

A Fan For All Seasons

His concern for all aspects of health and well-being was well established: he was also the founder of the St John Ambulance Brigade of Ireland. Due to the prominence of the brigade during the 1916 Easter Rising, Dr Lumsden was knighted for his services in attending to all sides' casualties during Easter week.

The Gate's football team took just eight years to come to prominence. In 1910, they won the Leinster Senior League and the Irish Intermediate Cup double. They would go on to win the Leinster Senior League on a further three occasions prior to joining the League of Ireland for its inaugural season. St James's Gate was renowned at the time of the first League of Ireland season. They had won the Leinster Senior League, the Leinster Senior Cup, the Irish Intermediate Cup and the Metropolitan Cup, all in the 1919-20 season, and it would perhaps have been expected that they would take the first title of the League of Ireland.

Bohs would present a challenge, too, and their fixtures against St James's Gate would prove to be crucial to the outcome of that first league title. The matches ended in two wins for The Gate, who won at Dalymount 2-1 and at home at St James's Park 1-0. The Gate also provided the league's top scorer, with Jack Kelly scoring eleven goals for the champions, over a third of their total goals scored.

Success didn't end there for The Gate, who went on to win the inaugural FAI Cup final against Leinster Senior League team Shamrock Rovers. The final went to a replay after a 1-1 draw in Dalymount. The replay finished in a 1-0 win for The Gate and on both occasions Jack Kelly scored for the team.

Eoghan Rice notes in his book, *We are Rovers,* that the aftermath of the replay was marked by crowd trouble. Rovers' fans who were 'incensed' by the result came onto the pitch and a fracas broke out between both sets of fans and players. The fighting continued as the teams made their way to the dressing rooms and ceased only when a shot was fired into the roof of the dressing room. While the cause of the trouble was disputed, Rovers Bob Fullam received some of the blame for provocation by repeatedly clashing with The Gate players. Fullam would go on to become a Rovers legend of their early league and cup triumphs.

For The Gate, this double celebration would prove to be the club's high-water mark. Surprisingly they did not go on to become a dominant force in the league, as some may have expected. The league title was not recovered until 1939-40 and a further

FAI Cup win in 1938 provided their only other trophy at this level. After finishing last in the league in 1943–44, they failed to gain re-election and dropped out of senior football for the next forty-six years, returning for a brief period in the First Division in 1990. This return, however, was short-lived and they had to resign after six seasons, citing financial difficulties.

The league was expanded to twelve teams for the following, 1922–23 season, but without Frankfort and YMCA as they failed to gain re-election. Six new clubs joined, including the first from outside of Dublin: Athlone Town FC.

There was another significant name on the list of six that would lay down an early marker by winning the championship on its first attempt: Shamrock Rovers. The club would go on to dominate the club scene like no other in both the league and FAI Cup. Shamrock Rovers made their debut in the 1922–23 season and romped their way to victory, losing just one game in twenty-two. That loss came against Shelbourne United. Along with Shelbourne United, the other three clubs were Midland Athletic, which was actually from Whitehall in Dublin and made up of railway workers, Pioneers FC and Rathmines Athletic.

The FAI Cup went north to Belfast in 1923 for the only time in its history. Falls League side Alton United lifted the trophy by beating Shelbourne 1–0 in the final. It was to be a decade littered with runners-up medals for Shels. While they captured the league title on three occasions, they finished as league runners-up five times and twice were losing finalists in the FAI Cup.

The top scorer in 1922–23 season would be that man of 1922 Cup Final fame, Bob Fullam. Fullam scored a remarkable twenty-seven goals for Rovers that season, to bring the title to Milltown Road. Fullam was an all-round forward with plenty of skill, as his goal records attests. Born in Ringsend, he began his career at Shels when they were in the Irish League and in 1921 he moved on to Rovers. Pictures of Fullam at the time show what a powerful forward he must have been, with a tough competitive image to match his ability. His goal-scoring abilities attracted attention from England and he joined Leeds United in 1923, playing with them for just one season, which saw Leeds win the Second Division Championship. Fullam played just seven times for Leeds and returned to Rovers to help them to the win their first league and Cup double in 1924–25 and the league again in 1926–27.

A Fan For All Seasons

International honours also came Fullam's way in the shape of two international caps for the Irish Free State, as the national team was known up until 1936, against Italy. There is an old anecdote about the second match against Italy, which took place at Dalymount. A free kick was awarded to Ireland and Fullam stepped up to take it. Fullam is said to have struck the ball so hard that when it hit the Italian wall, it knocked Mario Zanello unconscious. The story goes that the shock of the Italians after seeing one of their compatriots rendered unconscious was such that they pleaded with the referee to prevent Fullam from taking any more free kicks in the time that remained. As with all good stories of this kind, they add colour to the legend of the player and I'm sure Fullam didn't mind the story being retold on many occasions.

Bob left Rovers for a season to try his luck in the US with Philadelphia Celtic, but was back with Rovers again in 1928. Over the next five seasons, he would go on to win a further league championship and three FAI Cup Finals. He also scored in the 1929 FAI Cup Final replay against Bohemian FC.

It was Bohemian FC who won the championship in 1923-24 and provided the top two scorers in the league, with Dave Roberts scoring twenty and Christy Robinson scoring twelve. Bohs won their entire set of home games that season and sixteen of the eighteen league fixtures in total.

For the strictly amateur club, this was a golden period for Bohemian FC. The men from Dalymount won five league championships in thirteen seasons. The club secured the double in 1927-28, which was a glorious season for Bohs that also saw them win the League of Ireland Shield and the Leinster Senior Cup. Their success saw them win every domestic trophy on offer that season.

Further glory, of the European variety, would be bestowed upon Bohemian FC in 1929 when they became the first, and to date the only, League of Ireland club to win a European tournament. Bohemian FC was invited to take part in the Aciéries d'Angleur Tournoi that August in Liège, Belgium. The city of Liège had regularly hosted international football tournaments since 1908. Bohs played four other Belgian teams – Charleroi Sporting Club, Standard Liège, Royal Tilleur and Royal Flemish – on their tour.

It may have been that Bohemian FC received the invitation to take part in that year's tournament in part due to the performances of the Irish international side that beat Belgium twice, in an especially convincing fashion. On 12 February 1928, Ireland beat Belgium 4-2 in Liège and then 4-0 at Dalymount on 30 April 1929. The game in Liège included four Bohemian FC players – Harry Cannon, Jeremiah Robinson, Jimmy White and Jack McCarthy – who captained the side.

The tournament games were played over four consecutive days in August, beginning with a 2-1 win for Bohs against Charleroi SC. They followed this up with a 1-0 win against Royal Flemish. Their third win was against FC Tilleur, whom they beat 1-0, and they rounded off their four matches by beating Standard Liège 3-2. The Bohemian FC history of this tournament on their website notes that this last match against Standard was 'to win what the *Irish Independent* referred to as the Royal Angleur Cup'. Sadly there is no mention of any presentation or ceremony for Bohs after the victory.

While winning the tournament was a great achievement for Bohemian FC, it was not the only significant aspect of the tour. In a letter to the Department of Foreign Affairs, Mr Patrick J. Byrne, who was a diplomat in Belgium at the time, remarked on two things that occurred during the Bohemian FC tour. The first was an incident that occurred at Bohs' opening match against Charleroi. While noting that Bohs received a warm welcome from the British Consul in Charleroi, the letter states that 'the proceedings were marred somewhat – from our point of view – by the heralding of the Bohemian team on the field under the colours of the Union Jack'. The letter also noted that three Bohemian FC committee members called to Mr O'Byrne's office in Brussels with the intention of requesting that the embassy be involved in a wreath-laying ceremony at the Tomb of the Unknown Soldier, which Bohemian FC wanted to conduct.

Mr O'Byrne went on to write that the ceremony was *'very dignified'* and that *'the team arrived with the wreath, which was a large floral harp in the Saorstát colours'*. Mr O'Byrne also lent Bohemian FC his office's flag, to be displayed before their remaining tour matches, lest another Union Flag incident occur.

The letter shows that although the football competition was the main reason for Bohs travelling to Belgium, they were also representing Ireland on the European stage. At the wreath-laying ceremony, they put football into perspective. Even though the Great War had ended nearly eleven years previously, there was still a keen sense of loss for those Irishmen who had been killed in the war and the Bohemian FC committee felt that this should be recognised at this time.

A Fan For All Seasons

Signs of the changing times were evident in the 1924–25 season. The league spread its wings further, with the addition of the first Cork side, Fordsons, and the first County Wicklow side, Bray Unknowns. But the league title continued to be the preserve of the Dublin clubs. The early years of the league's history were characterised by the abundance of Dublin clubs, which entered, dropped out and re-entered the league. Some clubs, like Dublin United, lasted for just one season. Others, like Rathmines Athletic, failed to complete their full league programme for a season.

Shelbourne won their first title in 1925–26, after being in the shake-up for the previous four seasons. The title was to be shared among the three Dublin clubs for the next six seasons, until Dundalk eventually broke the Dublin stranglehold in 1933.

The goalscorers were definitely the kings during the early days and some pretty good figures were returned. Billy Farrell at Rovers scored 49 in two seasons. Billy was part of the legendary 'Four Fs' in the Rovers' forward line, which also included Bob Fullam, John Fagan and John Joe Flood. He was a prolific striker and to date remains the highest-scoring Rovers player to win the top scorer of the season accolade, with twenty-five goals in the 1924–25 season. Alex Hair was a Scot who had played for Partick Thistle and Preston North End before joining Shels. In 1930–31, he scored twenty-nine goals, as Shels claimed their third title, and in doing so he set the record for goal scoring in the league, which would stand until 1936, when Jimmy Turnbull from Cork scored a staggering thirty-seven goals, setting a new and as yet unbeaten record.

The 1932–33 season was to see the first league championship won by a club from outside of the capital. The FAI Cup had already gone to Athlone, Belfast and Cork, but it was Dundalk that would capture the first league title for the provincial clubs.

In 1930–31, Dundalk had been runners-up to Shels and were beaten FAI Cup finalists, loosing after a replay against Shamrock Rovers. They finally made the breakthrough with that league win, thanks to some very special players.

Henry Hurst was a left half who played over 350 times for The Lilywhites. He arrived in Dundalk from England and spent eleven seasons at the club. After their league success, the local newspaper, *The Dundalk Democrat*, noted his excellent heading ability and hard work in midfield, commenting that he *'plays till he falls'* and that he was a *'gentleman on and off the pitch'*.

Club captain Gerry McCourt was an inside forward who had played with Glenavon in the Irish league prior to arriving at Dundalk's Athletic Grounds. Originally from Lurgan, he joined Dundalk in 1930 and played with them until an injury ended his career some seven seasons later, in 1937. He would surprisingly make further five appearances in 1940 due to a player crisis and even managed to score another goal in that run, which brought his total for the club to 90.

The Dundalk FC history book records him as having a never-say-die attitude and states that he was always a fair and clean player. In another wonderful tribute, which would be welcomed by any sportsperson, he is described as a person who *'never knows when he is beaten … has brought the game out of the fire more often than anybody … uses his brains always … [and is] the best servant the club ever had'*.

Although it would be thirty years before the league championship returned to Dundalk, they did have some success in the FAI Cup in between, with three wins in the ten years between 1949 and 1957. These wins augmented their first win in 1942, when they beat a wonderful Cork United side who were going for the double. Dundalk's real glory days in the league were still some time away, but it is fitting that the most successful provincial club should also have been the first to steal the title away from the city and bring it to 'The Town'.

It wasn't until the 1934-35 season, when five of the ten teams in the league were from outside Dublin, that the league started to become a truly national competition. After Dundalk's championship win, the title returned to Dublin for the next three seasons, with two for Bohs sandwiching Dolphin's only championship win in 1934–35.

Dolphin was runner-up in the FAI Cup final on two consecutive occasions, in 1932 and 1933. In both finals, they were to fall to Rovers, who were on their record run of six straight cup wins. The last of these, in 1933, was to go to a reply after a 3-3 draw in the first match. That first final was notable for the three penalties awarded, two to Dolphin and one to Rovers, all of which were converted.

Dolphin had a number of noted players in their ranks at the time, including, Jimmy Bermingham, Joe Kendrick, Willie Fallon and Alex Stevenson. All would go on to win caps for the national side and Stevenson would become the only player to date to win an Irish international cap while playing for Glasgow Rangers.

A Fan For All Seasons

Despite the quality of their players and their recent success, Dolphin resigned from the League of Ireland just two seasons later.

The title travelled west for the first time in 1936–37, when it was won by Sligo Rovers. No Dublin club made the top three that season: Waterford were runners-up, with Dundalk in third place. Sligo had been elected to the league as recently as 1934, having been formed a mere six years previously in 1928. Their championship year was to start with eleven consecutive wins, which was half the league programme.

Jimmy Surgeoner was the Sligo player-coach at the time and had joined the club from Ballymena midway through the previous season. Sligo hit a bit of a difficult patch after their first defeat of the league season, going down 8-2 to Waterford, who would go on to finish in second place. They lost again in the next match, against Drumcondra and managed to secure just three wins in their next six matches.

However, their blistering league start ensured that this dip in form did not ultimately cost them the title, which was secured for the Bit O' Red with a 4–3 away win against Cork. A hat trick by Jack Symonds made the ex-Cork player a hero on the day, with Billy Harrigan grabbing the fourth goal for Sligo.

Another hero for Sligo that season was an Englishman by the name of Harry Litherland. Litherland scored a club record of 19 league goals that season, including 2 in Sligo's record league victory of 9-0 against Dolphin at the Showgrounds. His record stood for over seventy years and was not surpassed until Eoin Doyle scored 20 league goals for Sligo in 2011.

Like Dundalk, Sligo would have to wait a number of decades for the title to return to the Showgrounds, but they were in the limelight once more in 1939, when they managed to sign former Everton forward Dixie Dean. Dean had come to fame in England due to his goal-scoring exploits, which included a league record of sixty goals in a single season in 1927-28 and his status as Everton's all-time record goalscorer. Dean and Sligo made it through to the FAI Cup final of that season against Shelbourne. Dean managed to score in the final, just as he had for Everton in the 1933 FA Cup final against Manchester City. The game against Shels finished in a 1-1 draw and Shels went on to win the replay 1-0, with the only goal scored by William 'Sacky' Glen. A small anecdote is told about this final: Dean's runner-up medal was apparently stolen after the game only to be returned to him some time later.

Dean returned to Dalymount in 1978 to see Sligo compete in the FAI Cup final against Shamrock Rovers. Sadly for both himself and Sligo, Shamrock Rovers won the final 1–0.

Shamrock Rovers were back, with consecutive league titles in 1938 and 1939. This complemented their tremendous run in the FAI Cup early in the decade, when, after winning five consecutive cups from 1929 to 1933, they won it again, for the seventh time overall, in 1936. Rovers gained the reputation for being the cup specialists, but their league form was good too and they would end the decade as the leading club in the country, having won six league championships and eight FAI Cups by 1940. Goalscorer in the 1939 final, William 'Sacky' Glen would play a huge part for Rovers during their early years until he joined Shels in 1938. Glen won four league titles, seven FAI Cups, five Shields and five Leinster Senior Cups with Rovers. His cup medal with Shels in 1939 would give him a record eight Cup-winner medals from ten finals. This record of wins would be matched by another Rovers legend, Johnny Fullam, some years later, when he won six FAI Cup medals with The Hoops and two with Bohs.

In a throwback to the opening season, St James's Gate won the title again in 1940, powered by the goals of Paddy Bradshaw, who scored twenty-nine goals that season. He had scored twenty-two goals in the previous campaign. Bradshaw joined The Gate in 1938, aged 26, and scored five goals during his debut match against Limerick. He quickly received international honours and earned five caps for Ireland, scoring four times.

Bradshaw still holds the record for the fastest goal ever scored by an Irish international. After just twenty seconds of his debut against Switzerland at Dalymount, he blocked an attempted clearance by the goalkeeper, resulting in Ireland leading 1–0. Ireland would go on to win the game 4–0, with Bradshaw scoring his second goal before the break. Bradshaw also played for the League of Ireland selection on three occasions and scored in each game.

A number of quality players including Bradshaw turned out for the League of Ireland selection during this early period. Teams that included the great Jimmy Dunne achieved victories against the Irish League in 1939 and 1940, and a win over the Scottish League in 1939. Dunne was now at Shamrock Rovers and had risen to fame by scoring in a record twelve consecutive league matches for Sheffield United. Dunne's record remains intact to this day.

A Fan For All Seasons

Dr Kevin O'Flanagan, that master of all sports – Gaelic football, football and rugby union – turned out for the League of Ireland selection in these matches while still at Bohemian FC. O'Flanagan had an amazing career, which included spells of football at Barnet and Arsenal, rugby union at UCD and London Irish and international caps for Ireland at both football and rugby union. He was later a member of the International Olympic Committee.

These milestones would lay the foundation for a remarkable opening period in the history of League of Ireland football. A number of great players had already made their mark, among them Fullam, Farrell, Flood, Roberts, Bradshaw, Glen and the O'Flanagan brothers. Teams had developed both at club and representative levels: Rovers with their Cup-winning run; Bohs winning everything in 1928 and their European adventure; and the progress made by the League of Ireland selection, losing just once in the five years from 1935 to 1940.

The initial dominance by the Dublin clubs had been punctured a little, with Dundalk, Sligo and Waterford all making progress in the league. There was, however, a club on the horizon that would blow the Dublin teams out of the water and usher in a new era. That wind was blowing in from the south and it would dominate the league for the next six seasons. The roaring forties would see Cork reign supreme.

Southern Stars
Cork United Dominant, 1940–41 to 1945–46

We all know how shy and retiring sports fans from the Rebel County can be. They are demure, quiet, self-deprecating Corkonians, whose earnest hope is that the best team wins, so long as they are wearing red. It is not for them to tell you at length why their hurlers will be bringing Liam back home in September, or that Cork Con and Dolphin are the real conveyer belts of rugby talent, and never would they mention that the best footballers come from the Leeside, like Cantwell, Keane and Irwin, to name but three. They also have pretty good Olympians, but no, no, they would never ramble on about that at all.

Sport is a religion in Cork city and county and the fans support their teams with a passion and fervour that is rarely matched around the county. Football is no exception to this and substantial crowds can be seen flocking to Turners Cross to see Cork City on a fortnightly basis. The compact little ground can become an intimidating cauldron of noise and hostility for away teams and fans alike. The Shed End, home of the most vociferous City fans, leaves the opposition keeper in no doubt about City fans' thoughts on his ability. But while there is always a partisan crowd, they reserve their strongest criticism for the home team. For anyone wearing the now green shirt of Cork City, there is a minimum level of commitment and desire demanded by the fans, usually somewhere around 100 per cent. Cork football fans are not afraid to let their standards be known – and rightly so.

For a city with a population of around 120,000 people, it may seem unusual that there is just one team to represent the city at present. A look at the history of football in Cork will reveal a little more about why this one-club situation has been a major theme running through football for the city. There have been seasons when the League of Ireland has been treated to a Cork derby, but they have been few and have usually resulted in both teams folding in a short number of years.

The first representative from Cork in the League of Ireland was a works team from the Ford Motor Company, called Fordsons. The club had started its life as Ford FC in 1921, the brainchild of former Ireland international and Belfast man, Harry Buckle. The club changed its name to Fordsons the following year and was sponsored by the Ford Motor Company. The Ford plant in Cork was well known for producing the Fordson Tractor and it is likely that this inspired the name for the plant football team and their nickname, The Tractors. Fordsons were established in 1922 and entered the League of Ireland for the 1924–25 season, becoming not only the first team from Cork to take part but also the first team from Munster.

They finished a respectable forth, ahead of established sides like St James's Gate and Jacobs, having won ten of their eighteen matches. Their real day of glory was to arrive the following season in the FAI Cup, when they made it through to the final at Dalymount Park on St Patrick's Day, having seen off Shelbourne, Athlone Town and Bray Unknowns along the way.

Standing between the Cork outfit and victory were the defending champions, Shamrock Rovers. The game was to attract a record crowd for a cup final, with nearly 25,000 people passing through the turnstiles. The cup travelled south for the first time after Fordsons won 3-2. Match reports on the game bemoaned the lack of quality and referred to the game as Fordsons' defence against Rovers' attack, an attack which included the famed four Fs: Fullam, Fagan, Flood and Farrell. The match started at a blistering pace, with the score standing at 1-1 after just three minutes. However, it would be the Fordsons goalkeeper O'Hagan and full back Carabini who would win the plaudits from the press for their display. With the score standing at 2-2 after Fagan and Barry had exchanged goals, Rovers were awarded a penalty kick. Bill O'Hagan saved Bob Fullam's effort and minutes later Paddy Barry was put through to score the winner for Fordsons and bring the cup back to Ballinlough Road.

Fordsons were a popular team and a report in *The Irish Times* the day after the cup final attests to this, noting the amount of Cork fans that had made the journey to Dalymount for the match. This travelling support no doubt added to the record attendance. They had also been successful prior to their FAI Cup win, having won three Munster Senior Cups and the Munster Senior League.

They proved to be quite an addition to the League of Ireland and achieved five top-four finishes in their six seasons in the league before their participation came to an abrupt end in 1930 when the management of the Ford Motor Company informed the team that they could continue to play only as a factory team and that their matches should be confined to local leagues. A decision was then made to break away from the patronage of Ford and to form a new club to enable their continued participation in the league. Gate receipts had been good for Fordsons, so even without the Ford sponsorship it was thought that the new club, Cork Football Club, would be a success.

Cork FC replaced Fordsons in the League of Ireland and went further in the league championship than Fordsons, finishing runners-up to Rovers in 1931–32. They took their home matches to the Mardyke and thus began this famous Cork venue's long association with football. Another team, Cork Bohemians, joined the League of Ireland in 1932 and for two years we had our first series of Cork derbies. Sadly, although Cork Bohemians were a reasonably successful junior team, having won a Munster League and Senior Cup double the previous season, they found the step-up a strain on finances. A series of ground moves from Ballintemple to Cork Greyhound Track and finally to Turners Cross did not help their plight and they resigned from the league in 1934 amid financial difficulties.

Things were going well, however, for Cork FC and they finished league runners up again in 1934. They also reached the FAI Cup final in 1934. It seemed like history was repeating itself for Cork football. Eight years after Fordsons' successful FAI Cup win, it would be Cork FC's turn to defeat another Dublin club, St James's Gate, by two goals to one.

A surprising slump in form the following season saw the club finish the league in last place necessitating an application for re-election. The application was successful and in an attempt to restore the club's form, and place back at the top of the table, a significant signing was made by the club. Enter Jimmy Turnbull.

Jimmy Turnbull isn't a name that springs readily to mind when talking about famous goalscorers in the League of Ireland. More recently, fans would point to Stephen Geoghegan, Jason Byrne and Glen Crowe, while fans of an older vintage will no doubt recall Alfie Hale, Brendan Bradley and Shay Gibbons. Good as the above players were, none of them hold the overall record for most league goals in a season. That record is Jimmy Turnbull's from his one season with Cork FC in 1935–36, when he scored a staggering thirty-seven league goals and sixty-three goals overall in the season.

Jimmy arrived at the Mardyke from his hometown club, Gateshead, having previously played for a brief spell at Barnsley. Jimmy was just one of a number of overseas players drafted in by the Cork FC board in an attempt get Cork FC back on track. The first hint that the signing might have been a masterstroke came in Jimmy's first competitive game against the champions, Dolphin, in the League of Ireland Shield competition. Cork routed the Dubliners by 10–3 and Jimmy claimed half of the total number of goals scored. While this cameo was spectacular, the side needed more time to gel together and a Shield challenge failed to materialise. Despite this, Jimmy managed to score fourteen goals in the competition.

It wasn't until near the end of October that the side began to click together and the goals came in an avalanche: 3 at home against Sligo Rovers were followed by 4 at Kilcohan Park against Waterford. Things were looking up for Cork and they began to stake a claim as possible title challengers. With six matches to go, Cork travelled to play Drumcondra, who had been enduring a tough season of little success. Despite this, Drums managed to turn over the title chasers by 2–1. Jimmy Turnbull was by now the name on everyone's lips and, despite not scoring on this occasion, received much praise for being 'always a trouble to the Drumcondra defence'.

Cork had their revenge the following week at The Mardyke, when they beat Drums by five goals to two in the FAI Cup semi-final to seal a final spot against Rovers. Jimmy was again to the fore, scoring another hat trick, and *The Irish Times* praised his 'leadership' and 'scoring abilities'. If further praise of his ability was required, you need look no further than the sub-headline in *The Irish Times*, which read 'Turnbull's artistry too much for Drumcondra's halves'.

The praise rolled on after a further 2 against Brideville. 'Another brace for Turnbull', was the comment in *The Irish Times*. Even with the goals flying in for Cork and for Turnbull, in particular, they were always just a shade behind the eventual champions, Bohemian FC.

Sadly for Jimmy in his record-breaking season, there would be no fairy-tale ending in the FAI Cup final against Rovers. The sides had met a few weeks earlier in an FAI Cup final rehearsal at The Mardyke and Cork had won by 3–2. An on-form Cork side should have won the match and it would have been fitting for Jimmy to end the season with a medal. But goals from Paddy Moore and Charlie Reid meant that the FAI Cup went back to Milltown for the seventh time. It was Jimmy who scored the Cork consolation goal.

That was to be Jimmy Turnbull's most prolific season in the League of Ireland. He departed that summer for Belfast Celtic, under the management of Elisha Scott, where the goals kept coming. There is an anecdote which holds that he left because the Cork FC board debated the merits of parting with £50, which was Jimmy's signing-on fee. While Cork debated, Belfast Celtic acted and snapped Jimmy up for The Grand Old Team.

Jimmy made a return to League of Ireland football after the Irish League was suspended due to the Second World War, joining Cork FC's successors, Cork City, and having a brief spell at Cork United before hanging up his boots. In the eighty years since he set his record of 37 league goals, only Waterford's Jimmy Gauld has managed to come close, scoring 30 in 1954–55, when The Blues finished as league runners-up to St Patrick's Athletic.

Given that there were just twenty-two league games during Jimmy's time playing, the likelihood of the record being broken today is remote. One other small fact to note about the accumulation of the goals is that Jimmy scored against every league club that season, usually saving his best for Waterford, against who he scored six times in two league games.

Along with the departure of Jimmy Turnbull, the club also lost Owen Madden and Jack O'Reilly to Norwich City. The decline of Cork FC began as, without the goals of Turnbull, the side struggled and the following season saw the club finish eleventh. It was same again in the 1937–38 season and by this stage the crowds had started to stay away from The Mardyke. Beset by financial problems, the decision was made for the club to go into voluntary liquidation in early 1938. Plunkett Carter, in his excellent history of Cork football, summed up the dire straits that Cork FC found themselves in at the time: *'An FAI Cup run was their only lifeline but their demoralised team, paying their own train fares, were defeated 3–0 by St James's Gate at the Iveagh Grounds.'*

A Fan For All Seasons

Alarmed at having no Cork side in the League of Ireland, the league committee accepted an application from new club Cork City to fulfil the remaining fixtures that had been set for Cork FC. The following season saw Cork City inflict a record defeat on the eventual league champions, Shamrock Rovers, beating them 7–0 at The Mardyke in the Dublin City Cup competition. This proved to be a false dawn and the side that promised so much failed to deliver on the pitch and finished the season in eleventh place. This had become a recurring theme for Cork sides over the last three seasons, as had the now customary financial difficulties.

The board made a decision to cut players' wages and a number left the club. Desperate to stem the decline, the board turned to an old face for help: Jimmy Turnbull was back at The Mardyke, but visibly past his best by now due to an ongoing injury. The decision backfired and Jimmy played just a handful of games for the club. If £50 would have broken the bank back in 1936, a £10 fine imposed by the league on Cork City was now going to completely destroy the Cork football team. Plunkett Carter again outlines the situation they found themselves in: a 'perilous financial position that led to their expulsion on 30 January 1940 because of their refusal to pay a £10 fine imposed on them as a result of their failure to pay Shelbourne a share of the gate receipts from a match at The Mardyke'.

In just over fifteen years, Cork football had witnessed the rise and fall of Fordsons, Cork Bohemians, Cork FC and Cork City – four clubs in one city. All the clubs experienced financial difficulties due primarily to two main factors: firstly, an over-reliance on star players who were paid unsustainable sums, which the clubs could not afford. The gates were good when the team was winning, but these clubs could not afford to have an off-season when the fans would not turn up. Also, subsequent attempts by the boards to address the payment of these players usually resulted in the player leaving the club. Secondly, and this was and still is completely outside Cork football's control, their geographical position on the island plays against them. Every away trip entails long journeys, to Dublin on perhaps five or six occasions a season, to Sligo, Dundalk and Limerick, and this is before any cup fixture is drawn. Given the cost of just running the club, it is easy to see how travel bills could mount up quickly.

With Cork City just the latest side to bite the dust in the southern capital, it was the turn of newly formed Cork United to try their hand at the League of Ireland. United would take over the league placing and standings of City for that 1939–40 season and finish fifth. Little did anyone know exactly what this club's impact on League of Ireland football would be – 'spectacular' doesn't come close.

Cork United took a few matches of the new 1940–41 season to get going but when they eventually gelled they went on a run of ten consecutive wins, which brought them into title contention, along with Munster neighbours, Waterford. This was just what the board of directors had hoped to achieve: Cork football back in contention for league and cup honours. Owen Madden and Jack O'Reilly were back in Cork football, this time wearing the red of United, along with a soon-to-be household name in Sean McCarthy.

The league season reached a dramatic conclusion, with both United and Waterford locked on thirty points apiece. If goal difference had been considered, Waterford would have been crowned champions. As it was, a play-off match was required to decide the destination of the championship. The game was fixed for The Mardyke on 11 May, but, incredibly, the play-off match never took place, owing to a dispute between the players and directors of Waterford over bonus payments. Seven Waterford players were dismissed when, after an emergency meeting of the Waterford board, it was decided that the players' demands of a £5 win bonus or £2 10s bonus for draw or defeat would not be met. The Waterford board had offered the players the £5 win bonus but they would receive the £2 10s if they drew only, which meant there would be no bonus if Waterford were defeated.

As a result of the dismissal of seven players, Waterford could not field a team to take on United at The Mardyke and thereby handed the championship to United. However, it was not what the board of Cork United wanted to hear. Fear of losing gate money prevailed over any title, which is perhaps not surprising given the financial difficulties incurred by all previous Cork football clubs. In an attempt to ensure the match went ahead, the Cork United board offered to settle the bonuses issue with the Waterford players on Waterford's behalf. This gives an indication of Cork United's reliance on gate receipts. The Waterford board rejected United's offer to cover the bonuses cost and withdrew from the play-off and the league on the principle that they could not be held to ransom by the demands of their players.

The stance of the Waterford players might be considered unusual given that they must have fancied their chance of winning the play-off final. They had already beaten United at The Mardyke earlier in the season. A few weeks earlier, the teams had met in the FAI Cup Final and drew 2–2 at Dalymount Park in front of over 30,000 fans. The replay was set for the following Wednesday evening, again at Dalymount Park. Waterford were to lose the replay by three goals to one in front of a much reduced crowd, owing to the mid-week evening kick-off. With all this in mind, would Waterford not have liked a shot at settling the score and perhaps taking the title, irrespective of the bonus demands of their players? The question can never be answered. United achieved the double and the first league championship for Leeside on a walkover.

Sometimes it is a little piece of luck that gets things moving in the right direction, but the real secret is knowing how to use that piece of luck. United took advantage of their break and recruited well for the next season, eager to cement their place at the top of Irish football. Billy Hayes joined the side from Huddersfield Town in England, along with a local lad, Florrie Burke, from Ballintemple. The signings, along with goals from Madden and McCarthy, worked as United retained their title and made it to another cup final. This time Dundalk would get the better of the Cork men, winning the FAI Cup for the first time.

The old adage is that league titles define the greatness of a side and United deserve to be included among the greats. They made history the following season by achieving their third successive league title and once again reaching the FAI Cup final against Drums. Another bumper crowd of over 30,000 saw Drums run out 2-1 winners.

You would think that the league success and cup final appearances would have allayed some of the financial concerns of the club. This was not the case, as once again the costs incurred by a Cork football team on players' salaries were remarkable. United was a professional outfit and paid their players accordingly. They also offered top salaries to attract the very best to The Mardyke. Such payments were simply not sustainable given the level of interest in the League of Ireland at the time. Crowds did turn up for the big games and the FAI Cup final, but the real difficulty for United's moneymen was not the home gate receipts, of which they kept 75 per cent, but rather the meagre 20 per cent of the away gate they received. This was particularly obvious when travelling to play clubs who were having poor seasons and attracting low gates, such as Brideville, St James's Gate, Bohemian FC, and Bray Unknowns.

Despite the glaring disparity in the finance department, United pushed on and after a surprisingly poor season in 1943-44, during which they failed to retain their title or reach the FAI Cup final, they bounced back in 1944–45 to take their fourth league title in five seasons. The goals of Sean McCarthy helped return the title to The Mardyke. Sean had been the league's leading goalscorer for the past two seasons and in this season he managed to increase his total by 10, finishing on 26. Sean left United the following season, heading north to Belfast Celtic, but this didn't stop United from taking another league title and again having the league's top scorer in Paddy O'Leary the following season.

It seems that the financial situation at the club was beginning to tell and United directors took to the match programme with a plea to fans to help the club continue to 'put a team on the field which all Cork fans can be proud of'. The request was a simple one: buy a season ticket. Sadly, season ticket-holders and all other fans of United would not see the championship return to The Mardyke again, after winning five titles in six seasons. That 1945-46 victory would be their last. They would, however, have one more glory day, winning the FAI Cup against Bohemian FC in 1947 after a replay. The end of World War II would signal the end of their dominance and the movement of players to England upon the resumption of the Football League. Billy Hayes went back to Huddersfield Town, Jackie O'Driscoll transferred to Swansea and rugby and football star Tommy Moroney moved to West Ham United, along with Frank O'Farrell.

The club that had been renowned as the home of the best in the country was now seeing its best travel elsewhere and the fans went with the players. The Cork football public had become used to a diet of success and found these leaner times too hard to stomach. They stayed away from The Mardyke and effectively reduced the clubs much needed source of revenue.

The sad end for what had been such a successful club came suddenly in October 1948, when the directors announced that the club had been dissolved and a liquidator appointed. As with all its predecessors, money proved to be the issue. The club had been making a weekly loss of over £100 and, after liabilities were taken in to account, had just £23 in assets. The note in *The Cork Examiner* outlined the details, along with a statement that 'certain proposals were made at the meeting which would provide for the continuation of league soccer in Cork and that shareholders present approved the move.'

Eleven trophies in eight years had proven insufficient for a club to survive in Cork. It was Groundhog Day again for football in the city and it seemed now to be a case of just what name the next Cork club in the League of Ireland would take and, more importantly, how long it would last.

A Fan For All Seasons

Athletic would be the latest suffix for a Cork football team and, remarkably, it was made up entirely of the United side that had just seen their club wound up. They took over United's position in the league and eventually finished second last that season. The perennial basement club, Bohemian FC, saved their blushes. Like United, Cork Athletic would also earn a league and cup double during their time at the top of Irish football. They were league champions in 1950 by a point over Drums and runners-up in the FAI Cup in their first full year, on the back of goals from Paddy O'Leary and John Vaughan. It would take three matches to separate them and Transport in the 1950 FAI Cup final, Transport eventually finishing 3-1 winners after two 2-2 draws. Athletic would go a step further the following season by winning the league again by a point, this time against Sligo Rovers, and beating Shels in the FAI Cup final by a goal to nil after a replay. A famous name would also appear on the Athletic team sheet during this period: Noel Cantwell, hero, legend and captain fantastic for the national team.

Cork Athletic had a penchant for the FAI Cup and appeared in the final in four consecutive years. Every one of their cup finals went to a replay. Beaten by Dundalk in 1952, they came back for the first all-Cork final in 1953, against Evergreen United, who had joined the league in the 1951–52 season. This meant that there were two football teams in Cork again and a return of the hugely popular Cork derbies. But as often happens, history repeated itself: Athletic folded in 1957 and Evergreen United underwent the regular Cork football name change in 1959 to Cork Celtic.

Cork Athletic had one last FAI Cup final appearance in that famous final of 1956. Athletic were 2-0 up, with about ten minutes to play, and contrived to lose the game 3-2. Philip Greene's anecdote about the Cork Athletic chairman rushing out to a local pub in Phibsborough to buy champagne with Athletic two up, only to arrive back with the champagne and his team beaten is a well-known story. It would be a while before there would be any call for champagne in Cork as the league title didn't return until 1971 and the FAI Cup next visited the city a year later in 1972. On both occasions, they were won by a wonderful Cork Hibernian side.

An interesting trait of the Cork clubs was their preference for buying former stars of English football. Although this was not exclusive to Cork, they certainly led from the front. Athletic went to players such as Raich Carter, once of Sunderland, Derby and Hull, who, in the twilight of a war-interrupted career, played just a handful of games. Jimmy Delaney, of Celtic and Manchester United fame, arrived in search of another national cup-winner's medal to go with his FA, SFA, and IFA medals, but sadly for him couldn't add an FAI Cup medal to his collection. Rodney Marsh, George Best and Geoff Hurst would all line out for Cork clubs during a period when it seemed that the sole requirement for league teams was to achieve a quick shilling with a star-name attraction over the gates of the ground.

St Patrick's Athletic, Waterford and Shelbourne also got in on the act, signing Gordon Banks, Bobby Charlton and Jimmy Johnstone respectively. While there is no doubt about those stars pedigree, they were sadly well past their prime during their League of Ireland appearances.

The era of domination by Cork clubs had come to an end in the early fifties, but what a successful period it had been. Seven league titles had gone down south in eleven seasons from 1941 to 1951, along with three FAI Cup victories. In thirteen seasons, from 1941 to 1953, there had been a Cork club in the FAI Cup final on eight occasions. Heady days for Leeside football and evidence, if ever it was needed, that maybe Cork really is the sports capital of the country.

The Golden Era
The 1950s – Saints, Rovers, Drums and Shels

The period between 1948 and 1965 arguably produced some of the best football, best teams and best players in the League of Ireland's history. The League of Ireland was resplendent with colourful characters and the vibrancy of entertaining matches. A classic rivalry developed between two powerhouses in Dublin, Shamrock Rovers and Drumcondra, which drew thousands of fans weekly to Glenmalure Park and Tolka Park. Two other great sides emerged in St Patrick's Athletic, who went from non-league to League of Ireland champions in a season, and Shelbourne, whose youthful, exuberant team won the championship and FAI Cup. Dundalk, Cork Celtic, Waterford and Limerick added a real challenge from outside Dublin to give the League of Ireland a true national feel and an added depth.

Players of the calibre of Paddy Coad, Paddy Ambrose, Johnny Fullam, Eddie Bailham, Shay Gibbons, Ronnie Whelan Snr, Dessie Glynn, Alan Kelly Snr, Eamonn Darcy, Donal Leahy, Jimmy Hasty and Ben Hannigan were all in their prime during this period. The range of quality players scattered across the clubs ensured that the competition was healthy, with only St Pats managing to retain the title in 1955-56.

Founded in 1929, Pats began life as a junior club playing in the Phoenix Park, which is just a short hop from the club's spiritual home of Inchicore in south Dublin. Although the club has played at different venues over the years, such as Chapelizod, Milltown and Harold's Cross, the bond between the club and its fan base in south-west Dublin and Inchicore, in particular, has remained remarkably strong.

The early part of the fifties was to be hugely successful for The Saints, who won the League of Ireland championship three seasons out of five, including on their debut season. Pats were one of the top junior teams at the time and had featured regularly in the later stages of the FAI Cup, proving to be quite a match for many league sides. The side dominated the Leinster Senior League in the late forties and early fifties, winning four league titles in row between 1948 and 1951. They were elected to join the League of Ireland, along with Cork side Evergreen United, for the 1951–52 season.

Pats had to play their home games at Shamrock Rovers' Glenmalure Park, but would take the league by storm in their first season on the back of goals from Shay Gibbons. Shay contributed 26 league goals that season, continuing on from where he had left off in the Leinster Senior League. This total represented nearly half of the total goals scored by Pats in the league that season. In addition to Gibbons, The Saints had Harry Boland and Willie Peyton in their ranks. They were also adept at putting on a show for their supporters on the way to the title, including a 4–3 win against Waterford at Kilcohan Park, with Boland scoring a hat trick.

It would be a great period for high-scoring games and just a week after that seven-goal thriller for Pats at Waterford, title chasers Shels would put six past Sligo Rovers at Dalymount to keep the pressure on The Saints at the top of the table. Another 4–3 result would be achieved in the Cup semi-final, when Cork Athletic got the better of Sligo Rovers. Add to this league results such as Waterford beating Bohemian FC 4-2 and Cork Athletic putting five past Limerick and it is clear that the age of attacking football was upon us.

As the league race reached April, the top two met at Dalymount, with Shels winning by 3-1 to take a one-point lead in the championship. Shels had just three games left to play while Pats had four. A 3-1 win over Dundalk for the Reds a week later led to *The Irish Times* headline, *'Shelbourne in line for League honours'*. Pats hung on grimly thanks to a derby win against Rovers by a goal to nil. A devastating 6-1 defeat at Tolka Park against Drums seriously dented Shels' title hopes, leaving The Saints just two points behind, with two games in hand. It now seemed possible that Pats would emulate both St James's Gate and Shamrock Rovers by winning the League of Ireland in their first season. They took on Sligo Rovers at Milltown and Shay Gibbons capped a memorable day by scoring twice as Pats ran out 3-1 winners, with Harry Boland cracking in the third goal.

A Fan For All Seasons

Pats were the favourites now and travelled to Limerick's Markets Field, where a win for them against Limerick, and a defeat for Shels, who played Bohs at Dalymount, would see The Saints crowned champions. Sadly for Shels, a 3-2 defeat against the amateurs of Bohemian FC would seal the end of their title challenge, but not before some late drama at Markets Field. Twice Limerick had led against Pats, with goal machine Shay Gibbons bringing The Saints back to level on each occasion. Gibbons completed his hat trick in the second half and it looked like Pats would hold on; however, a last-minute penalty was awarded to Limerick. Limerick inside left Sean Cusack took the penalty kick and struck the post, sending the title to The Saints for the first time.

It was fitting that a hat trick from Gibbons should clinch glory for his side. In addition to his league winner's medal, the former Gaelic footballer also finished the season as the league's top scorer. In The Saints' second league-winning campaign, he would grab 28 league goals, yet still not finish top scorer. Gibbons finished just two goals shy of Jimmy Gauld's 30 league goals for Waterford. However, in that first league season, he also won the first of his four senior international caps for Ireland against Germany. His contribution to St Patrick's Athletic cannot be underestimated, as he led the line for The Saints with remarkable skill and ability.

Both with head and foot, Shay was a natural goalscorer and one of the league's very best. He remained with The Saints for most of the fifties and finished as the league's leading scorer on two further occasions, adding two more league-winner medals to his collection.

Pats charge to their first league championship in 1951-52 season served notice to the other league clubs. They managed to finish a respectable sixth the following season, but imploded the year after, finishing in second-last place, winning just four matches. They did manage an FAI Cup final appearance, but lost out to Drums by a goal to nil. Many might have felt that this season of hardship would have heralded a return to the Leinster Senior League for the upstarts from Inchicore. Thankfully not, as once again, powered by the goals of Shay Gibbons, Paddy O'Rourke and Joe Martin, the club won back-to-back titles in 1954-55 and 1955-56, losing just seven times in those two seasons. The enormity of this feat cannot be underestimated when set against the quality of the opposition across the league. Pats became the only side in this period to win back-to-back championships. Neither Waterford, nor Shamrock Rovers, sides which contained some of the best players around, could manage to halt The Saints' march during this time.

The Saints had a pretty good side themselves and, in addition to the goalscorers, had Tommy Dunne, Longo White, goalkeeper Dinny Lowry and the veteran player manager Alex Stevenson, once of Everton and Rangers. However, there were some blips on the way for The Saints in their second league-winning season, including the concession of ten goals in a fortnight, being hammered 5-0 at Dalymount against Rovers and then losing 5-1 in the FAI Cup at Kilcohan Park. The Saints managed to get themselves back on track and, with a probable league decider against Waterford on the horizon, the League Committee decided to move the fixture to Dalymount for crowd safety reasons.

In front of over 20,000 fans, Pats exacted revenge on The Blues for forcing them out of the cup and as good as clinched the league title, with a 4-1 win. In an encore of his feat at Markets Field, Gibbons again scored a hat trick for his side when it mattered most. Luck was also on hand again for The Saints as Waterford were forced to play the second half with ten men, due to an injury to one of their forwards. With the score at just 1-0 to Pats, luck, or a short-sighted referee, stepped in again as Waterford had a clear penalty appeal for a hand-ball offence denied.

Within minutes of this decision, Gibbons was celebrating his second goal and Pats were in the driving seat for the match and the title. His hat trick came with a fifteen minutes to go. The final goal was described by Frank Johnstone in *The Irish Times* as *'worth the admission money'*. Pats wrapped up the title the following Wednesday evening, playing again at Dalymount, beating Bohemian FC 2-1. It was a remarkable journey back from second last the previous season to champions again.

Their duel throughout that season with Waterford would develop into another good rivalry of the time, culminating in a cup final showdown in 1959, which went to a replay after a 2-2 draw. The Saints would come out on top, winning their first FAI Cup by 2-1, and again it appeared to The Blues fans that Lady Luck wore a red-and-white scarf, as upon the awarding of a penalty to Waterford, Dixie Hale sent the ball out of the ground and with it Waterford's chances.

The nadir of this Pats team was reached a year later, when they retained the league title at the Showgrounds in Sligo. This time Shamrock Rovers had come through to challenge them, but The Hoops ran out of steam towards the end of the season. It would take thirty-four years before the pennant was back in the hands of a St Patrick's Athletic captain; however, the fifties had given Pats' fans a brief taste of success thanks to a wonderful team.

A Fan For All Seasons

While The Saints were bringing joy to Inchicore, there was another club that would also bring thrills and spills, as well as big crowds, to their home ground on Dublin's north side. No less successful than The Saints, they had won their first two championships a little earlier, in 1948 and 1949, and their distinctive club colours of yellow and blue were known across the league by fans of all clubs. They were the first club to have pitch-side advertising and to install floodlights at their ground, Tolka Park. They were first club side to progress on an aggregate scoreline in European competition. Simply named after their home district in Dublin, the team in question is, of course, Drumcondra.

Drumcondra were founded in 1924 by a group of five men who would go on to become known as 'The Big Five' at Drums. Tom Cribben, Andy Quinn, Christy Purcell, George Ollis and Tom Johnston were the men who got things started for Drums. Unlike many other Dublin clubs, which were formed out of 'street teams' and 'pals' kickabouts', Drums presented an early example of professionalism to football in Dublin as they set about finding both local players and those from further afield to play for their newly formed club. While the level of ability and experience of the new players varied greatly, the one thing they all shared was a common belief in the benefits of playing together as one team, with a collective spirit that would be the hallmark of Drumcondra FC.

Drumcondra won the FAI Cup final in 1927 as a non-league team, beating Brideville after extra time in a replay at Shelbourne Park. They also won the FAI Intermediate Cup that season to complete a wonderful cup double. The club would make it to the FAI Cup final again the following season but would lose out to Bohemian FC, who achieved their first league and cup double that year. Within two seasons of that first cup win, Drums would be playing in the League of Ireland and would remain part of the league for the next forty-four seasons.

Drums had success in the early forties with two FAI Cup final victories. In 1943, they beat that great Cork United side by 2-1 in front of over 30,000 fans at Dalymount Park. They also came close to wrestling the league title from United in 1945-46, finishing just two points behind them. However, it would be the FAI Cup final in 1946 that would sow the seeds for one of the greatest rivalries in League of Ireland history. In that final, Drums came up against Shamrock Rovers, who were going for a hat trick of Cup Final victories. The game at Dalymount was played out in front of over 34,000 fans. Such was the enthusiasm of fans that all stand tickets at Dalymount had sold out by the Tuesday of cup final week. Drums' accomplishment of a 2-1 win in the final was described in *The Irish Times* the following Monday as 'the most difficult thing for a League of Ireland team – that of beating Shamrock Rovers in the final of the FAI Cup'. Drums had fought back from being a goal down to go on and win, despite Rovers being considered to have had the better chances in the match and better all-round play. But this fixture was still a few seasons away from the epic that it would become and it was Shelbourne that Drums struck up a rivalry with first.

After winning the FAI Cup final in 1946, Drums were runners-up in the league again the following year, this time by the smallest margin possible, as Shels beat them to claim their fifth title. Over the next few years, the two sides would be regularly in the running for league honours. Drums finally clinched their first title in 1947-48. Drums raced in to an early lead in the championship by winning their first six matches, including a 4-3 win at The Mardyke against United. No harm was done to their title credentials as they had been behind twice in that game and by mid-January *The Irish Times* was already calling them league champions elect.

They lost their 100 per cent record at Tolka the following week when salvaging a draw against Limerick, followed by their first loss at Dundalk a week later. Suddenly it seemed as if their early season form was deserting them as they crashed to a 4-1 defeat at Tolka against defending champions Shelbourne. *The Irish Times* headline from a few weeks back was looking a little premature as both Limerick and Dundalk were now right on Drums' coat-tails in the league race. A big crowd had gone along to Tolka to see Shelbourne thoroughly deserve victory, which might have been greater if their forwards had taken more of the chances that presented themselves on the day.

With four matches left to play, there was just four points separating the top five. Shels had managed to drag themselves back into contention to retain the title with a derby win against Rovers. Drums' awful slump in form continued as they were beaten again, this time by Bohemian FC. Added to this bleak run of results was a run of injuries, for Giles, Watters, Mulville and Clarke. The weather was also bleak, as heavy snowfall ensured the cancellation of a number of league fixtures, including Drums' journey to Milltown.

The unexpected rest seemed to do Drums good as they went on to beat Shels in the FAI Cup second round by a goal to nil. They also had one of their injured players back, Kevin Clarke, who turned in a man-of-the-match display at half back.

A Fan For All Seasons

Spurred on by this result, a spirited Drums overcame Waterford by three goals to two, with Kit Lawlor saving the day by scoring the winning goal. There could be no doubting the spirit, resolve and commitment of this Drums team, which was intent on a come back from seeming to have thrown the title away. By mid-March, while Ireland were securing a Triple Crown in the Five Nations rugby championship, Drums were securing a point at home against Cork United and were now within two points of the title.

The team's never-say-die attitude was in evidence in the rearranged game against Rovers. Drums fought back from being 3-1 down, with just six minutes to play at Milltown, to grab a draw. With players such as Kit Lawlor, Kevin Clarke and Benny Henderson on the team, Drums always kept on, right to the end of every match. The vital single point need for the championship was finally achieved at Markets Field against Limerick and gave Drums a total of eighteen points from fourteen matches. Dundalk and Shels finished joint second on seventeen points.

After two seasons of finishing runners-up in the championship, the league pennant was finally on its way to Drumcondra and the chance of a double was still on the cards as Drums were set to meet their old pals Rovers in the FAI Cup final.

Unfortunately for Drums and Benny Henderson, in particular, it wasn't to be their day. With the game in injury time Drums were thrown a lifeline when they were awarded a penalty for handball. Benny Henderson stood up to take the chance of drawing the game. His spot kick failed to beat Collins in the Rovers goal and the chance was lost. However, Drums could look back on a great season during which they had overcome injuries to key players, a mid-season slump in form and the weight of history in reaching the ultimate goal of League of Ireland champions.

Their rivalry with Shels would continue the following season as both battled it out for league honours. Drums ran out 4-3 winners when the sides met at Shelbourne Park in mid-February. The following week at Tolka, the battling spirit of Drums players and some fans was in evidence as a goalmouth incident in the FAI Cup tie against Limerick led to an all-in melee including players and fans alike. Drums won the fight and the match. Dundalk and Shelbourne would battle out the FAI Cup final after pushing Drums in the championship race, with Dundalk comprehensively beating the Reds by 3-0.

That league championship would be the last time Drums would see the pennant at Tolka for nearly ten seasons. They would be frustrated in their efforts to make it three in a row by a Cork Athletic side that beat them to the title by a point and even Dessie Glynn's 20 league goals, the best in the league, could not help them win the title the year after.

Dessie Glynn had joined Drums in January 1949 from legendary schoolboy club, Johnville. Johnville had been the starting point for many famous League of Ireland stars, including Ronnie Nolan, Tommy Dunne, Tommy Hamilton and Gerry Mackey, all of whom went on to win League of Ireland championship medals. A local lad from Drumcondra, Dessie played in nearly every position for Drums during his seven-year stay. His ninety-six goals in just under 150 appearances is testimony to his skill as a goalscorer. He also scored five goals in a single game against Transport on 24 November 1951. Dessie's fifth goal in that match came from the penalty spot, and according to legend, Dessie struck the ball with such force that it burst the Tolka Park net and knocked out a spectator. While no mention of this is recorded in the match report, it adds a little spice to the legend.

In 1953, a man from Dundalk arrived at Tolka to buy Drums from the club's owners, the Hunter family. Drums had finished runners-up in the league once again the season before. Their new owner would go on to change the face of football in Ireland. Sam Prole was a wealthy businessman who had ideas for Drums. One of his first was to erect a roof on the reserved enclosure; one of his best was to install floodlights at Tolka Park. This idea, unique among League of Ireland grounds at the time, was greeted with glowing praise. *The Irish Times* commended Mr Prole as he *'took a chance and the crowds are rolling up week after week'*. This comment appeared a few days before one of Drums famous floodlit friendly games, this time against Wacker of Vienna. Sam Prole also brought in his son Roy, to assist in the running of the club.

While the installation of the floodlights would have an early effect on the bank balance of Drums, it would also have long-term benefits when it came to the hosting of European games involving Drums. Unlike other clubs, Drums could play their mid-week European games at Tolka without having to travel to Dalymount for the fixture. In 1953, this advantage could not yet be perceived, as competitive European football was still some years away. However, like Wolverhampton Wanderers in England, Drums could now hold friendly games against Europe's top touring sides under floodlights in Tolka and reap the financial benefit.

A Fan For All Seasons

While Drums were undergoing a rebirth of sorts, their old rivalry against Shelbourne was being replaced by a rivalry against Rovers. This pairing would go on to become probably the best of all League of Ireland rivalries and certainly the best Dublin derby, a classic north side–south side showdown. How the crowds loved it and for many fans of that generation the fixture defined the League of Ireland. It was the fighting spirit of Drums against the classical swagger of The Hoops. However, a meeting in an FAI Cup final nearly discouraged fans from watching the two sides again.

Drums were the defending FAI Cup holders when they met Rovers in the 1955 FAI Cup final at Dalymount. Drums had overcome Waterford by two goals to one in the semi-final after a replay. Dessie Glynn scored the winner from the penalty spot, just minutes before giving away a penalty himself. Luckily for Drums, the penalty from Al Casey and the follow-up shot from Jimmy Gauld were both saved by Neville and they held on to get through to the final again. The attendance at that Wednesday night replay was in excess of 24,000, evidence of the growing following that Drums were attracting. There had been no trouble for Rovers in their semi-final match, as they comfortably beat non-league Longford Town.

The build-up to the final focused on the fact the Rovers had beaten Drums in five of their six meetings so far that season. Drums had been The Hoops' bogey team, having beaten them in the semi-final the previous year, but Rovers had finally turned the tables on Drums and this FAI Cup final was to be no exception. With this Rovers team noted for their attacking flair and Drums' great semi-final battle with Waterford still fresh in the mind, many spectators expected a classic final befitting such strong sides. It wasn't to be.

In front of over 33,000 fans at Dalymount, the Drums' defence held out until twelve minutes before time, when Liam Tuohy decided the final with the only goal of the game, achieved with a diving header. The goal came after a clearance from Drums found the crowd on the terrace. Disgruntled by the lack of quality on the pitch, the fans held onto the ball and wouldn't give it back, despite the referee Arthur Ellis's appeals. A new ball had to be called for by Ellis and after the resultant throw-in to Rovers, they scored to win the cup. The match was also marked by the crowd's slow handclap throughout the second half. Although the fans had come to watch their team win, they had also come to see quality football and they left the twenty-two players on the pitch in no doubt as to the fans' thoughts on their performances. In what had turned out to be something of a let-down for Drums, their only bright light was Benny Henderson, who tried to force an equaliser late in the game with a twenty-five-yard shot that flew just wide. Given the dire performances of both sides, it is probably just as well that Benny's shot didn't go in as the fans may well have voted with their feet on the merits of attending a replay.

Thankfully, this final display would be a one-off and the fans gave both sides the benefit of the doubt. By the 1956–57 season, the fixture was truly one to savour. With the sides meeting on no less than eight occasions, there was plenty of action to keep the rivalry alive.

When the sides met in their first match on 27 August 1956, in a Shield game at Milltown, Rovers ran out 2–1 winners in an entertaining game, which saw both sides praised for their display of 'attractive football' in *The Irish Times*. The early signs of greatness were on display for two of the protagonists, one in green-and-white hoops and the other in gold and blue, Liam Tuohy and Alan Kelly.

Liam Tuohy's class as a footballer is undoubted. The man from East Wall had a wonderful career at Rovers and went on to win eight senior international caps for the Republic of Ireland, scoring four goals. After a move to Newcastle United, Tuohy returned to Rovers and the medals kept coming. In all, he won four league championship medals and eight FAI Cup medals. In addition, he scored one of the best goals ever seen at Dalymount, when he scored for the League of Ireland XI against the Scottish League with a fantastic header. He was a constant thorn in the side of Drums and was forever popping up to score goals which would break Drums fans' hearts.

Alan Kelly was in goal for Drums at the beginning of a career that would see him become the national team's first choice goalkeeper winning forty-seven caps, and go on to play for Preston North End over 440 times. The man from Bray faced down Tuohy on a number of occasions during his two years at Tolka and picked up a league and FAI Cup winners' medal during his time there.

Other players such as Mackey, Coad, Nolan, Glynn, Fullam, Rowe and Lawler shone in an all-star cast and over 18,000 flocked to Milltown to witness that first Shield match.

Nearly a fortnight later, it was round two in the Dublin City Cup final at Dalymount. With the game level at 1–1 in extra time, the referee, an Englishman by the name of Bond, unmistakable due to having just one arm, abandoned the match due to 'failing light'. The big crowd that had turned up had been treated to some fine football, even if there was no final outcome. Drums raced into the lead when, after thirty-five seconds, Dessie Glynn scored from a corner.

The match was set up perfectly, with Rovers having to display all their elegance and balance in trying to rescue the game. Thankfully for The Hoops, Tommy Hamilton was on hand to equalise with ten minutes to go and send the game into extra time. The match reports of the time, while usually noting Glynn and Fullam of Drums, amongst others, made specific mention of the skill of Alan Kelly in goal throughout the game. Remarks and comments on his handling, shot-stopping and reading of the game hinted at what an excellent goalkeeper he was and would remain throughout his career.

The drama continued a week later, again in front of a huge crowd that turned up to see the replay of the abandoned Dublin City Cup final. By now, the reputations of both sides preceded them and it was once again Rovers' slick attack against Drums' steel defence. This clash of ideologies, which was beginning to define the League of Ireland, was taking the usual league season story to a new and more cerebral level. The match was once again level at the end of ninety minutes, at a goal apiece.

The sides were also level on corner kicks, an archaic method of separating teams that finished level in a cup-tie. On some level, it must have seemed that by referring to the corner count, the most attack-minded team would have the most and therefore be awarded the match. However, administrators did not take the weather in Dublin into account when they were dreaming up this rule.

The game went into extra time and with the score still level towards the end of the second period, it was Rovers who led, not on the scoreboard, but on corners, eight to seven. Drums were pressing desperately trying to find a winning goal or at the least a corner to draw level. A cross came in and rebounded off a Rovers player. It flew up into the air and was drifting towards the dead-ball line. Drums would have a corner. Or so they thought, until a gust of wind caught the ball and kept it in play. Never had the elements played such a huge part in deciding the outcome of a cup final. Drums were beaten by Rovers – and by the elements too.

It was back to league action when the pair met at Tolka Park in November. Rovers were outplayed for long periods by an attack minded Drums but somehow The Hoops managed a draw. While Drums were well known for their commitment and spirit, they certainly didn't have a monopoly on these and The Hoops knew how to dig in when necessary too. For all their attacking play and attractive football, Drums could only manage a draw. Rovers continued to hold the Indian sign over Drums as they again got the better of them in front of 20,000 at Dalymount over Christmas in the Leinster Senior Cup final.

The two were also battling it out for the league title along the way and met at Milltown in January. This was a red-letter day for Rovers as they took Drums apart by five goals to nil and all but sealed the league title. Tuohy was once again ready and willing to inflict damage on Drums and, along with the rest of the Rovers team, *'proved that all conditions come alike to this very fine combination'*. **The Irish Times** went on to eulogise about Tuohy's display, noting that in previous matches between the sides this season, Bunny Fullam of Drums had usually *'shared the honours with Tuohy'* but that on this occasion Tuohy *'ran rings around Drumcondra's right back'*. It was certainly a day to forget for those in gold and blue as they made their way back to Tolka without any points and with their league title challenge firmly checked. Rovers would indeed go on to win the title by five points from Drums.

The 1957 FAI Cup final brought glory to Drumcondra FC as they eventually beat Rovers for the first time that season and exacted revenge for their hammering at Milltown and defeat in the FAI Cup final two years before. Thanks to goals from Fullam and Coleman, and one particularly fine save by Kelly, the cup was heading back to Tolka. Drums finally clicked against The Hoops and, unlike the match in Tolka earlier in the season, they didn't let them off the hook. The season had finished with both the league and cup shared between either half of this great combination. Drums now had a taste for beating Rovers and did so again in the Top Four semi-final a few days later. Much like the buses that travel up Drumcondra Road, two usually come along together.

Drums would go a step further the following season by winning the league title, with Rovers finishing runners-up. The crowds were now coming in droves to see this fixture and on Sunday, 26 January, the league fixture between the two had to be abandoned at Tolka. Such were the numbers packed into Tolka that the crowd was forced to sit around the edge of the pitch. With Rovers leading 2-1, Tommy Hamilton, trying to round Alan Kelly in goal, tumbled into the crowd that surrounded the dead-ball line and the Drums keeper's goal. Due to the proximity of the crowd to the pitch, fans surrounded the players and officials. It turned out that the referee was awarding a penalty to Rovers. Cue pandemonium in the goalmouth as Drums players and fans surrounded the referee to protest.

A Fan For All Seasons

Despite appeals over the loudspeaker to clear the pitch, the fans remained and the referee had no choice but to run for cover and abandon the game as tempers became more inflamed. The final announcement on the loudspeaker was to advise fans that the match had been abandoned. Incidentally the League Committee decided that the result should stand and allocated a win and two points to Rovers. Thankfully, from Drums' point of view, this decision didn't go on to cost them the league title as they finished two points ahead of Rovers.

Drums would win the title again in 1960-61, with the goals of Dan McCaffrey helping to bring the title back to Tolka. McCaffrey would score twenty-nine times in the league for Drums that season, including five goals in one league match against Sligo Rovers at Tolka. Drums looked all set for a league and cup double too, until St Patrick's Athletic beat them in the FAI Cup final by two goals to one. The unfancied Saints battled against a howling gale and the new league champions to bring the cup back to Inchicore for only the second time, despite McCaffrey giving Drums an early lead with another goal for the club. Longo White managed to score an equaliser for The Saints and then, just as he did in the 1959 final against Waterford, Willie Peyton stepped up to score the winner for The Saints. Drums' double was denied and it was to be their last chance of achieving this level of success.

Drums and Rovers would be back for one more shake-up in the league, with Drums gaining the upper hand in 1964-65. However, this would be their last league title and within ten years, the great name of Drumcondra FC would disappear from the League of Ireland, not to be seen again.

While Drums always seemed to win less than they should have, the same could not be said for the football aristocrats at Milltown. It could almost have been believed that the hooped shirts alone won matches, such was their ability to get results in games where they were undoubtedly second best. Four league championships and five FAI Cup wins during this time were testimony to Rovers success and this is not even classed among their 'successful' periods, such as their six consecutive FAI Cup wins or four consecutive league titles. One thing this period is remembered for, however, is the style and flair with which Rovers sides played and entertained thousands of fans every other week at Glenmalure Park and at many other grounds around the country. The period is also remembered for all the bicycles that would become a common sight outside Glenmalure Park in Milltown every Sunday that Rovers were playing at home.

Rovers are always known as the FAI Cup specialists due to their record as twenty-four-time winners. By 1969, they had won the cup twenty times in forty-eight years. It was as though the glamour of the big day out suited The Hoops and their cavalier style of entertaining and attacking play. The league championship had proven to be a less frequent visitor to Milltown and until Paddy Coad took over in 1949, they had won the pennant on just six occasions. Paddy Coad was a somewhat reluctant coach and it took all of the persuasive ability of Rovers chairman, Joe Cunningham, to convince Coad to take the role after the unexpected death of Jimmy Dunne. It was one of the best moves that either man would make in football.

Paddy put together a young team that would go on to become known as Coad's Colts. The Colts were to have tremendous success and it wasn't long before their brand of play had thousands making their way up Milltown Road to see The Hoops. The league championship would also be making its way there soon.

After a gap of fifteen years, the title arrived back in 1954. Under Coad's guidance, both on and off the pitch, and with players such as Paddy Ambrose, Noel Peyton, Liam Tuohy, Gerry Mackey and Ronnie Nolan, Rovers became league champions on the final day, with a home win against their title contenders, Evergreen United. As would be the case on many more occasions, Liam Tuohy was on hand to score the winner, which came after a defensive mix-up in the Evergreen United rearguard. Coad won praise for his ability to bring through so many young players and return the title to Milltown. *The Irish Times* commended him and his side on their efforts, noting that his *'long term policy in the coaching of his young team has, at last, been fittingly rewarded'*. The huge number of Rovers fans who turned out at Milltown would probably have agreed, but this was just the beginning of a period that would include four consecutive League of Ireland Shield wins.

Rovers lost the league title in 1955 to St Pats, not that they gave up the title without a fight. They turned on the style when dispatching The Saints by five goals to nil towards the end of the season in front of 22,000 at Milltown but it wasn't enough to keep the league pennant flying at Milltown. Rovers did make it back to the final of their favourite competition however, the FAI Cup. Rovers would renew their rivalry with Drums in the FAI Cup final at Dalymount and run out 1-0 winners. They were back again in the final in 1956 for that classic game against Cork Athletic.

Frank Johnstone described the 1956 FAI Cup final in *The Irish Times* as the *'best Cup Final I have ever seen'*. As 35,000 looked on at Dalymount, it seemed that

A Fan For All Seasons

Rovers would relinquish their hold on the cup, with Athletic two up with a quarter of an hour left to play. Rovers had been on the attack for most of the game and it could be argued that this game did more for Rovers than any previous league title or cup win. Irish people, and Dubliners, in particular, love a team that never knows when it's beaten, a side that never gives up. They feel a certain affinity with a team that is fighting against the odds and proving others wrong. Rovers were in just that position on that Sunday afternoon. Certainly, the fact that they always played attacking football, whether they were ahead or behind, would have inspired the admiration of most football fans.

Rovers began to fight their way back into contention after an Athletic defensive error and a slice of luck. A defensive clearance rebounded off Liam Tuohy and broke to Tommy Hamilton, who slipped the ball into the net to put Rovers back in the game. Three minutes later, they were back on an equal footing after a handball in the Cork Athletic box led to a successful penalty kick from Liam Hennessy. It was now two all and game on. Rovers attacked in a green-and-white wave and forced a series of corners. Athletics' cup final dream was rapidly turning into a nightmare. The horror show was complete when in the third minute of injury time, Ronnie Nolan headed the winner from captain Paddy Coad's corner.

The comeback was complete and the most celebrated FAI Cup final in history had just been won by Rovers – and in some style too. Their commitment to their attacking strategy was admirable and it is probably a credit to Coad that even with time running out and a two-goal deficit, they continued to play what Frank Johnstone described as 'real football'.

With successful back-to-back FAI Cup wins and a league runners-up spot to show as their reward, it would be a league championship again in 1957. Rovers were starting to play with a swagger. The visits of Rovers to other league grounds seemed to bring out an added edge in the teams they were meeting. Clubs began testing themselves against The Hoops as a measure of how good they were.

The Rovers home fixture was an 'occasion' now for other league teams. Rovers seemed to take this in their stride. They put four past Evergreen United, St Patrick's Athletic and Bohemian FC and took two points away from Oriel Park. No one had an answer to the artistry of this green-and-white machine. They regained the title once again at Milltown, with three games to spare. By this stage, they had won fifteen games and remained unbeaten in the league. They had also amassed a

40

staggering sixty-three goals, scored in just nineteen games. The Hoops lost their unbeaten league record in their penultimate game at The Mardyke, yet even here they went down with a fight, losing by the odd goal in seven.

Rovers finished runners-up in 1957–58 to their north-side rivals Drums, but they then regained the championship in 1958–59. Paddy Coad had delivered three league titles and two FAI Cups, as well as a number of other trophies, including four League of Ireland Shields. The delight this team would bring to fans would be the bedrock of Rovers support over the next decade. However, it would be five seasons before the championship was back at Milltown. By that stage, Paddy Coad had left and it was Seán Thomas who guided The Hoops to glory. They also had an unprecedented and, to date, unequalled winning run in FAI Cup finals, proving once again that Rovers' real love was always 'The Cup'.

By the end of the fifties, the Colts had begun to break up, but the replacements were not bad either and they would write a whole new chapter in Rovers' glorious history. Their players continued a tradition of achieving international representative hours while wearing the hooped shirt, such as Shay Keogh, Gerry Mackey, Tommy Hamilton and Noel Peyton, all Colts in the green of Ireland.

The early sixties heralded a small renaissance for Rovers' original rivals, Shelbourne, as the club from Ringsend began to recapture their glorious pre-League of Ireland days. Dublin's premier club, before the foundation of the league, had been somewhat conspicuous in its absence when the trophies were being handed out. Sporadic league championships, including a surprise win in 1952–53, were supported by one single FAI Cup back in 1939. This return was meagre, to say the least, considering their first twenty-five years of existence had yielded twenty-four major trophies.

The upturn in Shels' fortunes was due to a successful FAI Youth Cup win for the club in 1959. The Shels manager at the time was Gerry Doyle and he was happy to promote many of the youth team to the senior side for the following season. The results of this belief in youth and the old adage, 'If you're good enough, you're old enough', were instantly apparent as the club romped through the FAI Cup competition to reach their first final in nine seasons. League results had been inconsistent, but once it came to the premier knockout competition, Shels were on the money.

A Fan For All Seasons

Their first-round match against Bohemian FC had been postponed due to heavy snow but this just put off the inevitable as Shels comfortably beat the amateurs by five goals to two, thanks to a hat trick from Jackie Hennessy. The second round saw Shels play another derby match, this time against old rivals Shamrock Rovers at Milltown. A cracking game resulted in a nine-man Rovers side earning a draw, when, after another Jackie Hennessy goal for Shels, Tommy Hamilton equalised for The Hoops. The replay was fixed for the following Wednesday at Tolka and Shels made no mistake this time, dispatching Rovers by 3-0, with Eric Barber scoring two of the goals. The scoreline in no way flattered Shels and while Rovers fans may have felt that their keeper, Eamonn Darcy, was to blame for two of the goals, it could also be said that the Shels performance was one of their best that season.

Eric Barber remains a Shels legend. He holds the club record for goals scored at 126. He scored in every round of this magnificent cup run in 1960. Eric was a member of the FAI Youth Cup winning team in 1959 and his value to the senior side was now markedly evident. Another member of that youth side was Tony Dunne, who would go on to have an amazing career at Manchester United, including winning a European Cup Winners medal in 1968. While Ollie Conroy was helping out up front for Shels, goalkeeper and future club chairman Finbarr Flood was keeping the opposition out at the other end, ably assisted by Freddie Strahan. Freddie Strahan was renowned for his defensive ability. He was also adept with a hurley and had won a Dublin minor championship medal with St Kevin's when he was sixteen. He also managed to score against England at Dalymount in 1964, making him the only player playing in the League of Ireland to score against England to date.

Shels rumbled on to the semi-final and again showed their talent by beating Dundalk by four goals to one. Barber was on hand with his customary goal and Flood again put in a fabulous display to send The Reds through to the final against Cork Hibs.

The final at Dalymount Park was more notable for Shels' dapper all-red kit than for the football on show as perhaps cup final nerves got the better of both teams. Thankfully for this young Shels team, they managed to weather the opening twenty minutes onslaught from Hibs and eventually settled down to play the style of football that had seen them reach this stage of the competition.

Eric Barber gave Shels the lead after running through the Hibs defence and then lobbing the ball over O'Brien in the Hibs goal. Barber had a hand in the second goal too, when, after challenging for a header in the Hibs area, the ball broke to Joey Wilson, who scored to seal a famous cup win for The Reds – their first in twenty-one years.

Shels goalkeeper Finbarr Flood would go on to become part of FAI Cup folklore for his performance in that final. He lined out for Shels with three broken fingers and still managed to keep a clean sheet. Flood, who had earned himself the sobriquet 'The Man in Black' after his emulation of USSR goalkeeper Lev Yashin, was hardly tested in the final and dealt comfortably with everything Hibs threw at him.

The FAI Cup final win was justification for Gerry Doyle and his mantra of giving talented young footballers a chance. Under his guidance, and with a little learning from defeats and setbacks along the way, The Reds would go on to claim the biggest prize two seasons later when they captured the league championship.

After twenty-two league matches, both Shels and Cork Celtic finished level on points. The last league fixture of the season was the meeting of the two at a packed Turners Cross. Cup final goalkeeping hero Finbarr Flood had moved on but it was still the man between the sticks that saved The Reds and forced the league title to a play-off decider. John Heavey made two outstanding saves in two minutes to first deny Paul O'Donovan and secondly to thwart Donal Leahy. Surprisingly, Shels took the lead against the run of play when Ollie Conroy pounced on a mistake by Kevin Blount, but Celtic eventually beat Heavey in the Shels goal to draw level. It was from then on that the nerves set in as the fear of making a mistake eclipsed any possibility of making a positive difference and the game deteriorated into a kick-and-rush hurly burly.

Despite the obvious potential for a play-off, the League Committee had failed to put any concrete plans in place. Due to the lack of preparation for this eventuality there was significant discussion on where the play-off games should be held. Had goal difference been used as a deciding factor, Celtic would have secured the league handsomely. Finally Dalymount Park was declared as the venue to decide the title.

However, before the league play-off match, Shels were faced with trying to retain the FAI Cup. In a final billed as the 'Cup Final of the Decade', it was Rovers who trounced the favourites by four goals to one, with over 32,000 looking on. That Shels took the lead and still managed to give up four goals is testament to how well Rovers played on the day. Despite the five goals, the match was described in

A Fan For All Seasons

The Irish Times as one that *'will go down as yet another in a long series of tame finals'* – hardly the stuff of legend.

That Shels, a team still full of young players, got themselves back on track for the play-off three days later, is remarkable. They managed to regroup after being humbled in the FAI Cup final and turned in a spirited display right from the start. Despite this, it was Celtic who had the ball in the net first, only to see Austin Noonan's effort ruled out due to an offside offence. The all-important goal for Shels came from three of their legends working together: Jackie Hennessy played a ball to put Ollie Conroy clear on the left and his cross was met on the run by Ben Hannigan, who swept the ball into the net to secure the championship. The team of youngsters had grown up and had now claimed both major trophies in three years. Their next challenge would be Sporting Club de Portugal in the European Cup, but for the moment being league champions was all that mattered.

Shels closed this short period of success with two more magic moments for the club. The first was winning back the FAI Cup by beating Cork Hibs again in the final in 1963 by two goals to one. Hibs managed to score first, but goals from Ben Hannigan and Jackie Hennessy turned things around for The Reds and they secured their second cup win in four years. The second magic moment came when they knocked Portuguese side Belenenses out of the Fairs Cup in 1964.

The time of Dublin clubs dominating the league championship honours was coming to an end. Now back with his hometown club, Paddy Coad was certainly up for the challenge at Waterford and was ready to do battle with his former employers at Milltown. A new side was coming to take on the capital establishment and they would leave everyone blue.

Call of Duty
Interleague Games

League representitive matches, or inter-league fixtures, are a rarity these days. The thought of the best players representing their respective leagues has a novelty factor that one can hardly imagine today. Gareth Bale turning out for a La Liga Selection or Sergio Ageuro lining up for the Premiership XI would be great to see, but given the crowded fixture calender of club and international matches, the thought is little more than wishful.

However, for a period up to the late sixties, such matches were a huge attraction, certainly when the League of Ireland XI were running out at Dalymount Park. The selection was a great opportunity for home-based players to win representative honours and to test themselves against the best footballers in Britain, with the Football League, Scottish League, Welsh League and Irish League regularly engaging in fixtures both home and away.

The split in Irish football in 1921 which led to the formation of two seperate associations also led to the discontinuation of international football matches between the Republic of Ireland and England, Wales, Scotland and Northern Ireland for many years. The International Football Association Board (IFAB) made up of the FA, Scottish FA, the FA of Wales and the Irish FA refused to recognise the authority of the FAI and so they refused to organise friendly matches against any FAI international side. It was not until England came to Dalymount Park for a friendly match in 1946 that any member of the IFAB, or 'Home Nations', played against an FAI selected team at full international level.

A Fan For All Seasons

Thankfully, there was no such rule for interleague representative matches and so they grew in importance and prestige for the League of Ireland selection and were a way of testing themselves against the best our near neighbours had to offer. The fans liked them too, with over 15,000 turning up for the very first fixture at Dalymount Park against a Welsh Football League Selection. These crowds continued to grow, with the 30,000 barrier breached on a regular basis at Dalymount Park. The fixtures had prestige and prior to European competition gave a reasonable indicator of the quality of the League of Ireland. Great results and occasions were enjoyed, and victories were achieved over all the IFAB member leagues. A number of these victories live long in the memory and in the folklore of the League of Ireland, such as surprisingly defeating the Scottish Football League in 1939, defeating the Football League in 1963 containing future World Cup winners for England, and drawing 2–2 with the Scottish league in 1964.

The League of Ireland XI would also play a number of games against club sides such as Celtic, Torpedo Moscow and Torino. They were invited to play the Basque Country in front of 40,000 at San Mamés in Bilbao in 1979. There were matches against Argentina in Buneos Aires's two famous grounds, La Bombonera, home to Boca Juniors, and El Monumental, home to River Plate in 1978 and '80. A tour of New Zealand was undertaken in 1982 and Olympic qualification was embarked on in 1987 and '88. Throughout the years, the selection has had a colourful history.

It all kicked off in 1924 at Dalymount, with the visit of the Welsh League on 10 February. The League of Ireland side contained five Bohemian FC players who would go on to become league champions that season with The Gypsies. The League of Ireland got a great start against their Welsh opponenets when St James's Gate player Ernie MacKay put the home side one up after just two minutes. However, a quick equaliser for the Welsh soon followed and, according to reports, from then on the Welsh side was vastly superior, scoring again to lead 2-1 at the break. With just fifteen minutes remaining in the game, Bohs' Dave Roberts was on hand to bring the League of Ireland level at two goals apeice. Roberts then got his second goal following a 'fair shoulder' charge on the Welsh keeper. Roberts charge had forced the Welsh goalkeeper to drop the ball over his goal line thereby giving the League of Ireland a 3-2 lead. The Welsh side equalised towards the end of the game to force a 3-3 draw.

The report on the game commented that the draw was a flattering result for the home team and that after ten minutes of effort and application, it became clear that the League of Ireland XI were a *'much inferior combination'*. It also bemoaned the attitude of the Welsh League players, who, the report stated, 'derived a disinclination to over exert themselves'. The match report would make you wonder why anyone went back to see another interleague game, but despite the perceived poor quality of the play, the crowd had been treated to six goals and an exciting finish. The ball was now rolling on this new and exciting type of fixture.

The first winning result for the League of Ireland XI came in March 1926, when they defeated the Irish League selection by three goals to one at Dalymount Park. The previous day, *The Irish Times* ran a preview of the fixture. In its commentary, it noted the strong selection of each side and hoped that the fixture would bring a 'settlement between the two bodies, which would be good for the game in every part of the country'. The piece opened with a note that it would be the first time 'since the rupture between the Leinster Association, and the governing body in the North' that an 'Ulster XI' would visit Dublin. The tone of the short article seemed to hope that perhaps a reunification of the bodies would emerge from the goodwill generated by the fixture.

The goodwill extended to the footballing public of Dublin, who gave the Irish League XI a wonderful reception as they ran onto the pitch at Dalymount. Nearly 20,000 fans had turned up to see this unique fixture. The League of Ireland sent out a strong selection, including the legendary 'Four Fs' from Shamrock Rovers, Farrell, Flood, Fullam and Fagan, and set about attacking from the start, with one goal disallowed and a Bob Fullam effort denied by the post. It wasn't long though before they took the lead with a Charlie Dowdall goal and the St James's Gate man made it two after nearly twenty minutes. The home attack was relentless in the first half and only the outstanding goalkeeping of Cliftonville's O'Beirne kept the Irish League within touch. The Irish League did manage to pull one back in the second half, described as a *'grand goal'* from a *'deft header'* in *The Irish Times*, but Billy Farrell headed a goal of his own to restore the home team's two goal advantage near full-time. The final score was 3-1 and, in keeping with the tradition of the time, both parties of players and officials set off for a reception at Jury's Hotel.

While the match itself is significant as the first win for the League of Ireland XI, the administrative side of the match was even more interesting. A reception for players and officials of both teams was held at Jurys Hotel after the match. It was hosted by the honorary president of the Football Association of the Irish Free State, Sir Henry McLaughlin KBE. Sir Henry was a Belfast man who had played for

Cliftonville. In his welcome address, he stated his hope that bonds had now been formed between the two parties that would *'never be broken again'*. Responding to this, Mr Booth, president of the Irish League, said that he looked forward to a time when there would be one league competition run for the whole of Ireland. He added that the players on display that afternoon formed an excellent basis from which a good International side could be selected. While the sentiments expressed where no doubt genuine, the hope never became a reality and both leagues and associations would continue on their seperate paths. In an ironic twist, the closing remarks of Sir Henry, who commented that 'Ireland was going to find her unity on the playing fields of Ireland', could not have been further from the truth.

The fixture would go on to become a regular for the next four seasons. It would be played in Belfast and Dublin on alternate occasions up to and including 1930, when the Irish League XI routed the League of Ireland XI at Dalymount Park by six goals to one, with Linfield's legendary Joe Bambrick scoring four for the Irish League. Bambrick had created history a few weeks earlier when he scored a record six goals in an international match for Ireland against Wales at Belfast.

This would be the last meeting between the sides for eight years. The resumption in Dalymount Park in 1938, which ended in a 3-1 win for the visitors, was the precursor to an eight-season series of home and away matches once a season, which began in 1940. The chief factor in this renewal can be attributed to the suspension of International matches during the Second World War. During this time, unofficial representative matches took place, with guest players lining out for local teams in Britain. These 'guests' usually played with club or regional sides, depending on where they were based during the war. One such guest at Linfield was future England manager Ron Greenwood, who was based in Northern Ireland with the RAF.

The Irish League was suspended during the war and a regional league structure was put in place. To add some variety to the regional restrictions in place in Northern Ireland and in addition to the league representative matches, the Dublin-Belfast Inter-City Cup was formed. This competition ran for eight seasons also. It was made up of six teams from each respective league and played on a knock-out basis. During the lifetime of the Inter-City Cup, it was Rovers who led the way, winning the competition on four occasions, including a 3-2 aggregate win over the hugely successful Belfast Celtic in 1946. Belfast Celtic were a renowned club in the Irish League, having won the Irish Cup in 1941, '43, '44 and '47, in addition to their four Northern Regional League titles under the guidance of Elisha Scott.

While the proximity of both leagues on the island lent to frequent inter-league and club matches at this time, there had also been games against those first opponents, the Welsh Football League, and visits from the Scottish Football League. A visit from a Yugoslav League XI in 1937 added a continental European flavour to Dalymount Park, but it was the first win over the Scottish Football League on St Patrick's Day in 1939 that really grabbed the football public's imagination at the time.

This was the first occasion that both league sides had met and a crowd of over 30,000 descended on Dalymount for the big game. The attendance testifies to the interest in the game, as there was racing at Baldoyle and the Railway Cup final at Croke Park competing for the public's attention.

The quality of the Scottish League selection may have provided an added incentive, as players such as Tommy Walker from Hearts, Alex Venters of Rangers and Celtic's Jimmy Delaney were among a star-studded line-up, some of whom were reportedly in high demand by clubs in England. A number of years earlier, Tommy Walker had been the subject of a potential world-record transfer fee offered by Arsenal to Hearts for his services. Alex Venters was in the middle of a season at Rangers, which would see him finish as leading goalscorer in the Scottish First Division, with thirty-five goals. For Jimmy Delaney, Celtic's outside right, the match was almost like a homecoming as both his parents were from County Laois. Jimmy would go on to play with and manage Cork Athletic in the mid-fifties. Jimmy won the Scottish Cup, the FA Cup and the Irish Cup during his career and was runner-up in the 1956 FAI Cup final, narrowly missing out on a wonderful haul of four different national cup-winners medals.

At this time, the Scottish players were well known for the stylish play and slick passing movements. Unfortunately for them, St Patrick's Day of 1939 would not be suitable for that kind of football, as there was a strong wind in continuous attendance at Dalymount. The League of Ireland XI adapted better to conditions and with ace marksman Paddy Bradshaw leading the line, they had the perfect target at which to send in high balls on the breeze. Bradshaw would finish that season as the league's top scorer, getting twenty-two goals for The Gate. The home side had a lot of class in their line-up too, including Jimmy Dunne of Rovers, Kevin O'Flanagan of Bohs and 'The Mighty Atom', Dicky Lunn from Dundalk.

The Scottish League opened well, with three chances for Jimmy Delaney to open the scoring. One of Delaney's efforts was a cracking shot that came back off the crossbar with Dundalk's goalkeeper Charlie Tizzard clearly thankful that the goal frame had come to his rescue. Rangers' Alex Venters, too, had brought his shooting boots, forcing a save from Tizzard and then seeing an effort go just wide of the post. The visitors' efforts were finally rewarded when Delaney got a ball past Tizzard after a Venters pass. The Irish side was 1–0 down at half-time and, despite a few chances for Bradshaw, it looked like the League of Ireland XI might just be outclassed.

An early second half miss by Kevin O'Flanagan from five yards out, with just the keeper to beat, didn't help the home team's chances. The reporter in *The Irish Times* described the miss in his match report the following day as *'one of the worst misses I have ever seen'*. But you couldn't keep the 'Flying Doctor' down and it was his cross and Johnstone's header some fifteen minutes into the second half which brought the home side level. O'Flanagan, like a player stung after his earlier miss, then had a shot rebound off the angle of post and bar which would have given the League of Ireland the lead. With the home team now comfortably on top of their highly regarded visitors, it fell to Paddy Bradshaw to score the winning goal from Dicky Lunn's high ball into the penalty box. Paddy won the ball and slotted it into the corner of the net. The final score of a 2–1 win for the League of Ireland XI sent the fans home happy and probably a little surprised.

There would be no rest for five of the victorious League of Ireland team as Dunne, O'Flanagan, Hoy, O'Reilly and goalscorer Bradshaw were all listed to travel to The Mardyke in Cork for an Ireland international friendly against Hungary two days later. Hungary had been runners-up in the 1938 World Cup final. Ireland achieved a creditable 2–2 draw, with a last-minute goal from Johnny Carey. The first Ireland goal was scored by Paddy Bradshaw, thus rounding off a busy few days in front of goal for The Gate man.

The next number of years would see the Irish League providing the regular opposition to the League of Ireland due to the Second World War. It would also be a pretty lean time for victories, with just six wins achieved between 1939 and 1953. In 1954 a selection from the Hessenliga in Germany would visit Dalymount to provide a different style of opponent. The Irish side recorded a fine 1–0 win in poor conditions. A further win against the same opponents would follow in 1956, but it was another game in September of that year that would keep the fans talking.

The Football League sent a side over to Dalymount, expecting to continue their run of always defeating the League of Ireland selection. The Football League had never been seriously troubled by the League of Ireland XI on any of the previous ten occasions on which they had met. In fact, some of the games had turned into routs, with the Irish selection twice conceding nine goals when playing in England and conceding six the last time they had played at Dalymount. The previews in that Wednesday morning's papers were not predicting any break in that pattern when the sides met that evening.

Seven Rovers players had been selected to start and it was felt that this, along with the good old 'Dalymount Roar', might unsettle the visitors. These were the straws which were being clutched. The Football League had not conceded a goal against the home side at Dalymount since 1947. Even a goal would give cause for cheer under the circumstances.

The Football League XI picked a strong side, full of internationals, and included stars like England captain Billy Wright, Duncan Edwards, Roger Byrne, Denis Violet and Tommy Taylor of Manchester United. A crowd of over 32,000 turned up at Dalymount to see the event and they weren't disappointed by the outcome. With the League of Ireland trailing by three goals to one with a quarter of an hour left, hardly anyone in the ground would have seen a way back. To make matters worse, the home side had been reduced to ten men due to injury. However, through determination and no little skill they managed to salvage a 3-3 draw on the night, ending the Football League's historic sequence of winning all fixtures between the sides.

It had started off well for the home side, who unexpectedly led after nine minutes due to a goal by Tommy Hamilton after Liam Touhy's first effort had been blocked by Reg Matthews in the Football League goal. Despite this brilliant start, the Football League responded quickly, with an immediate equaliser from Albert Quixall. A header from Tommy Talyor some minutes later had the visitors in front by two goals to one. The Irish side conceded a further goal from Denis Violet just before the break to leave them 3-1 down.

Despite the halftime score, the number of Rovers players on the home side gave the team a cohesion and a confidence working as a team that the Football League lacked. It was this spirit and skill which would stand to them in the second half.

Nowadays, whenever there is mention of Irish footballers at club or international level, the terms 'hard-working', 'committed' and 'tough' are used, especially by visiting team managers and media. With this in mind, it is worth noting an extract from *The Irish Times* report the following day: *'There was a rich football ability displayed throughout by the home eleven ... combined with sound defence and a constant bid to play pure football'*. I wonder how often any of those adjectives have accompanied an appraisal of an Irish footballer recently. The hackneyed tags of 'hard work' and 'commitment' are the very least that is expected of any Irish footballer when they play. By settling for these tags as glowing attributes of Irish footballers, we are contributing to the stereotype and ignoring the real talent and standards that were the benchmark in the past and should be the benchmark for the future.

It was 'rich football ability' which drove the League of Ireland on in the second half. The football was fast-flowing and exciting, but not without the odd scare along the way. Reduced to ten men, it was the team's spirit and cohesion which eventually saw the League of Ireland XI rescue the match with fourteen minutes remaining. Tommy Hamilton from Rovers was again involved, when his long ball was fumbled by Reg Matthews, who was under pressure from Shels' Dermot Curtis. The ball broke to Liam Touhy, who slipped it into the net. The team was 3-2 down, with just under a quarter of an hour to play. The crowd willed the home side on for the equaliser and the Dalymount Roar was in full voice. Sometimes when a goal is scored, an important goal, there seems to be a collective intake of breath before the cheering starts. It's almost like a sixth sense is invoked to fill our lungs to capacity before greeting the goal with all the fervour and appreciation we can muster. Dermot Curtis was to have the hero's moment and the acclaim of the Dalymount Park fans when, with ten minutes to go, his strike from a distance was misjudged by Matthews and found the back of the net, which evoked an earth-shuddering roar of delight from the terraces.

Such was the joy and overwhelming surprise at the result that a little poetic licence was taken in the following day's match reports, with descriptions lauding the draw as the best ever result achieved by an Irish team – a slight exaggeration compared to the wonderful Ireland team that defeated England in Goodison Park in 1949, but the sentiment was well intended.

Four wins over the next seven years for the League of Ireland selection would see the crowds start to decline at Dalymount. This period also included the selection's record defeat as they went down by eleven goals against the Scottish Football League at Celtic Park. As always though, the sight of a team in white shirts would draw the crowds back to Dalymount and in October 1963 the Football League were again the visitors on what would turn out to be the League of Ireland XI's greatest night.

Over 30,000 turned up to see a Football League selection which included Jimmy Armfield, Ray Wilson, Bobby Moore, Ian Callaghan, Martin Peters and Roger Hunt. The League of Ireland selection had come in for criticism when it became apparent that Dundalk, who were the league champions, would have no representation on the starting team. Nonetheless, the home selection was still pretty strong, with ten of the starting eleven coming from the five Dublin clubs, Waterford's Peter Fitzgerald being the odd man out. Shels, Rovers and Pats had dominated the FAI Cup over the previous five seasons and both Drums and Shels had been recent league champions. While the match previews hinted at a possible shock in the result, this was based mainly on some good performances by the Irish clubs in Europe in the preceding weeks rather than any analysis or assessment of the League of Ireland starting eleven as a team.

However, the whole team rose to the occasion – none more so than Drums goalkeeper Eamon Darcy – but it took a while for them to settle into any kind of pattern of play and they were nearly punished after half an hour. An attempt to play-offside by the home defence resulted in a mix-up and left West Ham's Johnny Byrne running towards the goal with just Darcy to beat. The Drums man came out to meet the onrushing Byrne. As Byrne tried to go around him, Darcy stuck out a hand and tripped him up, resulting in a penalty kick. Byrne himself decided to take the kick and put the ball to the goalkeeper's right.

Darcy guessed correctly and got a hand to the shot deflecting it on to the post, from which the ball came back into this arms. A legend holds that luck had nothing to do with Eamon's great save. According to Eamon's team mate on the night, Tony O'Connell, Eamon had been talking to Drums Roy Prole. Prole had seen the Football League side train and watched them taking penalty kicks. Byrne took one during training and Prole advised Darcy of this before the match. Whether or not Eamon would have recalled this piece of information, with all the noise and tension of waiting on Byrne to strike the ball, is unsure, but it is a nice piece of folklore, which appeals to all lovers of the underdog.

So the home side's goal remained intact, to the relief of the Dalymount crowd. But Byrne was not to be denied a second time. A Roger Hunt cross found Byrne in the box and his header beat Darcy to give the Football League a deserved lead. Darcy came to his side's rescue again before half-time when he brilliantly saved an effort from Hunt. As had been the case during the same fixture in 1956, it took until the second half to see the best of the League of Ireland side.

The Football League was still playing better football, but it was the home side who were now providing all the excitement for the fans. Tony O'Connell hit the upright after beating Jimmy Armfield. O'Connell was involved again when, after beating the Football League full back, his cross was cleared by Moore to Eddie Bailham, who fired an unstoppable shot into the net to draw the sides level and send the crowd into ecstatics. The League of Ireland then hit the frame of the goal again, this time when Paddy Robert's free kick hit the crossbar, but none of the home players in the box could take advantage of the opportunity.

While Eamon Darcy is considered the main hero of the match for his saves, including the penalty from Byrne, Tony O'Connell is also deserving of hero status as he hit the post, had a hand in the equalising goal and generally gave his marker, Armfield, a torrid night's work. The winning goal came after a free kick was awarded for Armfield pulling O'Connell down. The ball was clipped into the Football League's box by Johnny Fullam. It came to Eddie Bailham, who in turn helped it on to Ronnie Whelan. The St Pats man took a touch and then placed it beautifully past Tony Waiters in the Football League goal. Cue pandemonium on the Dalymount terraces. A lucky photographer captured the moment Whelan struck the ball from behind the goal, a lovely left-footed drive across Waiters' goal, with the keeper driving to his near post. Memorable goals would run in the Whelan family.

There was still time for the Football League to have another chance and Hunt hit the crossbar with just minutes remaining. The tension on the terraces had reached an unbearable level. Would the home team be denied a famous win, just like the national side in their match against England back in 1957, when England's John Atyeo scored an equaliser in injury time? John Meighan, the match referee, blew for a late free kick to the Football League, which most of the crowd thought was the final whistle. The pitch was invaded and had to be cleared before the remaining seconds could be played out. The final whistle was greeted with a thunderous roar from the Dalymount Park crowd. It was said that the range of the sound was only comparable to the sound of silence that greeted the final whistle after Atyeo's equaliser. Not only did they hear the 'Dalymount Roar' at the Pillar that night; they heard it all over the city.

The only disappointing aspect of this wonderful match was the absence of any television cameras. A great opportunity was missed to commit some of the finest League of Ireland players to film on their greatest night. For the record, the victorious League of Ireland XI team of part-timers and one amateur was made up of Eamon Darcy (Drumcondra); Willie Browne (Bohemian FC {Amateur}); Freddie Strahan (Shelbourne); John Keogh (Shamrock Rovers); Paddy Roberts (Shelbourne); Johnny Fullam, Jackie Mooney and Eddie Bailham (All Shamrock Rovers); Peter Fitzgerald (Waterford); Ronnie Whelan Snr (St Patrick's Athletic); and Tony O'Connell (Shamrock Rovers).

Of course, all great victories are accompanied by great stories. In this case, there is a great story relating to Ronnie Whelan, the winning goalscorer. The story goes that Ronnie, who was working an evening shift that week, asked for Tuesday and Wednesday night off to train and to play the match. His shift boss agreed to the Wednesday night off only. Ronnie went along to Dalymount and played on Wednesday, scored the winner and had his name all over the following morning's papers. Life was sweet. He arrived for his Thursday evening shift and was informed that senior management wanted to see him. If Ronnie thought it was to congratulate a now famous employee on a job well done, then he was sorely mistaken. He was advised, in no uncertain terms, that he didn't actually have permission to be absent from work and that if he ever did the same thing again, he would be fired on the spot. Poor Ronnie, brought back down to earth with a bang.

The League of Ireland XI would continue to perform well for the next twelve months and followed up their win over the Football League with a win and then a draw against the Irish League.

The next big game to draw the crowds was in September 1964, when the Scottish League were the opposition. Thankfully, this time the RTÉ cameras were in place to capture a 2-2 draw and probably one of the best goals seen at Dalymount Park. Philip Greene was behind the microphone and out of his seat describing the build up to the League of Ireland XI's second goal: *'Nolan to O'Neill ... O'Neill now for the League of Ireland ... O'Neill twenty-five yards out ... Crosses ... Touhy, the header ... Oh, what a goal! Oh, what a goal! Oh, what a goal! ... Oh, listen to that crowd roar ...'* And what a goal it was. Frank O'Neill picked up a ball after Ronnie Nolan had dispossessed Partick Thistle's Davie McParland out on the touchline. Frank delivered a beautiful cross into the box, where Liam Touhy got in front of his marker and sent a flashing header into the net. That made it 2-0 to the home team and sent the crowd wild. There is a great television shot just after the goal as the camera pans out. The fans in the old wooden stand at Dalymount are visibly on their feet applauding the goal. Unfortunately, two goals from Motherwell's Joe McBride brought the Scottish League level and the game finished in a draw.

This was to signal the end of the glamour associated with the League of Ireland XI at Dalymount and sporadic wins against the Irish League were the only results of note from then on. There was a sprinkling of glamour in April 1978, when the League of Ireland XI travelled to Buenos Aries to play an Argentinian team including Passarella, Ardiles and Villa in preparation for the 1978 World Cup Finals. They were defeated by three goals to one. Synan Braddish from Drogheda United grabbed a late consolation goal at La Bonbomera. A footnote to this game was a substitution made by Menotti, the Argentina manager, who replaced Ricky Villa with a little guy called Diego...

Another trip to Argentina followed in 1980 when the League of Ireland played at El Monumental, home of River Plate FC. The visitors lost by a goal to nil against the World Cup holders, with Maradona beating Sligo Rovers's Alan Patterson after twelve minutes. Despite this, both Patterson and Dundalk's Tommy McConville turned in fine displays for the League of Ireland. A humbling was in store when they next travelled to South America in 1981, this time to take on Brazil. The Irish side lost by six goals to nil.

The eighties did not bring much cheer to the selection, with just four wins in the decade. Two wins were gained against Irish League selections in front of sparse crowds at Tolka Park and Oriel Park, with the attendance for both games combined totalling less than 2,000 people. There was a rare away win in Dunedin against New Zealand after a brief tour in 1982, with the only other win that decade coming in an Olympic Games qualifier at Dalymount against France.

The League of Ireland took part in the qualification round in a group which included Sweden, France, Hungary and Spain. Along with that 3-0 win against France, there were draws away, against both France and Spain, 1-1 and 2-2, and a further 2-2 draw in the home match against Spain at Tolka Park.

The great nights of the League of Ireland XI became a distant memory for fans and the inter-league games slowly disappeared from the calendar. The selection would have some more days out in the nineties, but these would be seen more as a fixture to attract a club from Britain over to play. Celtic, Leeds United, Manchester United and Liverpool all visited. The last interleague game was against the Irish League in Terryland Park in November 2000. Less than 400 people turned up in Galway to witness the game. Ten years later, the League of Ireland XI would be revived to play Manchester United in a friendly at Aviva Stadium, losing 7–1.

Rather than finish the story of the League of Ireland XI on a sad note, I'll let Philip Greene have the last word as he reacts to the League of Ireland scoring at Dalymount by capturing the excitement of the fans present: *'The League of Ireland lead … Oh dear, what a night, what a night …'*

European Nights, Part 1
Tickets in Hand, with Rovers Leading the Way

European competition is the greatest measurement of the strength, or weakness, of any football league. This perennial search to find the champion club of Europe from the Champions League, along with the best of the rest, in the Europa League is looked forward to by all fans, irrespective of their club's current plight. It gives each league a sense of perspective amongst it peers. It gives fans a welcome break from their domestic fare and an opportunity to sample something a bit different, exotic even. The allure of the unknown, and in some cases unpronounceable, foreign clubs sends fans scurrying for their atlases as much as for their scarves. For the giants of European football, such as the Premiership, La Liga, Serie A and Bundesliga, it lends support to and affirms their place as the top leagues in Europe and, by virtue of snobbery, the world.

The League of Ireland has never had such delusions of grandeur about its status amongst the leagues of Europe. Delusions of adequacy would suit just fine. But although neither the big-eared European Cup nor the no-handles Europa League trophy have made their way to an Irish club trophy cabinet yet, there have been some memorable evenings since our first European league adventure in 1957.

Irish sports fans love European competition. It's always seen as a chance to show everyone else just how good we think we are. You need look only to the success of the Irish provincial rugby teams, who have won six European Cups between them, to see tangible proof of this belief. We love the away day, the opportunity to take on the big guns from Europe.

The chance for the League of Ireland to pit its wits against the best in Europe arrived in September 1957 and it was none other than Shamrock Rovers who led the way. This participation in the European Cup showed remarkable foresight on behalf of the Rovers' board and management and their courage alone should be applauded. While this was a golden period for the league, it was a quantum leap for a part-time club to go travelling around Europe playing football matches without any real idea of how they would fare.

Thankfully for Rovers fans and luckily for the Rovers treasurer, the teams were segregated into three geographical regions at that time. Rovers found themselves in the Western Europe pot, along with ten other clubs. A draw was conducted, so the first four teams pulled from each of the regional pots would play a preliminary round and the winner would go through to the first round proper. Given that there were eleven teams in the Western Europe pot, a further four teams were drawn for the preliminary round.

Clubs such as Benfica, Ajax, Rangers, St Etienne and Manchester United were all in the pot with The Hoops. Rovers were both unlucky and lucky at the draw in Paris: unlucky insofar as they were one of the teams drawn and so did not receive a free pass to the first round proper, but lucky in drawing perhaps one of the most popular, brilliant and thrilling teams of the time, Manchester United.

Not only were Rovers playing their first match in this still relatively new European Champions Club Cup, but the match would be against United, a team that included our very own Liam Whelan. United were champions of England for the previous two seasons and Liam had played a major role in that success. While Rovers fans were delighted at the big draw and the chance to see top-quality European football, I'm sure the Rovers board and management were not too disappointed at the thought of entertaining United and the bumper gate that it would attract.

So it was to Dalymount Park and not Glenmalure, which was considered too small for the fixture, that nearly 45,000 people made their way on 25 September 1957. Rovers were one of our top sides at the time and attracted good crowds at Milltown. They boasted a number of household names, such as Paddy Coad, Paddy Ambrose, Ronnie Nolan and Liam Tuohy. However, it would be fair to say that a number of folks turned out in Dalymount to see the local boy done good, Liam Whelan of Home Farm and Manchester United.

A Fan For All Seasons

The match had a 5.45pm kick-off, as there were no floodlights in Dalymount – such was the innocence of football at the time. The crowd packed in for what was expected to be a memorable evening. I am sure that the sense of occasion was not lost on Liam either, as he sat in the dressing room at Dalymount. It was a chance to play at home again, but this time with his club, of which he was an integral part and which was taking England by storm. He would also be playing in front of his family and friends.

One of United's first chances fell to Liam. Given that he had been United's top league scorer the previous season, you would have bet on him putting it away. It was a chance to score in his hometown, in front of people he had known since childhood, and show how far he had come, but Liam missed his chance and it was Tommy Taylor who scored the first goal after half an hour.

While United were well on top in the first half, Rovers were still holding their own and at half-time they were just a goal down. This was no small feat, given the calibre of opposition. However, luck, which plays such a crucial role in all big events, was to take a hand. There were no floodlights at Dalymount and, given the time of the year, it was bound to get dark early. With this in mind, there was some concern about whether the match could be played to its conclusion with a reasonable amount of light. The teams had come to an agreement to forgo the half-time interval and simply swap ends.

This proved to be a turning point and a 1–0 half-time deficit turned into a 6–0 rout, with Liam scoring two goals, Taylor getting another and Berry and Pegg making it six, as Rovers ran out of steam.

Despite the result, the occasion had been a tremendous success and the attendance had justified the Rovers directors' decision to go into European competition. The return leg at Old Trafford finished 3–2 to United and a modicum of pride was salvaged. Now that Joe Cunningham and Rovers had opened the door, it allayed some of the fear felt by other teams in entering in to European competition.

Drumcondra had a go in the European Cup the following season, against Atletico Madrid, a side who would make it to the semi-final against that great Real Madrid side of Di Stefano, Gento and Puskas. Poor Drums would be chastened by an 8–0 defeat in the Metropolitano and a 5–1 defeat at Dalymount. For the nearly 20,000-strong crowd that turned up at Dalymount for the return leg, it was also a glorious chance to see Vava, the great Brazilian double World Cup winner and final scorer in 1958 and 1962. He scored in both games against Drums too. Drums would have their best moment in Europe a few years later.

But it was Rovers who bounced back for the league in 1959 and secured a reasonable away result when they went down 3-2 against Nice, with goals for Rovers from Tommy Hamilton and Liam Tuohy. A crowd of almost 35,000 turned up for the return leg at Dalymount to see Bill Hennessy give Rovers the lead and put them in the driving seat, with the chance of a play-off. The away-goals rule was not in vogue as yet. Unfortunately for The Hoops, a Nice equaliser proved to be their undoing and they bowed out 4-3 on aggregate.

The seeds of European football had been sown in Dublin and this was shown by the nearly 100,000 people who had turned out for the three home European Cup ties over the previous three seasons.

Some of Europe's best would travel to Dublin to play European ties over the next few years, such as Barcelona's visit to play Shelbourne in 1963 at Dalymount in the Cup Winners' Cup. The legendary Sándor Kocsis was on that Barcelona team, along with Jesús María Pereda, who would score in the 2-0 win for Barca at Dalymount. Pereda would go on to get a hat trick in the 1966 World Cup qualifier against Ireland in Seville in October 1965, which would force the tie to go to that seminal play-off in Paris. Ireland had won 1-0 at Dalymount the previous May.

Jock Stein's Dunfermline had played St Pats in the Cup Winners' Cup in 1961, winning 8-1 on aggregate. The big names kept coming, with Valencia, Rapid Vienna, Real Zaragoza, Vasas Budapest, Nuremburg and Bayern also visiting with star-studded selections.

However, Drumcondra FC, in the Inter-Cities Fairs Cup, provided the League of Ireland's year zero. On Wednesday, 17 October 1962, they secured an aggregate win and progressed to the next round, which was the first time any League of Ireland club had done so. Drums were drawn in the first round of the competition against Odense from Denmark, with the first leg to be played at home on 3 October. Drums had proper home advantage, playing under floodlights at their home in Tolka Park. Unlike many other League of Ireland sides, which had to use Dalymount Park for European nights, Drums could rely on knowing every blade of grass on the Tolka Park pitch and use the tight, enclosed space to their advantage.

A Fan For All Seasons

In front of their own fans, Drums raced in to a 3-0 half-time lead, with Billy Dixon getting two either side of a Jimmy Morrissey goal. Odense grabbed one back through Bruun with a quarter of an hour to go, but Jimmy McCann reinstated Drums' three-goal cushion five minutes later to leave Drums with a very healthy 4-1 lead going into the return leg in Denmark two weeks later. The Drums fans were pretty happy with what they had seen at Tolka and it was a welcome reversal of the score-line inflicted on Drums the previous season at home by 1. FC Nürnberg in the European Cup.

All seasoned League of Ireland fans will understand that when it comes to European competition, our clubs like to take the most circuitous of routes in their attempts to win. Drums were no exception to this time-honoured tradition of trying our best to blow things from a good starting position. Now, with a three goal lead going into the return, it might have been expected that once Drums weathered the initial opening from Odense, then things would fall into place nicely. Odense ahead 2-0 after ten minutes told another tale, however. A Robert Prole own goal after three minutes was followed by a Petersen goal to double Odense's lead a few minutes later. It took goals from Sonny Rice and Jimmy Morrissey, his second in the tie, to get Drums back on level terms by half-time. Fans might have imagined that a 6-3 scoreline at half-time would put an end to Odense's stubborn resistance, but a further two goals from Odense ensured that tensions were high right to the finish. The final score of 4-2 to Odense ensured an aggregate win of 6-5 to Drumcondra. History had been made in Denmark. The rollercoaster aspect of the tie would reflect Drumcondra's forty-four seasons in the league. It is sad to reflect that the first club to win a tie in Europe is no longer part of the league, but at that time it was celebrations all round and anticipation of who was to come in the next round.

For their sterling efforts against Odense, Drums were rewarded with a second-round draw against FC Bayern to be played in December. The Drumcondra match programme cover placed the 'Munich' in brackets. The Bundesliga would be established the following year, after an amalgamation of the old Obersliga structure by the German Football Union. Bayern were perhaps still a little way from being the top club we know today. At that time, 1860 were the top team in Munich, winning the old Obersliga South that season and in light of this Bayern didn't even make it to the first season of the Bundesliga proper. Despite this, Bayern proved far too good for Drums in the first leg at the Grunwalder Stadion, winning by six goals to nil. However, it should be noted that five of the six goals Bayern scored that night came after half-time.

Drums had been brought back down to earth with a bang and it would take a lot to bounce back for the second leg at Tolka on 12 December. But on that Wednesday evening, pride was restored when a Billy Dixon goal earned Drums a 1-0 victory on the night and gave the Drums fans an early Christmas present. Their European adventure had come to an end, but they had been trailblazers in their achievements and finished at home on a high.

The early days of European competition provided a giddy sense of anticipation. Drums had shown that anything was possible on any given night, be it significant defeat or a spirit-lifting victory. Over the next four seasons, three matches would define the early exploits of League of Ireland clubs in Europe: they were Shamrock Rovers against Valencia in 1963, Shelbourne against Belenenses in 1964 and finally Rovers against Bayern Munich again in 1966. These three matches, individually and collectively, sum up what might have been for the League of Ireland clubs. They also demonstrate that the teams were not that far away from tangible success. Given a break of the ball or any piece of good luck, things could have been different for the clubs involved: we could have been talking about the catalysts for Irish clubs in Europe today and not eulogising heroic missed chances from yesteryear.

Shelbourne, however, did take their chance when it was presented to them in the form of a play-off match in the Fairs Cup in 1964. Shels were drawn to play OS Belenenses from Portugal in the first round of the Fairs Cup. Portuguese opposition was slightly more exotic than when Drums faced Odense and Belenenses were considered to be slightly more difficult opponents. After all, they were playing in the same league as Benfica, who had Eusebio and had won two European Cups already, and Sporting Club, who were the current Cup Winners Cup holders.

Shels managed a creditable 1-1 draw away in Lisbon. They then played out a scoreless draw at home, meaning that the tie had to go to a play-off. Luck favoured Shels when they correctly called the toss of a coin to decide where the play-off match would be held.

Dalymount Park was to host the play-off game on 28 October. Looking at footage of the match over fifty years later, it's great to see Dalymount packed and to hear Philip Greene's excited commentary. Greene almost comes through the microphone at you, as he always did. He always seemed so surprised and excited by every goal. His commentary on the opening goal was no exception. When a long ball down the field found Eric Barber on the left-hand side of the penalty box near the end line, he clipped a lovely cross into the six-yard box, where the inrushing Ben Hannigan headed the ball against the post and into the goal. As Ben jumped up and ran to celebrate, it seemed that Greene almost missed the fact that after hitting the post, the ball had gone in. But then, almost apoplectic with delight, he exclaimed: *'Ball hits the upright … It's in the net! It's a goal! Ben Hannigan has scored for Shelbourne. They lead! A vital early lead goal!'*

The crowd were right behind Shels and the second goal came after the ball was won in midfield and pushed on to Eric Barber. Barber cleverly back-flicked the ball towards the oncoming Conroy. The ball instead hit a Belenenses defender and fell into Conroy's path. As another defender came out to meet Conroy, he unleashed a wonderful shot from just inside the box, which flew past the keeper into the net. Greene again is wonderful: *'Conroy's through, he shoots … It's a goal! It's a goal! Conroy has scored for Shelbourne'.* It's almost like having a fan in the commentary box, so much so that you can almost here the concern in his voice when Belenenses pull a goal back just before half time. *'Teodoro shoots…oh there's a goal…there's a goal for Belenenses…nine minutes left in the first half and the score is two to one…'*

The goal was not to be enough for Belenenses, as Shels held on for a wonderful victory for both themselves and League of Ireland football. They had followed in Drums' footsteps in achieving progression through a European tie. The tension towards the end must have been immense for both players and fans, not to mention poor Philip Greene. Shels' reward for progression would be a second-round tie against Atletico Madrid, but unfortunately the journey would end there after two 1-0 defeats signalled the end for Shels.

With all this excitement involving two Dublin clubs, Shamrock Rovers did not want to be left out of the fun. They were drawn in the 1963 Fairs Cup against Valencia. The first leg was at Dalymount, in front of a packed house. There is a great picture of a moment in that game when Rovers were on the attack. The still shows a Valencia defender clearing the ball from danger as Jackie Mooney bears down on him. The moment is illuminated by one of the giant floodlights at Dalymount and it appears as if it is shining only on precisely that part of the pitch where the play is. The rest of the stadium is drowned in a sea of blackness. Despite Rovers' best attempts that evening, they were to lose out to a single goal, but would bounce back in the return at the Mastella, where they held the lead at half-time by two goals to nil thanks to Liam Tuohy and Jackie Mooney. Unfortunately, Valencia scored twice in the second half to level the match on the night and advance 3–2 on aggregate.

While the Valencia game may be considered one that got away, it doesn't come close to the heartbreak that must have been felt after the final whistle when Rovers played Bayern Munich in the second leg of their 1966 Cup Winners' Cup second-round match. Rovers had comfortably beaten Spora Luxembourg in the first round 8-2 on aggregate and now faced a Bayern side that included Sepp Maier, Franz Beckenbauer and Gerd Muller among their stars.

At the time, Rovers were in the middle of their amazing run of FAI Cup wins and had completed a hat trick of cups with a wonderful side, which included Mick Smyth, Johnny Fullam, Frank O'Neill and Liam Tuohy, to mention just four. The first leg at Dalymount took place on 9 November 1966. The German side were up 1-0 at half-time, thanks to a goal from midfielder Dieter Koulmann. However, this Rovers team was made of stern stuff. Drawing on their experience of having beaten Spora Luxembourg in the previous round and drawing against Real Zaragoza a year before in the Fairs Cup, they managed to grab an equaliser in the second half. The equaliser was scored by Billy Dixon, who having also scored against Bayern in 1962 when playing for Drums, once again found German defending to his liking as he brought The Hoops level. Billy would go on to score another important goal for Rovers later in the season, when he scored the winner in the first live televised FAI Cup final against St Pats. But the goal that night against Bayern sent the fans in Dalyer into raptures and reminded Bayern that they would not have it all their own way.

With a draw in hand, Rovers travelled to Munich for the second leg a fortnight later. It appeared that Bayern had learned their lesson from Rovers' spirited equaliser at Dalymount. The hosts raced to a two-goal lead after just eight minutes, with goals from Dieter 'Mucki' Brenninger and Rainer Olhauser. It seemed like the Germans were secured passage to the quarter-finals.

Despite being two down at half-time, Rovers were not done. They came charging back in the second half to level the game, with goals from Bobby Gilbert and Liam Tuohy. As Philip Greene later commented, it was the fighting spirit and never-say-die attitude, which Rovers sides had always displayed, that drew him to support The Hoops: *'They could be two down with ten minutes to play and either win 3-2 or get beaten 3-2 … It was magic … It was charisma.'*

Rovers certainly showed a lot of fighting spirit and charisma in the face of one of Europe's great clubs. As the match stood, it was 3-3 on aggregate and Rovers were heading through on the away-goals rule. The rule had been introduced the previous year for the Cup Winners' Cup. Rovers were all set to cross the Rubicon and eliminate one of the greats. It was time for the League of Ireland to make its mark on European football and who better than Rovers to be in the vanguard, ten years after seeing Manchester United put six past them in Dalymount? It was the part-timers' moment to shine.

Gerd Muller had other ideas, however. 'Der Bomber' popped up with just minutes remaining to salvage a third goal for Bayern to win the match and break Shamrock Rovers' hearts. Muller, as was so often the case, was in the right place at the right time and that night he helped to spare Bayern's blushes and win the tie 4-3 on aggregate. Paddy Mulligan was on the Rovers team that night and his words summed up the game: *'We were so close to getting into the European Cup Winners' Cup quarter-final.'*

Bayern progressed and went on to win the Cup Winners' Cup final in Nurnberg that season, beating Rangers in the final 1-0 after extra time.

If you look back at that period of European football, from 1957 to 1967, it is clear that League of Ireland clubs were able to hold their own on a number of occasions against the best in Europe. Certainly, there were some ugly results, such as Drumcondra's 1958 match against Atletico and Waterford's 1966 clash against Vorwaerts Berlin. In both ties, double figures were breached on aggregate.

However, in Rovers' two games against Spanish opposition during this period, just the odd goal on aggregate prevented progression: 3-2 defeats to Valencia and Real Zaragoza had included a 2-2 draw at the Mastella and a 1-1 draw at Dalymount respectively. Incidentally on both occasions Rovers were knocked out of the Fairs Cup by the team that would finish runners-up in the competition.

Shelbourne also had two matches against Spanish opponents during this time, facing Barcelona and Atletico Madrid. Shels put up a commendable opposition to these two European giants. Barcelona had won the Fairs Cup twice and been runners-up in the European Cup, while Atletico had won the Cup Winners' Cup in 1962 and were runners-up the following season. Shels' 2-0 aggregate defeat to Atletico was a sign that if the correct structures and belief had been there, there could have been more exciting nights in Europe for Irish clubs.

After Rovers' near miss in Munich, it would be thirteen years before a club came as close again to a European quarter-final, when Dundalk played Celtic in the European Cup. There would be some good nights in between, but nothing to match the drama of Munich.

Super Hoops
Six Cups in a Row for Rovers

For many League of Ireland clubs, winning the Football Association of Ireland Senior Challenge Cup at any time is a moment of great achievement and pride for the club. Victory on the big day, in front of a big crowd, lingers long in the memory of players and fans alike. This sense of accomplishment is amplified when a club hasn't won the Cup for a long time, as was the case for St Pats in 2014. Pats bridged a fifty-three-year gap when they beat Derry City and brought the cup back to Inchicore after appearing in, and losing, seven previous finals since their 1961 win over Drumcondra.

It was a great occasion for The Saints fans who warmly welcomed the cup back to Richmond Park amid scenes of laughter, tears and a little disbelief. So many had felt that they would never see the club regain the big trophy and the outpouring of emotion at the final whistle was a release after years of bitter disappointment and pent-up frustration. The emotion was also felt in the commentary box, where former manager Brian Kerr, who was working on the game for RTÉ television, was barely able to hide his delight in seeing his former club triumph.

There is one club, however, for whom winning the FAI Cup has become second nature, a club so synonymous with the cup that knocking them out of the competition was once described as the hardest task in Irish football. Shamrock Rovers started their love affair with the cup from the very beginning, making it to the first final as a non-league club. They went down to league champions St James's Gate, but only after a replay at Dalymount Park. It was during the late 1920s and early 1930s that Rovers' name became synonymous with FAI Cup folklore as they won five successive cups from 1929 to 1933. At that time it might be said that the glamour of cup final day and the big occasion held greater appeal with the football public. The exploits of Rover's 'Four Fs' had become well known in football circles. It was hard to imagine that the feat of winning five in a row would ever be equalled, let alone surpassed, but perhaps only a club like Rovers could re-write the record books in their favourite competition.

Until the 1980s, Rovers managed to win the Cup at least once in each decade and up to 1987, when they beat Dundalk 3-0, a Rovers captain had lifted the trophy on no fewer than twenty four occasions. Sadly for younger Hoops fans, the FAI Cup hasn't made its way back to the Rovers dressing room since. The thought of so many years between victories would have been laughable in decades past, especially in the 1960s, when Rovers owned the cup, beating all previous records set and winning seven finals including completing their record six in a row.

It was Sean Thomas who guided Rovers at the beginning of their record-breaking run when winning the 1964 cup final against Cork Celtic. Thomas had been at the club since taking over from Albie Murphy in 1961. He had managed to lead The Hoops to cup final glory in his first full season in charge against Shels. Now, three years into the job, he had delivered Rovers' first title in five seasons and the 1964 cup final would be a chance for the first double since 1932.

Thomas had recruited well at Rovers following the break-up of the famed Coad's Colts team of the fifties. Along with returning club captain Liam Tuohy, Thomas had brought in Pat Dunne, Frank O'Neill and Johnny Fullam, players who added both steel and flair to a side already containing Ronnie Nolan and Paddy Ambrose.

During his first period with The Hoops, Pat Dunne won six medals and starred in one of Rovers' most memorable European nights against Valencia at the Mastella, where Rovers managed a 2-2 draw. In his second season with Rovers, the team lost just once in the league campaign and won five of the six competitions they entered, the Top Four Cup being the odd one out. A transfer to Manchester United earned him a Football League Division 1 league championship. From Old Trafford he journeyed south to Plymouth Argle. After three seasons in Devon with Argyle, he returned to Milltown and made over 150 appearances for the club. Pat also won five international caps for Ireland, including that memorable win over Spain at Dalymount in 1965.

A Fan For All Seasons

For Frank O'Neill and Johnny Fullam, both returning from England, their time in the League of Ireland would yield an avalanche of winner's medals. Both players won forty medals between them, with Frank slightly ahead on twenty-one. Frank was also on the winning team in each of the six-in-a-row cup successes, a record he shares with another Rovers legend, Pat Courtney.

Frank had spent two years at Arsenal, playing mostly in their reserves before returning home to Rovers. A product of the Stella Maris club, like his teammate Pat Dunne, his play at outside right would thrill Rovers fans, in particular, and all football fans over the next twenty years. He was a creator and scorer of goals for club, country and league selections during his career. He scored in consecutive cup finals and in European competition for Rovers. He also caused Spanish goalkeeper Jose Iribar a huge amount of 'anguish', according to Philip Greene's commentary, in Dalymount in 1965. Frank took a free after John Giles was fouled on the touchline. The free kick was followed in by Noel Cantwell who caused panic in the Spanish penalty resulting in Iribar dropping the ball in to his own net. Philip Greene summed the goal up wonderfully, *'a good one, they're in after it...it's a goal! It's a goal! Iribar... Iribar has put through his own goal. Look at him! Look at him in anguish!'* Frank was also on hand for the League of Ireland XI when he sent a beautiful cross onto the head of Liam Tuohy who scored the second goal against the Scottish League at Dalymount in 1964. Frank had flair and skill and lit up grounds whenever he played. His twenty Ireland caps, all won while playing for Rovers, are a reflection of his skill and remain a League of Ireland record.

Adding the steel to this Rovers side was teak tough Johnny Fullam at wing half. In 1969, a knee injury prevented him from joining Frank O'Neill and Pat Courtney as a winner of six consecutive cup finals, but he was back again the following season, this time in the red and black of Bohemian FC, to claim yet another winners' medal. After a spell at Bohemian FC, with Sean Thomas, he returned to Milltown and picked up his eighth cup winners' medal when The Hoops beat Sligo Rovers in 1978. Acknowledgment of his reliability and consistence came by way of eleven international caps for Ireland, ten of which he won while at Rovers.

By any standards, this Rovers team was good and contained the right balance of players to achieve success. As they set out to win the FAI Cup in 1964, and to achieve their first double in decades, no one could have foreseen how they would come to dominate this competition. But like many periods of dominance, Rovers' began with a false start, when they met Cork Celtic in the final. A rather ordinary 1–1 draw was played out at Dalymount, with Jackie Mooney giving Rovers the lead, only for Donal Leahy to equalise with ten minutes left to play. The game would go to a replay.

Evidence of the following Rovers were now attracting could be seen by the 30,000 fans that crammed into Dalymount for the relay. While Celtic was commended for their gallant display, it was Rovers who won the day, thanks to two goals from Eddie Bailham. Bailham's winner arrived three minutes from the end of a titanic struggle and was a great strike with his left foot from the edge of the box. Jackie Mooney received the ball into his feet and almost seemed to mis-control it, but his touch sent the ball into the path of Bailham. Eddie then sent a first-time shot past the diving Kevin Blount and into the Cork Celtic net to win the cup and the double for Rovers.

It was a glory, glory season for Rovers, but there would be one dark cloud on the horizon and it would appear on 8 May 1964. Sean Thomas, who had guided Rovers to a League Championship, FAI Cup, Dublin City Cup, League of Ireland Shield and Leinster Senior Cup glory that season, resigned from the club. There had been rumblings about difficulties between Thomas and the Rovers board, but no one in League of Ireland circles had expected that this would lead to Thomas walking away from Milltown. That the board accepted his resignation says a lot about how entrenched positions and opinions had become over time. Thomas moved on to Dalymount and Bohemian FC, taking over from their previous coach, George Lax. Thomas became Bohs' first 'manager', replacing the coach and selection committee employed by the amateur club up to that time.

Although Thomas was gone from Milltown, the show went on and Rovers wasted little time in appointing club captain, Liam Tuohy, as player manager. The following season would see The Hoops met Cork Celtic at the semi-final stage of the competition. This was a tough test for Rovers as the match was played at Flower Lodge in Cork. However, despite the partisan home crowd and Celtic racking up twenty-one corners in the game, Rovers ran out 3–0 winners and were set to meet Limerick in the 1965 decider. The Blues overcame the odds and beat Drumcondra at Dalymount to book their place in the final.

As with the previous year's cup final, the sides could not be separated on the day and Limerick managed to force the game to a replay. Noel Dunne's crouching header against the run of play would retain the cup for Rovers in the replay, but, as Seamus Devlin pointed out in his match report for *The Irish Times*, it was a match where *'one could honestly echo that old football cry, 'Lucky Rovers'*. While Rovers' play was not up to their usual slick standards, Ewan Fenton's Limerick team played the game of their lives and were desperately unlucky to lose this game. After the concession of Dunne's goal near the hour, Limerick tore into Rovers and it required all of Mick Smyth's ability to keep the Rovers goal intact. In one last desperate throw of the dice from Limerick, both Fenton and Al Finucane moved into the attack to try to salvage an equaliser, but it wasn't to be on this occasion. Although Limerick had lost the game, they had won a lot of admirers for the manner in which they took the game to The Hoops and while it may seem like hollow praise, the description of their efforts as *'One of the greatest displays by a losing side'* was meant as a genuine compliment after an excellent performance.

Not that Rovers or their hordes of fans minded how the cup was won. The trophy had been retained and the club moniker of 'Cup Specialists' was beginning to be accurate once again. Another man who didn't mind how it was won was Rovers player Paddy Mulligan. Although at the club since 1963, Paddy had missed out on a cup winners medal the previous season, as he was not selected for either of the games against Cork Celtic. The man from Beaumont would, however, go on to be a regular on the Rovers side and picked up a further three FAI Cup winners medals with Rovers before a transfer to Chelsea in 1969.

While with Chelsea, he was in the squad for their European Cup Winners' Cup Final against Real Madrid. He managed to make a brief appearance in the first final as a replacement for John Hollins, but didn't get onto the pitch for the replay, which Chelsea won 2-1. After ten years in England, with Crystal Palace and West Bromwich Albion, he returned to Milltown for a brief spell, where he ended a playing career which had seen him win fifty caps for Ireland, ten of which he had won in the hooped shirt.

Another player collecting his first Cup winners medal in 1965 was Mick Smyth, the goalkeeper. Mick had returned home to Dublin after a brief spell in England. He started out his career with Rovers' rivals Drumcondra, but would go on to have great success with Rovers in the FAI Cup. He also had a long and successful spell with Billy Young's Bohemian FC side and picked up a third league winners medal with Athlone Town to add to his two from Bohemian FC.

The 1966 FAI Cup final would be a repeat of the previous year's final as Rovers once again came up against Limerick. This was the only similarity in a game which stood out for the remarkable lack of quality football displayed by both sides.

The year 1966 also marked the Golden Jubilee of the 1916 Easter Rising. The game was preceded by a ceremony to mark the jubilee and was attended by over 200 veterans of the Rising and Uachtarán na hÉireann, Éamon de Valera. The crowd of over 26,000 was treated to a dull game that was in marked contrast to the final and the replay of the previous year, which had drawn so much praise. Such was the demand for entertainment from Irish football fans at the time that the poor fare on offer was greeted with slow handclapping from the terraces and it was remarked in the following morning's match report that the fans should have been thankful that they had been spared a replay.

The game saw former Rovers forward Tommy Hamilton line out for Limerick, hoping to put one over on his old club. Unfortunately for Tommy and the rest of the Limerick team, they never really got the opportunity to shine, with a disallowed goal in the second half their only real chance. Had it been allowed, the goal would have brought Limerick back on terms, as they had fallen behind to a Tony O'Connell goal after an hour's play. The disallowed goal, from Eddie Mulvey, was the result of a mid-air charge on Mick Smyth, which ended with the goalkeeper being pushed over the goal line with the ball in hand. However, the referee felt that the challenge was a little too robust and awarded a free out.

A lot of praise was given to Rovers' young forward Brian Tyrrell for his hard work during the game. He had celebrated his birthday the previous day and rounded off a great weekend in style with a cup winner's medal. Within a few days, he would leave Rovers to sign for Australian side Sydney United.

Frank O'Neill secured victory for The Hoops with Rovers' second goal from a twenty-five-yard free kick. This secured three in a row for Rovers and ensured the green and white ribbons would stay on the big trophy for another year.

Nearly thirty years after the first live televised FA Cup final in Britain, the FAI Cup final got the television treatment in 1967. This was a seminal moment for domestic football in Ireland and for RTÉ, in particular. The final also attracted the worst attendance in the history of the competition, with just 12,000 fans paying in to Dalymount Park. The attendance must have come as a great shock to the FAI, given that this was the annual big day out for clubs and that the fixture included Rovers. The game was also a derby match with St Patrick's Athletic. All of these factors make it easy to understand the FAI's concern about letting the cameras in again.

The match itself was notable for Rovers' comeback in the second half. The Hoops trailed a defensive but determined Pats by two goals to one at half-time. The Saints had gone ahead after a mistake by Mick Kearin allowed Noel Dunne to nip in and clip the ball over Mick Smyth's head. Unfortunately for Peter Farrell's team, and for Dougie Boucher, in particular, the concession of a penalty for a handball less than ten minutes later allowed Frank O'Neill to bring The Hoops back level. In a rare attack, Saints grabbed the lead again, with Noel Bates heading past Smyth to send the Inchicore men into the break in front.

Whatever Liam Tuohy said at half-time had the desired effect as Rovers came out in the second half with all guns blazing. Mick Leech drew the sides level again shortly after the restart and from then on it was clear that there was only going to be one winner. The Saints managed to hold out until the eightieth minute, when Billy Dixon, who was due to be married the following Monday, grabbed the winner and dashed Pats' hopes of halting Rovers' run of cup final wins.

Match reports noted the determination of Dixon throughout the game, commenting that he may not have wanted his honeymoon interrupted by a midweek replay. As it was, Billy and the Rovers team didn't have much to worry about, as Pats' defensive tactics could not be altered in the last ten minutes. Noel Dunne did force Mick Smyth to bring off one great save, but it was Rovers, through Frank O'Neill, that had two great chances to extend their lead towards the end.

On went the Rovers' Cup-winning juggernaut and the build-up to the 1968 Cup final against league champions Waterford was dominated by two questions: firstly, would Peter Thomas, the Waterford goalkeeper, be deemed fit to play? Secondly, would the veteran Rovers player manager, Liam Tuohy, take his place in the starting line-up for The Hoops?

Thomas had been dogged by a knee injury, which had kept him out of the side during the previous week's demolition of St Pats in the league. While the rest of The Blues made their way to Dublin in preparation for the final, Thomas remained in Waterford, receiving treatment in the hopes of a speedy recovery.

The Tuohy question was raised because of a poor run of form from Damien Richardson. Liam had been the twelfth man for much of the season and only time would tell if the legend would return to the pitch on the big day.

Seamus Devlin, writing for *The Irish Times*, sought out two well-respected football men for their opinions in a preview piece on the Friday before the game. Both Arthur Fitzsimons and Sean Thomas had differing opinions on the merits of each side, with Fitzsimons firstly praising Waterford's 'competency', but doubting 'their ability to come from behind'. Thomas was more effusive in his remarks about The Blues as he considered them 'the most complete football team playing here in Ireland at present'. When asked about Rovers, both men praised their ability to rise to the occasion and their fighting spirit. Thomas was a little more cautious in his assessment, saying that he didn't 'think they have been playing quite as well as in recent years'. When it came to calling the winners, Thomas was in no doubt that Waterford would complete the double, Fitzsimons was more measured, noting that the opening goal would be key for either team.

The final was one of the most anticipated finals in years. Waterford had shown their brilliance by winning the championship and Rovers were going for five in a row in the cup. There was a great sense of anticipation as a crowd of over 35,000 crammed into Dalymount Park to witness the spectacle.

The game itself would be a slight disappointment, but it would be remembered for Johnny Fullam's sterling efforts in defence and Mick Leech's two goals as The Hoops ran out 3-0 winners. This scoreline would not have been immediately evident during the first-half performance and it took all of Fullam's ability and experience to keep The Blues at bay and guide this young Rovers side through some torrid times. Liam Tuohy declined to name himself in the starting line-up and Damian Richardson held his place. The Blues dominated the early exchanges. They were unlucky to see a Mick Lynch's effort hit the upright with Mick Smyth beaten and unlucky again when John O'Neill's header also struck the post. Thanks largely to the Rovers captain, the sides went in level at half-time.

The second half saw a change in the Waterford approach, which cost them dearly. Gone was The Blues' footballing superiority as they engaged in more robust tactics, which resulted in eleven frees against them during the second half. As for Rovers, they just kept on fighting away. It was a long pass from Mick Lawlor to Mick Leech that eventually broke the deadlock. Leech still had a lot to do, but, like all quality goalscorers, he calmly slipped the ball underneath the advancing Thomas, who had been passed fit to play. Leech's celebration after scoring and his teammates' reactions show how much the Rovers side valued the breakthrough. After enduring Waterford's first-half efforts, they were now in front with a simple, yet beautifully taken goal. The Hoops fans also sensed the significance of the lead goal and came onto the pitch to join in the celebrations.

The cracks began to appear in the Waterford team and a blocked Mick Lawlor effort looped out of reach for Peter Thomas and gave Rovers a 2-0 lead. This summed up The Blues' luck, who having hit the post twice now saw the same kind of deflected shot go into their own net. Just before the end, Mick Leech got another chance in the box and passed the ball underneath Thomas to seal a 3-0 victory for The Hoops and keep the FAI Cup in Milltown. Who could stop this run? The league champions and one of the League of Ireland's greatest ever sides had tried and failed.

It took some time for the next challenger to be decided – four games to be precise, as Limerick and Cork Celtic went to three replays of their semi-final before Celtic emerged victorious.

Celtic made it to the 1969 final and came as close as anyone yet to stopping The Hoops' run of victories. After a John Carroll goal had given the Cork side the lead, they managed to hold out until nine minutes from time. The refrains of 'Lucky Rovers' could be heard in the ether around Dalymount Park. After a save by Celtic goalkeeper Tommy Taylor, the ball broke to Pat Courtney, who crossed it back in and onto the head of Paddy Mulligan. It appeared that the effort from Mulligan was going wide, but in a valiant attempt to preserve his goal, the unfortunate John Keogh put the ball into his own net and brought Rovers level. It was so close for to glory for Celtic who had to make do with a replay the following Wednesday evening.

Celtic had blown their chance of swiping the FAI Cup out of the trophy cabinet in Milltown. Rovers were in no mood to relinquish their trophy and turned in what was probably one of their best final performances in this long run. Mick Leech was the man who got things going for The Hoops and his two goals in the first half left Celtic with a mountain to climb. There was no respite for Celtic in the second half as goals from Mick Kearin and Damien Richardson ensured that Rovers made history and broke their own record of five successive cup wins. The sole consolation for Celtic was a Frank McCarthy goal, which left a final scoreline of four goals to one. Rovers were again praised for their attacking instincts and fluid movement. Celtic were also commended for their sporting play, despite the heavy defeat and, as Seamus Devlin remarked, Celtic 'never resorted to tactics other than those strictly in accordance with the book'. It was cold comfort for the Cork side that had come so close in the first game.

Back at Milltown it was business as usual as the cup returned to what seemed to be its permanent home, decked in green and white. Perhaps even Rovers' chairman, Joe Cunningham, was looking for a change of winner. With his bookmaking business, he must have felt that Rovers' consistent cup final wins were becoming far too safe a bet for the punters.

Their old rivals Shelbourne FC finally ended Rovers FAI Cup winning run when The Reds knocked The Hoops out of the competition at Milltown. Shels' Brendan Place and Brian Delargy each scored to bring the curtain down on a chapter of cup history and ensure that Rovers would not be appearing in that season's cup final. The Hoops had gone in at half-time leading by an Eric Barber goal, despite Shels having the better of the game. Rovers' luck held out until fifteen minutes from the end, when an error in judgement from Mick Smyth in goal, after a Johnny Campbell corner, gave Brendan Place the chance to equalise after a scramble. Campbell was on hand again two minutes later as the flying Delargy met a high cross and his header flew past Mick Smyth to give Shels the lead. Rovers did manage to stir themselves for one last attempt to force a replay, but Paddy Roche in goal for Shels was on hand to ensure The Reds won the game. Rovers were out of the cup for the first time in nearly seven seasons. For many, it seemed almost apocalyptical that Rovers would not contest the final as it was hard to imagine anyone other than the men from Milltown winning the trophy.

While Shels had done everyone else a favour by eliminating Rovers, they could not go on to win the FAI Cup themselves. Bohemian FC would bring the trophy back to Dalymount but only by finally overcoming Sligo Rovers after two replays. However, even though Rovers were not involved in the 1970 final, there was a green-and-white connection on cup final day as the victorious Bohs team included former Hoops players Johnny Fullam and Ronnie Nolan, under the guidance of Gypsies manager and former Hoops boss, Sean Thomas.

The Sky Is Blue
Waterford Rock Kilcohan, 1966 to 1973

The mid-sixties heralded a period of domination by a wonderful side that entertained thousands of fans at Kilcohan Park. Waterford FC were just embarking on their first League of Ireland championship winning season in 1965 with League of Ireland hero and local man, Paddy Coad, in charge. Paddy was born in 1920 and went to Del La Salle school in Waterford, where his first sporting successes were at both hurling and table tennis. However, it would be through his involvement in football that Paddy would go on to earn fame nationally.

Coad had returned to live in Waterford after a hugely successful period as both a player and coach at Shamrock Rovers. He had lined out for Waterford between 1937 and 1942, with a brief spell at Glenavon which was cut short due to the outbreak of the Second World War. He first took up the managerial reins at Waterford in 1960 and would say until 1963. During this time he guided the side to a league championship runners-up place in 1962–63, with the help of goals from the league's leading scorer that season, Mick Lynch.

It may have seemed to Waterford fans like a case of *déjà vu* as the team had finished runners-up to Pats in the league in 1955 and then third in 1961 and 1959. They had also been beaten by Pats in the Cup Final after a replay at Dalymount in 1959. The side was good but it just couldn't seem to come out on top during this period.

The team finished second last in 1963–64, gathering just nine points and losing on seventeen occasions. Bohemian FC finished rock-bottom after achieving just seven points and one win. New manager John Phelan, who had been involved with Waterford's Cup win in 1937, resigned in September 1964. In a statement, the board cited training practices and the players' low levels of fitness among the reasons for the decision. The statement also noted that the club lacked a 'grand' training plan. The statement is rather scathing in its remarks on the coaching team but it is difficult to see how Phelan could have met the board's wishes without their committed backing and support.

The board turned to Paddy Coad again, who came back for a second spell, but the 1964-65 season was to be something of a disappointment as his side finished joint last with Limerick. There was no sign then of the wonderful achievements that were just around the corner for the club and the fans.

However, with the addition of players like Jimmy McGeough and Johnny Matthews, things started to move in the right direction. Peter Fitzgerald's return to the club and later Alfie Hale joining new goalkeeper Peter Thomas saw things looking up for The Blues. The transformation in Waterford's fortunes was radical in that 1965-66 season and The Blues put together thirteen consecutive league wins. Mick Lynch also returned from a spell at Drumcondra and he, along with Shamie Coad, Paddy's brother, would finish as top scorers in the league that season.

Those seventeen and fourteen goals, from Lynch and Coad respectively, would account for over half Waterford's goals scored and see the title travel to Kilcohan Park for the first time in the club's history. Mick Lynch would play a leading role on that historic Sunday afternoon when the title was won. This was all the more remarkable given that he had collapsed towards the end of a recent cup game against Rovers. It was his two goals, coupled with one from Seamus Casey, that would see Waterford win 3-1 at Drogehda United's Lourdes Stadium. Coad was clearly delighted at being the first manager to bring the championship back home to Waterford and in addition they had pipped Rovers to second place. 'This victory has really crowned my football career,' Coad said, adding that 'to bring the title back to my native Waterford leaves everything else in the shade'.

Another local man who shared in the delight of that first league win was Peter Fitzgerald, who was in his second spell at the club. Peter was a centre forward and one of six brothers who went on to represent the Waterford club. Peter won five senior international caps for Ireland while a player at Leeds United and was a member of the League of Ireland XI, which defeated the Football League at Dalymount Park by two goals to one in that famous 1963 game.

A Fan For All Seasons

Jimmy McGeough would play a major role in Waterford's success in that first league title season and throughout his stay on Suirside, which lasted until he left for Lincoln City in 1972. Jimmy joined Waterford from Derry City, who were then playing in the Irish League and with whom he had won both an Irish league and an Irish Cup. Not only was Jimmy noted for his wonderful displays in midfield, which would earn him eleven winners' medals across many competitions; he also had a reputation for being a bit of a joker with a quick wit.

This was in evidence when he was asked a question at a Larne FC club function. Jimmy had gone on to manage Larne FC for a season in 2004-05, guiding them to an Irish Cup final. When asked by BBC journalist and former footballer Jackie Fullerton how McGeough ended up at Larne, he deadpan replied that he 'got the train'. A hugely popular member of that Waterford side, Jimmy was described as a 'nutter' by teammate Johnny Matthews and one of the best players he had ever played with, in an interview for the *Munster Express* newspaper.

While there was a northern influence in midfield, there would also be a Coventry City connection which would go on to lay the foundations, not only for that initial league success, but for the great days and championships that lay ahead. In March 1966, a loan signing was secured for Waterford. This player would join Waterford on St Patrick's Day under the impression that his loan spell would last just six weeks. The six weeks eventually turned into thirteen years and would go on to become a career decorated with medals.

Johnny Matthews was born in Coventry and joined his home-town club in 1965. The Coventry City manager at the time, Jimmy Hill, agreed to the loan move and in the last seven games of that championship season in 1966, Matthews scored on two occasions. Matthews' loan deal turned into a permanent transfer the following season and he went on to become a legend at Kilcohan Park. He also picked up a league winners' medal for those seven games in the 1965–66 season.

Matthews was central to Mick Lynch's first goal that secured the title for The Blues against Drogheda on that historic Sunday afternoon in Co. Louth. Johnny remains the record goalscorer for Waterford, having scored 147 goals in just over 300 appearances for the club. One of those goals in particular stands out for both it's importance and for the cool, calm mentality it took to score: an equalising penalty against Cork Hibs in the league decider at Flower Lodge, which helped bring the title back to Kilcohan Park in 1972.

While he is rightly proud of his collection of league medals, which consists of six for Waterford and a further one for Limerick, Johnny commented in an interview that one of his regrets is never having won the FAI Cup. He was runner-up on three occasions with Waterford. Strangely, although he was Waterford's record goalscorer, he never finished any league season as the league's leading scorer. Despite this, Johnny is rightly remembered as an integral part of the golden Waterford era by both The Blues fans and all fans across the league.

The other Coventry City connection would go on to change the face of goalkeeping in the League of Ireland. Peter Thomas joined Waterford from Coventry City in 1967. Instead of long kick-outs, Thomas was noted for throwing the ball out to players when starting an attack. This became a useful weapon in the Waterford arsenal. Thomas was not a tall man, but he made himself big when forwards were bearing down on goal. He won five championships in six seasons with Waterford and in his first season with the club conceded just eighteen goals. During this period of dominance, he said, 'If I can't get it into my hands, then no one can'. He wasn't far off the mark with that comment.

Times were moving fast in Waterford and although great players joined the team, the great man himself, Paddy Coad, left in 1967, after Waterford finished fifth, eleven points behind champions Dundalk. However, the fans kept coming through the gates in droves. In 1968, after a league match at Kilcohan Park, the club moved to place an attendance limit on spectators in the ground. The limit was set at 9,000 people due to the 'uncomfortable conditions which spectators experienced'. The very idea of such a move is unthinkable today.

Martin Ferguson was appointed as player manager in the summer of 1967, but he was relieved of the managerial role the following January. Ferguson, who is the brother of Manchester United manager Alex Ferguson, and the Waterford board agreed upon the departure by 'mutual consent'.

This mid-season blip did not stop the Waterford team from continuing their march towards recovering the title. The board brought in Dubliner Vinny Maguire as player manager on a contract until the end of the season. When asked to comment on his appointment by *The Irish Times*, Vinny said, *'We'll go on winning'*, and that is just what they did, including a record result against Sligo Rovers that February at Kilcohan Park. Such was the power of this Blues side that match reports described Waterford's 9-0 defeat of Sligo Rovers as *'slaughter in cold blood'*.

A Fan For All Seasons

The chances that were missed by Waterford prevented what could have been one of the greatest wining margins in League of Ireland history. Maguire's men put on a display led by recalled centre forward and veteran goalscorer Mick Lynch, who scored four goals and turned the clock back to his leading scorer days during Waterford's first championship. Lynch had been recalled after a month's lay-off and was on the team because Al Casey was due to be married the following day. Alfie Hale got in on the act with two goals and there was one each for Johnny Matthews, Shamie Coad and right-winger John O'Neill.

The goals kept coming, including a 4-3 win against Drums and another goal fest to celebrate receiving the championship pennant at Kilcohan Park when Pats were beaten by six goals to one.

With the championship came a return to European football. Waterford had a taste of this in 1966; however, the 12-1 aggregate defeat to East German army team Vorwaerts Berlin had left a disappointing taste in Waterford mouths. This time around, though, it would be a far bigger occasion as The Blues drew defending European Cup holders Manchester United. United included in their ranks Charlton, Best, Law, Crerand, Stiles and Irish international full back Tony Dunne. Shay Brennan, United's other Irish full back would miss the game, but would go on to join Waterford as manager a few seasons later.

Sir Matt Busby was at the peak of his powers and in keeping with his reputation for attention to detail, paid a visit to Kilcohan Park to see The Blues' first match of the season, some four weeks before the first leg of the European Cup tie. What Sir Matt witnessed, beyond the throng of autograph hunters and well-wishers, was The Blues demolition of Cork Hibs by five goals to nil.

The draw for that season's European Cup took place in July in Geneva and United had been drawn out of the hat first, giving them home advantage for the first leg. According to Don Kennedy, the Waterford chairman, United were instructed by UEFA to play their first leg away due to a clash with Manchester City also playing at home in a European competition first-leg tie.

This was a stroke of luck for Waterford, who decided that the home leg would have to be moved to Dublin. The question was, would Dalymount be big enough for the crowd that was expected to turn up to see the European Champions? It was decided to approach the Irish Rugby Football Union to ask permission to use

Lansdowne Road in order to accommodate as many people as possible. The match would be the first football match to be held in Lansdowne Road in over forty years and the first ever Irish club match to be played at the venue.

Such was the crowd who turned up to the all ticket match that the official attendance cannot be pinned down with any certainty. What is certain is that fans took whatever means necessary to get into the ground to see the tie. There are many reports of fans scaling walls and barbed wire to get inside the ground. Tales are told of touts desperately looking for tickets to sell. Ground admission cost 4 shillings and touts were offering up to £2 to anyone who would sell them these little pieces of golddust. The television cameras capture the immense crowd well, showing plenty of fans sitting along the touchline. On several occasions, the crowd spilled onto the pitch, including once to mob United forward Denis Law on securing his hat trick. Matt Busby pointed out afterwards that these invasions were down to 'enthusiasm' and that his team were accorded a 'wonderful reception'.

While the tie was daunting for Vinny Maguire and his league winners, it was seen at the time as a huge reward for winning the league. All last season's hard work was rewarded with this glamour tie. It was an early indication of the mindset that would afflict Irish clubs in Europe for most of the next four decades. However, for the Waterford players, the thrill of taking to the Lansdowne Road pitch against the champions of Europe would remain with them and they thoroughly enjoyed the occasion and it would be a memorable evening for the 48,000 plus crowd that watched the game.

The game itself had a 5.45pm kick off as there were no floodlights at Lansdowne Road at the time. It started well for The Blues, with an Alfie Hale effort being cleared by Bill Foulkes, but the European champions weren't in the humour to take things easy and the 'Law Man' struck after eight minutes to put United one up. It could have been worse some quarter of an hour later when Best had a second goal for United disallowed for offside. A truly brilliant save by Peter Thomas, who dived low to his left, prevented a second for Law after half an hour.

The save was world class as Thomas was actually moving to his right, tracking a cross in to the box from George Best, but somehow managed to dive back to his left and turn the ball around the post for a corner. This save, coupled with another on his near post from a Best shot, shows what a great keeper Thomas was and how vital he was to the success of Waterford.

However, the game was really settled just before half-time, when Law was on hand again to head home United's second goal. Two down at half-time, The Blues put in a better performance in the second half, with a fine display from Alfie Hale in particular. The tie itself was sealed by Denis Law's hat trick after fifty-five minutes, when he again beat Thomas following a Best pass. A chance for a fourth for Law came and went, with a missed penalty hitting the upright. Waterford did manage to give their fans a reason to cheer when Johnny Matthews scored just after the hour mark, following up on a blocked shot from Al Casey. Waterford were unlucky not to get another near the end, when Alfie Hale's headed effort rebounded off the crossbar, with United substitute goalkeeper, Jimmy Rimmer, well beaten.

The game had ended 3-1 to United, but despite the result, The Blues players were upbeat and had enjoyed the experience of trading punches with the European champions. Vinny Maguire, who had commented that he had hoped for a draw, was delighted with the effort shown by his side, remarking that he *could not ask more*. Alfie Hale noted that he hoped the fans had enjoyed the occasion and both he and winger John O'Neill highlighted how good they thought United had played, saying that the team's skill had been emphasised greatly out on the pitch with them.

Matt Busby had compliments for The Blues too, remarking that he had no hesitation in saying that Waterford were a very good team. He was also effusive in his praise for the ground and the crowd. Busby's generosity in his remarks did not extend to taking the foot off the pedal in the return leg at Old Trafford. Waterford were ruthlessly dispatched by seven goals to one. Al Casey scored The Blues' only reply.

An incident in that second leg has gone down in League of Ireland folklore. Al Casey was on the receiving end of a full-blooded challenge from Irish international full back Tony Dunne. As Al lay on the ground, with Dunne demanding he get up, Al remarked, *'It's okay for you to say that ... I'm in work tomorrow while you'll be out playing golf'*. Such was the nature of European games for our clubs: honest effort and application by part-timers who had to fit in the demands of earning a living while living out dreams of playing at venues such as Old Trafford. With this in mind, who could deny them their moment against World Cup Winners, European Cup Winners and European Footballers of the Year?

The United match firmly behind them, Waterford returned to their bread-and-butter, the league championship chase. The high scores from last season continued, with a 7-0 thumping of Limerick at Kilcohan Park in October. Limerick would recover to go on and lead the championship for a spell that season, with Rovers and Dundalk in pursuit. It seemed that even the weather couldn't stop Waterford's bid to retain the championship pennant, as they put five goals passed Shels in February on an ice rink of a pitch at Tolka Park, all before half-time. They opened up a five-point lead at the top by the end of March, beating Drogheda United 3-2. Drogheda had beaten both Rovers and Dundalk in the preceding weeks, so these two points for The Blues were significant. The title was finally retained after an Alfie Hale goal secured a draw in their last match of the season at Richmond Park against St Pats.

Alfie Hale would play a significant role for Waterford throughout his career. He would have four spells at The Blues, mixed with time spent at Aston Villa, Doncaster Rovers and Newport County in Britain. Alfie, who started out at Waterford in 1957, made a scoring debut appearance for The Blues on St Patrick's Day against Bohemian FC. This would be the first of over 150 League of Ireland goals that would see him into the top ten all-time league scorers. Alfie returned from English League football to Waterford and set about helping Waterford towards league success. He finished as joint leading league goalscorer on two occasions in 1972 and '73, with twenty-two and twenty goals respectively.

Alfie's dedication to Waterford also extended to a spell in the manager's seat in 1969-70, when he guided the team to their third successive league title and the club's fourth in five seasons. He reverted back to playing only upon the arrival of new player manager Shay Brennan in August 1970. The former Manchester United and Irish international agreed to join Waterford after over 350 appearances for the Red Devils, during which he won two league titles and a European Cup.

Shay Brennan's first season as player manager at Waterford would see The Blues finish just one point behind new champions and great rivals, Cork Hibs, in the league standings. The Blues had made a valiant effort to achieve a record fourth consecutive league title, a feat which had eluded even the great Cork United side of the forties. In the penultimate round of matches, Waterford travelled to Flower Lodge and beat Hibs by a goal to nil. They needed another result to go their way to take the championship race to the final weekend, but disappointingly for The Blues, Drogheda United were unable to do them a favour by beating Shamrock Rovers at Lourdes Stadium. The Hoops ran out 3-1 winners. Hibs would go on to beat Rovers in a play-off for the pennant in Dalymount a fortnight later by three goals to one, securing their first league title.

A Fan For All Seasons

While the loss of a history-making four in a row hurt The Blues, it prompted them to steel themselves to recover the title which had by now become something of a fixture in the Kilcohan Park trophy room.

Sunday, 16 April 1972, will be always remembered as one of the most dramatic days in League of Ireland history. Waterford travelled to Flower Lodge, the home of their great Munster rivals, Cork Hibs, for a match that would either decide the outcome of the league campaign in The Blues' favour or send the season into a play-off weekend. The scene was set and a stellar cast was available for the showdown, with Bacuzzi, Herrick, Marsden and Dennehy among the Hibs' eleven and Thomas, O'Neill, Hale and Matthews included for The Blues. A crowd of 25,000 packed into the Cork venue to witness the affair.

It was Hibs who were first to strike after just two minutes, when John Lawson's volley past Thomas put them ahead and sent the partisan home fans into raptures. Hibs hadn't lost at the Lodge all season and it appeared from the early exchanges that this record would remain intact. Things were made harder for Waterford when midfielder Jimmy McGeough had to be replaced by veteran Vinny Maguire and some minutes later they were down to ten men for the rest of the match when Paul Morrisey left the field injured. Hibs took full advantage and a Dave Wigginton goal ten minutes before half-time appeared to have Hibs well on their way to forcing a league-deciding play-off. It was 2-0 to Hibs at half-time and to most of the crowd it seemed that the game was wrapped up for Hibs.

Another chance went by for Hibs to secure the two points, when Peter Thomas brought off a fine save just after half-time from Wigginton. But Waterford had not been three-time league champions for nothing and in the second half they displayed the football, courage and commitment needed to retrieve the situation. It wasn't until nearly ten minutes from time that Waterford managed to pull one back when Humphreys scored a goal after a pass from Matthews. It was 2-1 and game on for The Blues. Unfortunately for John Herrick, a challenge from Jackie Morely resulted in a handball by the Hibs man and Matthews did not miss the resultant penalty. The draw would secure the title and, with a stunned Flower Lodge crowd looking on, the comeback was completed in injury time, when a free kick from John O'Neill found the head of that Waterford goal machine Alfie Hale. He beat Brady in the Hibs goal to seal the win and the title. It was a stunning comeback by a legendary team and it meant the pennant was back at Kilcohan Park for another summer.

Hibs came in for some criticism after the game when their style of play in the second half was questioned by *The Irish Times* journalist Seamus Devlin. For Devlin, Waterford had deservedly won on their footballing ability. He had a sharp rebuke for Hibs' perceived 'kick-and-rush brand' of football in the second half and noted that Waterford were 'always that much smoother, even when reduced to ten men'. That the title was secured with those ten men spoke volumes for the side and the spirit which was pervading the club. Shay Brennan's men had delivered when it mattered most and away from Kilcohan Park too. Would there be no end to the domination of the championship by The Blues?

The following season would see Waterford play Hibs again on the last day of the season, but on this occasion Hibs were not the other side in contention for championship honours. That fell to those men form the north-west, the Brendan Bradley-inspired Finn Harps. Harps had emerged in a short period of time as challengers to Waterford's dominance. Harps had only had League of Ireland membership since 1969. Harps went toe to toe with The Blues throughout the season, but a 2-0 win against Hibs at Kilcohan Park secured the title once again for Waterford. This was a particularly satisfying win as it was the first of Waterford's league successes to be secured at their home ground, in front of their home fans. Harps kept up the chase to the end, winning 2-1 in Markets Field against Limerick, but it wasn't enough and the Donegal side had to reflect on a season which saw a valiant effort fall just one point short of glory. Harps would have their day in the FAI Cup following year.

What a record Waterford had in scoring sixty-seven league goals and only conceding twenty-one. They had now won six titles in eight years and had dominated the league scene during the late sixties and early seventies. Brilliant footballers had played their part. They had been lauded in the press for their flowing, attacking football and the Waterford public had taken to them and their success. Yet for all their league dominance, the FAI Cup remained elusive. Not since 1937 had the FAI Cup been seen on Suirside and that would remain the case throughout The Blues' golden period. Twice the chance of a glorious league and cup double was foiled. Firstly by Rovers in 1968, when nearly 40,000 fans turned up at Dalymount to see Rovers collect their fifth consecutive Cup, after winning 3-0. Then in 1972 against the team they had pipped so dramatically for the league title, Cork Hibernians. A Miah Dennehy hat trick, the first in FAI Cup final history, sealed revenge for the men from Flower Lodge in the final at Dalymount Park.

A Fan For All Seasons

That championship in 1973 actually signalled the beginning of the end of this wonderful period for Waterford football. The title would not be seen again at Kilcohan Park. The newly formed League of Ireland Cup was won in its first season by The Blues the following year against Finn Harps, but given the diet of success that the fans had been used to, this was a disappointment when coupled with a fifth-place finish in the league.

The FAI Cup did arrive back in Waterford when in 1980 they beat St Patrick's Athletic by a goal to nil at Dalymount. The great goalkeeper Peter Thomas finally got his cup winners medal to accompany the man-of-the-match award that his display so richly deserved. Manager Tommy Jackson and that Blues side had achieved something that the greats, like Coad, Brennan, Matthews and Hale, had not managed in a Waterford shirt and, despite the best efforts of The Saints, the FAI Cup finally had Waterford's blue ribbons attached.

This cup success would be the last time one of the two big domestic trophies travelled to Waterford. The club would fall away in challenging for league titles, with just two runners-up appearances over the next thirty-six years. The glory days became a memory, but what great memories that side gave to all that saw them play around the country. Super football from a super side that surely ranks as one of the best, if not the very best, that the League of Ireland has seen.

8

Bohs Go Pro
Thomas and Young Bring the Trophies Back, 1969 to 1979

For seventy-nine years, the watchword at the Bohemian Football Club had been amateurism. Since their foundation in 1890, The Gypsies had been loyal adherents to the essence of the Corinthian spirit. Their foundation during the Victorian era ensured that the ethos of healthy minds in healthy bodies was a guiding principal at the club and it served them well from the outset. They were regularly among the recipients when it came to the awarding of trophies; Leinster Senior League, Leinster Senior Cup and IFA Cup honours all came to Dalymount before the foundation of the League of Ireland. Bohs would also be a force in the new league and were league champions no less than five times up to 1936.

While the early years had been kind to Bohemian FC, in January 1969 things were looking bleak for the club. The previous season had seen them finish last, in twelfth place, and had followed on the heels of Sean Thomas's departure from the club to take up a position with Boston Shamrocks. Thomas's departure was a massive blow to the club, given the miracles he had worked since coming to Dalymount in 1964.

Thomas had arrived at Dalymount for the 1964–65 season, after sensationally quitting double-winners Shamrock Rovers in May. He set about working his magic at Dalymount by refreshing the team with new players from junior and minor football. Jimmy Conway was spotted playing with Stella Maris and was signed up by Thomas, along with Bobby Wade. Coupled with the experienced Bill Browne and Billy Young, Thomas guided the club to a third-place finish in his first season.

A Fan For All Seasons

Still amateurs and having finished last the previous two seasons, with just two league wins, Thomas' achievement was almost the equal to anything accomplished at Milltown.

Third place was secured again the following season, but the season ended with the loss of a number of key players, such as Turlough O'Connor and Jimmy Conway, both of whom went to Fulham, while Kevin Murray and Larry Gilmore went north to Oriel Park and Dundalk. The amateur status was now beginning to restrict the ability of the club to grow and develop. However, Sean Thomas's abilities once again shone through as Bohs overcame the loss of a number of their quality players to finish runners-up to Dundalk. It was defeats to Pats and Drogheda towards the end of the season that prevented them from mounting a real challenge for title honours. Nevertheless, the turnaround in those three short seasons had been significant, with a huge amount of the credit going to Thomas. In much the same way as he left Rovers, his departure from Dalymount came as a shock. He announced that he was 'packing his bags' for Boston and the fledgling American League. It was a hammer blow to The Gypsies, which perhaps served as a wake-up call to some to get a discussion going on the future direction of the club.

Pat Murphy took over for the start of the new season, but the magic was missing and Bohs were back to their old habit of finishing last. By April 1968, Thomas was back from Boston and back at Dalymount. The poor form continued, prompting an Extraordinary General Meeting in December 1968 to discuss how the club could tackle its current plight. The majority of members at the meeting seemed to feel the need to urgently change the amateur status of the club. This prompted the resignation of some of those who were determined to keep the status quo. Bohemian FC were not just facing a difficult time on the pitch; the struggle off the pitch was equally tough, as members both for and against a break with the old ways put forward their cases.

In January, there was a small article in the 'Sports Log' of *The Irish Times* entitled *'Plea for Bohemians to stay amateur'*. It outlined some reasons why the club should retain its amateur status and was written by a 'fan of thirty years'. The fan is not identified, but some of the sentiments expressed are solidly made, while others are a little wistful. One of the more unusual points made in the piece comes at the beginning of the article when the author reflects that football has become more popular and has penetrated universities and colleges, but that it has encroached on the cricket season. Tough times indeed for the cricket scene. The article also held that a move to professionalism would not guarantee Bohemian FC success and pointed to the club's three terrific seasons under Thomas. How much of this revival was down to Thomas's ability as a coach alone could be ascertained by considering the results achieved when he wasn't there, notwithstanding the loss of star players to other clubs.

The article also pointed out that although the club was amateur in status, this did not mean that it had to have an amateurish approach to football. The writer cites the employment of Thomas on a full-time basis as evidence of the club's understanding of how football had changed. The article concludes with a call to arms to preserve the amateur ethos and holds that any deviation from this would be to sacrifice the 'basic duty of fostering the game'.

All very honourable sentiments, but after nearly thirty years without a senior trophy, perhaps it was time for a change, time to go in a new direction and be as brave as the founders of the club had been in 1890. I wonder what founding members like A.P. Magill, H.P. Bell and Frank Whittaker would have made of the situation.

The second Extraordinary General Meeting of the season was called for Friday, 21 February 1969, to be held at St Saviour's Hall on Western Way, where a vote would be taken to determine the direction of the club. The initial enthusiasm of the majority of members seemed to be flagging and it was not certain that the quota of three-quarters of members approving the change could be reached.

What was certain was that Bohemian FC was losing money and at a rapid pace. It was estimated that the club had lost £2,000 the previous season and was on target to lose the same amount again for the current season. They were also £20,000 in debt. In addition, there had been a reduction in the number of fans coming through the turnstiles. The situation was looking bleak. A recent match at Dalymount against Shelbourne had yielded gate receipts of just £60, so the 'revenue' had to be supplemented by £15 from the Bohemian FC treasury to ensure that Shelbourne received their guaranteed dividend from the receipts. It was painfully obvious to all that the current situation could not continue, even from a purely financial point of view. Yet still there were those who clung to the old ways and ideals, even though they were so clearly out of step with modern times.

The prospect of a move to professionalism seemed to hinge on the club's possible loss of league status. Bohs had already gone through the process of applying for re-election to the league and were suitably chastened by president of the League of Ireland Sam Prole's comments at the time, who stated that they needed to *'put their house in order'*. In an excellent article prior to the members' vote, Seamus Devlin cautioned those reluctant members, who he labeled the 'conservatives', to remember that other league clubs might not look too favourably on carrying a sinking ship like Bohs. He went on to warn readers that the pitch at Dalymount Park itself might no longer be reason enough to keep Bohs in the league, given the recent opening of Lansdowne Road to football once again. Those who felt that Bohs might not retain their league status were urged to consider the expense of having a big ground like Dalymount in Division B, where the chances of carrying out any development would be remote in the extreme.

At the meeting on Friday, 270 members of the Bohemian Football Club turned up to hear arguments for and against a change in status. When the vote was taken, a huge number, 205 members, voted to change the rules and open the club to professional players. Liam Rapple, vice-president of the club, remarked that the vote was unlikely to result in any immediate changes at the club. 'It is something we should not rush in to', he remarked. While this was possibly said out of deference to those members who wished to retain the club's amateur status, it was obvious to all that the current plight of the club could not be allowed to continue indefinitely.

Sean Thomas, the first team manager, had to be 'informed' of the decision of the members. Thomas was not a member, but this reflected the old-style rules and regulations which were still adhered to by Bohs in 1969. Thomas remarked that the vote would mean 'an end of frustration for me and whoever may come after me'. He also echoed Liam Rapple's sentiments that change would be 'very gradual'.

Perhaps those 'conservatives', as Sean Devlin called them, would have preferred more members to be like Dr Brendan Menton, honorary secretary of Home Farm Football Club. Remarking on the Bohemian FC members' vote, Dr Menton said that the decision would make Home Farm more determined than ever to win a place in the League of Ireland. Home Farm, like Bohs, were very much an amateurs' club and it may have been felt that, with the changes to come at Dalymount, there would still be room for an amateur club in the League of Ireland.

Farm had tried on eight previous occasions to win League of Ireland status while playing in Division B. Dr Menton also made the point that the advent of professionalism at Bohemian FC would possibly see a reduction in players moving from Home Farm to Dalymount, which had once been a relatively frequent occurrence as the best of Home Farm's players could move into playing League of Ireland football with Bohs and still remain amateurs.

While it was felt that the changes at Bohemian FC would be made slowly, the first noticeable change came less than a month after the members' vote. Sean Thomas wasted no time in taking advantage of the new dawn at Dalymount and snapped up winger Tony O'Connell from Dundalk. Tony had taken the revolutionary step of buying out his own contract with Dundalk to enable the transfer to Bohemian FC to go ahead. Tony was contracted to play just the five remaining games left in the season.

Having had such a successful time with Shamrock Rovers, the acquisition was something of a yardstick to Bohs fans of the calibre of player that Thomas wanted at the club. And Thomas wasn't finished: he signed up former Pats goalkeeper, Dinny Lowry, just two days after O'Connell. Both players would go on to make their debut the following Sunday at home against Dundalk, where they managed a creditable 1–1 draw. Things would never be the same again.

In August 1969, as the first full season of professionalism approached, Liam Rapple, now president of Bohemian FC, felt it appropriate to reiterate that while the club was undergoing changes, it remained committed to the idea of fostering amateur football. This commitment, he said, was a principle held dear by the founding members. In what may have been a revealing comment about the members' vote, he said that they had chosen to 'adopt a middle course by the infiltration of professional players'. Infiltration was an unusual choice of word considering the Bohemian FC members decision.

While the dust was still settling in the members' room at Dalymount, Sean Thomas was sweeping out any remaining cobwebs in his reform of the club. By this time, he had signed seventeen players on professional contracts and while Liam Rapple insisted that there was always room for amateurs at Bohs, his assertion was looking a little weak as the number of professionals in the ranks grew.

Tony O'Connell and Dinny Lowry stayed on after the end of their first season and were joined on the players' list by veteran Rovers man Ronnie Nolan. Ronnie had joined Bohs as a coach two years previous, but this didn't deter the wily Thomas from including him on the playing staff now that he had the opportunity to do so.

A Fan For All Seasons

In possibly his best move at Bohemian FC, Thomas also secured the services of the legendary Johnny Fullam from Rovers for £2,000. From then on, the club became known as 'Johnny Fullam's Bohemians' and the former Rovers legend would go on to play over 170 times in red and black. For a man synonymous with the FAI Cup, having played in five of the previous six finals, it was fitting that Bohs should reach the FAI Cup final during Fullam's first season at Dalymount.

Their first full year of professionalism had minimal impact in the league campaign and led to just eight league wins and an eleventh-place finish out of fourteen. It was an improvement though and after dismissing Dundalk with a Ben O'Sullivan goal in the FAI Cup semi-final at Tolka Park, there was a real chance of silverware and glory.

Facing The Gypsies was Sligo Rovers, who were out to win the FAI Cup for the first time in their history and bridging a gap of thirty years since their last FAI Cup final appearance. It would take three games to decide the eventual destination of the 1970 FAI Cup, with a second replay required for only the second time in the competition's history. The last occasion this had occurred was in 1950, when it took Transport three games to overcome Cork Athletic.

The deciding game itself was played on Sunday, 3 May, in brilliant sunshine on a bone hard pitch. It was Sligo Rovers who took the lead after fifteen minutes, thanks to Johnny Brookes. They held the lead up to the interval. Sean Thomas again showed his prowess as a football man. He replaced Mick Kelly with Jackie Clarke, a gamble that paid off handsomely as the change allowed captain Johnny Fullam to exercise control over the proceedings. Along with Tommy Kelly and the veteran Ronnie Nolan, who would collect his seventh cup winners medal, Bohs took control in the second half.

The equaliser was scored by Fullam after good work by Johnny Doran. With just five minutes on the clock in the second half, Doran won possession and crossed a ball over to Fullam, who turned it past Tom Lally in the Sligo Rovers goal. Twelve minutes later, Fullam was again involved in what would be the winning goal. In tandem with Tommy Kelly, Fullam was dominating the play in midfield and a cross found Tony O'Connell, whose shot beat Lally for Bohs' second goal. The club's first professional was about to secure their first silverware in twenty-nine years.

Both Fran Swan and Tony O'Connell went close to adding to Bohs tally but a 2-1 scoreline finally settled the issue in favour of The Gypsies. It must have been a sweet moment for Johnny Fullam when he received the FAI Cup as Bohs captain. Johnny had cruelly missed out on Shamrock Rovers' sixth straight FAI Cup final win the previous year due to injury, but here he was again, in the thick of the action when the medals were being handed out. For Johnny, it seemed that even if the colour of his jersey had change, the outcome was seldom different in the FAI Cup final.

One thing Johnny didn't manage to claim that day was the man-of-the-match award, which went to Tommy Kelly. Along with a silver tray, there was a £50 voucher for Longford sports firm Donlons Limited, a prize which is truly reflective of a bygone time.

The success was a just reward for those members of Bohemian FC who had courageously voted to amend the club's rules. With Sean Thomas in charge of the team's affairs, Bohs could make up for lost time. Thomas would also bring quality players like Mick Martin and Gerry Daly through to first-team football at Dalymount. Top four finishes would follow over the next three seasons and Thomas again put Bohs back at the business end of League of Ireland football. However, that FAI Cup win in 1970 would be his only major trophy success at Dalymount and in 1973, he left the Bohs hot seat. His replacement, Billy Young, continued the good work started by Thomas and delivered Bohs' first league championship in thirty-nine years just two seasons later.

Billy Young was a Bohemian FC man through and through: player, club captain and manager. He would serve as manager at Dalymount with distinction for sixteen years and bring the glory days back to Bohs. In his first season in charge, Bohs finished runners-up in the championship to Cork Celtic. In his second season, Bohs stormed to the title, taking the championship by a massive nine points from Athlone Town. Bohs also won the League of Ireland League Cup and completed a great season for a great side, which included Mick Smyth, Eamonn Gregg, Johnny Fullam, Noel Mitten, Turlough O'Connor, Pat Byrne and Gerry Ryan.

The team had developed a habit of producing 1-0 victories over the season. This trend would continue on a Sunday afternoon in late March when a Sean Sheehy goal, against title challengers Athlone Town, proved enough to bring the title back to Dalymount after thirty-nine years. It was a great achievement for Young, who had built on the foundations already in place, but had managed to finally deliver the title after seasons of falling short.

A Fan For All Seasons

Remarking on his title side's achievement, Billy Young noted that they had *'won the Championship with basically a young team'* and hoped that their feat could *'bring other clubs around to the realisation that it is so much better to develop one's own talent rather than buy success on the transfer market'*. An admirable sentiment and one which was easy to make in the wake of the club's success; however, the immense contribution of veterans Smyth and Fullam could not be overlooked, despite the contributions of young guns Gregg, Daly, Sheehy and Mitten.

For the former Shamrock Rovers Cup-winning goalkeeper Mick Smyth, this was his first league winner's medal in a career that had begun nearly fifteen years earlier. It was a fitting reward for one of the league's outstanding goalkeepers and complemented his five FAI Cup winners' medals from Milltown. Mick would go on to win two more league titles: another at Dalymount and then one at Athlone Town with his old comrade Johnny Fullam. A sixth Cup win was to come, with Bohs in 1976, along with three League of Ireland Cup wins, one with Bohs and two with Athlone Town. He finished his career back at Rovers in 1983, having amassed sixteen winners' medals in twenty-three years and one International cap for Ireland in 1968 against Poland.

The name of Eamonn Gregg will always be closely associated with Bohemian FC. A tough and skilful defender, Eamonn won nine international caps for Ireland, all while wearing the red and black of Bohs. In over 180 club appearances, Eamonn won two league titles, an FAI Cup and two League Cup medals before leaving Dalymount in 1980. He was back ten years later as manager and achieved success in bringing the FAI Cup back to the club in 1992. A 1-0 win against Cork City at Lansdowne Road, courtesy of a Dave Tilson goal, bridged a sixteen-year gap for the club.

Gerry Ryan's form in his short time at Dalymount helped earn him a league title and FAI Cup winners medal and also resulted in a move to Derby County. Gerry would move on from the Baseball Ground to Brighton, where he would be part of the 1983 FA Cup final squad that played Manchester United. Gerry was named as substitute for Brighton and in a small coincidence another Bohs old boy, Ashley Grimes, was named as substitute for United. In another coincidence, Grimes would replace Ryan as a substitute for Bohs in the 1976 FAI Cup final win.

Bohs had given notice of their title credentials earlier in the year upon reaching the League Cup final, which was then in its second year, having replaced the League of Ireland Shield competition. They met Finn Harps at Oriel Park in the final, which finished in a 1-1 draw. In a game full of incident, match referee Eamonn Farrell booked four players and dismissed one, Finn Harps' Gerry McGranaghan. There was an own goal from Johnny Fullam and a host of chances missed by Bohemian FC before Noel Mitten scored for The Gypsies. The game ended amid angry scenes from spectators, who had been incensed by some of the referee's decisions, with both was verbal abused and cans being flung in his direction. The replay was set for Tolka Park on 9 January. Johnny Fullam made up for his own goal in the first tie by grabbing the winner with just seconds remaining in extra time to win the game 2-1.

A Niall Shelly goal was enough to 'illuminate the dark', to quote Peter Byrne's description of the 1976 Cup Final. Bohs beat Drogheda United by a goal to nil in an insipid contest at Dalymount and would go on to finish league runners-up the following season.

After a league title-winning season dogged by injury, the championship season of 1977-78 would see Turlough O'Connor make up for lost time and finish as the league's top scorer with twenty-four goals. The man from Athlone, whose second spell with Bohs it was, would grab over 120 goals in red and black and see himself placed fourth in the list of all-time league goalscorers, with 178.

By this time the team had been refreshed, with Pat Byrne, Eddie Byrne, Fran O'Brien and Padraig O'Connor all commanding regular places. However, when Bohs met Rovers in mid-March, it was under the shadow of the loss of both Pat Byrne and Eddie Byrne, along with Fran O'Brien, to American League outfit Philadelphia Fury. Mick Leech was brought in from Rovers to assist Turlough O'Connor and Joey Salmon in the goal search, but the disruption caused a delay in what should have been a swift confirmation of the title. A draw at St Mel's against Athlone Town was followed by a defeat at Richmond against Pats. However, their second title in four years was secured at Dalymount with a 2-0 win against the defending champions, Sligo Rovers. How fitting it was the Turlough O'Connor, club captain, should score both goals.

The first was a quick shuffle of the ball from left foot to right before shooting to the far corner, past Sligo Rovers goalkeeper Alan Patterson, and the second was scored from the penalty spot. As Peter Byrne pointed out in his match report, the relief was evident on O'Connor's face as he went up to the director's box to receive the league trophy. His relief reflected the toll taken by the last month at Dalymount, which had seen Bohs capture the title, despite the disruption caused by player transfers. There was little doubt that Bohs were the best team in the country at the time, but they had made their supporters sweat for the championship.

The following season marked ten years of professionalism at the Bohemian Football Club and what a successful period it had proven to be. Another League Cup victory was secured and this brought the collection of silverware to six senior trophies. Two League Championships, FAI Cups, and League Cups. For Billy Young, it was a huge achievement, accomplished despite the loss of key players at various times due to injury and transfer. Young had shown himself to be an astute manager and although that League Cup in 1979 would be his last trophy with Bohs, he continued to keep Bohs at the forefront of Irish football. League runners-up on three occasions and beaten cup finalists twice in consecutive years was scant return for his further efforts at Dalymount. Thankfully for Bohs, Young was there to nurture the club through the early years of professionalism and he richly deserves recognition as one of the Bohemian Football Club greats.

Commendation must also go to those 205 members who, it must be hoped, enjoyed the rewards that their brave decision a decade earlier had delivered.

Four Cup Finals
Hibs, Harps, Farm and Francis

If there is one major thing Irish domestic football lacks, it is a sense of occasion surrounding the FAI Cup final. Despite nearly every other sport treasuring their showpiece occasion and using it to promote their game, the Football Association of Ireland can seem remarkably timid when it comes to promoting the FAI Cup Final. Initially played on St Patrick's Day, the Cup Final has moved about a bit on the calendar and has never really cemented a place in the hearts of Irish football fans, let alone the nation at large. The first Sunday in May,

May Day bank holiday and now any Sunday in November have all been tried, without any regular success. Certainly there have been times recently when the attendances hinted at something like the glory days of the mid-forties to mid-sixties. The 36,000-strong crowd that went along to see Sligo Rovers defeat Shamrock Rovers in 2010 at Lansdowne Road ranks as one of the highest attendances for a cup final ever. However, unlike the FA Cup final in England, with its classic finals, such as 'The Matthews Final' in 1953, Jim Montgomery and Sunderland beating Leeds United in 1973 and Wimbledon's 'Crazy Gang' upset of a vintage Liverpool team in 1988, the FAI Cup has remarkably few landmarks to chose from.

That there is a noticeable lack of 'shocks' or 'upsets' in the history of the FAI Cup final is perhaps a tribute to the fact that the better team has generally won the final. Take the wonderful Shamrock Rovers side of the sixties and the earlier vintage from the late twenties and early thirties. Indeed, probably the best comeback in the final came from Rovers in 1956, when, with ten minutes to go and 2-0 down, they defeated Cork United 3-2. Shelbourne, too, had an excellent cup tradition throughout the nineties, winning the cup three times and finishing runners-up twice. During that time, they also played a memorable final replay against Pats at Dalymount, defeating The Saints and preventing the double going to Inchicore.

Three FAI Cup final moments of note occurred in the mid-seventies, while 1990 saw a fairy-tale story unfold. Miah Dennehy ensured his name was in the history books, with the first ever FAI Cup final hat trick for Cork Hibernians in 1972 when they defeated Munster rivals Waterford. Finn Harps' brilliant team of the mid-seventies got their reward in 1974 as Harps brought the trophy to Ulster for the first time. Home Farm's win in 1975, when they beat their more illustrious north-side neighbours Shelbourne, was to be the last time an amateur club lifted the trophy. The fairy tale of St Francis captured the imagination in 1990, when The Liberties area of Dublin descended on Lansdowne Road to see if the junior club could complete their amazing journey.

The name of Dave Bacuzzi will always be linked with the wonderful Cork Hibs side of the early seventies. Bacuzzi was originally from London and had played with Arsenal, Manchester City and Reading before receiving a telegram inviting him to 'Cork Island', instead of 'Cork, Ireland', to become player manager at Hibs. Bacuzzi, who had won an English Second Division championship with Manchester City, came from a strong footballing family. Dave's father Joe played for Fulham and he also won a Second Division championship during his time at Craven Cottage. Dave joined Hibs in July 1970 and was assisted by Austin Noonan, who had been in charge the previous season. Noonan had led Hibs to the League of Ireland Shield after a 1-0 win against Munster rivals, Waterford. Dave would go one better in his debut season when Hibs beat Shamrock Rovers to win the League Championship after a play-off at Dalymount Park. Goals from Dave Wiggington and two from Miah Dennehy would bring the title back to Flower Lodge for the first time. There was a great buzz about Hibs and this was reflected in the attendances at Flower Lodge, especially when Waterford or Shamrock Rovers were the visitors.

Powered by the goals of Tony Marsden and Miah Dennehy, Hibs went seeking back to back titles in 1971-72 season. Their rivals would be their neighbours from down the coast, Waterford. After an epic struggle in the league, the title went to Kilcohan Park by four points. While Hibs had been fighting it out in the league, they had also reached the FAI Cup semi-final again. This time, they were eager not to suffer the same fate against St Patrick's Athletic as had befallen them against Drogheda United twelve months previous. Thankfully for Hibs, a goal from Sonny Sweeny was enough to see off The Saints' robust but limited challenge in a game memorable mostly for goal chances missed. Sonny's goal would set up a chance at revenge for Hibs, as Waterford had won through to the final after beating Dundalk in the other semi-final. The showdown was set for 23 April at Dalymount.

In front of over 22,000, the game remained scoreless at half-time. Waterford, desperate to win the cup after so many disappointments in the competition, kept on probing away at Hibs through Alfie Hale and John O'Neill, while Hibs were happy for the most part to soak it all up. Unfortunately for Waterford, Hibs got their first goal after a Waterford attack broke down. Dennehy picked the ball up and set off on a run that took him towards the right-hand side of the penalty area. As Vinny Maguire tried to get back, Dennehy had an extra yard of pace, but seemed to have taken the ball too far to the end line. Just when it looked like the ball would run out, Dennehy clipped a lovely shot past a surprised Peter Thomas in the Waterford goal to give Hibs the lead.

Dennehy's second was about strength and persistence as he fought for a long ball downfield with Vinny Maguire again. Dennehy got the better of the Waterford defender and when he reached the penalty spot, he shot. Thomas managed to get fingertips to the ball and deflect it onto the post. The ball spun out and across the face of the goal, but Dennehy had continued his run and was there to slam the ball into the empty net.

The third and final goal came with a well-placed shot from twelve yards past Thomas when the Waterford defence was caught badly out of place. Thomas had rushed out to challenge Tony Marsden, who was through on goal, but the keeper could not get back into position in time to stop Dennehy securing the cup for Hibs. It was the first ever hat trick in the FAI Cup final and it had been accomplished in just nineteen second-half minutes. Miah Dennehy was carried shoulder high off the field at the end by the jubilant Hibs fans, who were delighted to see their side triumph against the team that had just taken their league championship crown. It was a triumph, too, for Dave Bacuzzi, who had now led Hibs to the two biggest prizes in Irish football in his first two seasons. Hibs would go on to retain the FAI Cup again the following season, adding to their ever filling trophy cabinet at Flower Lodge. The League of Ireland Shield against Shamrock Rovers and a Blaxnit Cup win, an all-island competition, against Glentoran would also follow under Dave's time in charge.

However, in April 1974, Hibs surprisingly decided not to renew Dave's contract. Given the success that the side had achieved, it was an unusual move and Dave moved on to take up a position with Home Farm. As for Hibs, the glory days were now behind them and financial difficulties at the club soon began to show. Attendance levels began to fall away and the strange decision was made to sign Rodney Marsh to try entice the fans back to Flower Lodge. Despite a fundraising drive to remedy Hibs' financial situation, the club resigned from the league in 1976 and their place was taken by another Cork side, Albert Rovers. Yet another Cork side had left the League of Ireland scene and a club which had once been synonymous with challenging for honours became a part of history.

While Dave Bacuzzi was getting settled into his new role at Whitehall with Home Farm, Patsy McGowan was in the thick of the action up in Donegal, with a wonderful Finn Harps team. Harps had finished runners-up to Waterford in the league campaign in 1972-73, with The Blues just edging them out by a single point. Harps welcomed back the goal machine Brendan Bradley for the 1973-74 season, a move which would pay dividends.

Brendan Bradley was born in Derry. He had made an impression in local leagues and was signed by The Candystripes at the age of sixteen. With few first-team opportunities at Brandywell, Brendan made the short journey to Finn Park and it was here that his goalscoring ability became evident. He was the league's leading goalscorer in his first two seasons and helped Harps to win the Dublin City Cup. This was Harps' first trophy at senior level. Brendan secured a move to Lincoln City in 1972, but a change in manager at the club, coupled with a surprising goal drought of twelve matches, resulted in his return to Ballybofey in 1973. Harps fans, unlike most League of Ireland defenders, were delighted to see him back.

Finn Harps' journey to Dalymount began at home against Home Farm. It was the visitors who took the lead at Ballybofey, thanks to Frank Devlin, and for a while it looked like the amateurs would cause something of a shock. However, order was restored thanks to goals from Terry Harkin, Declan Forbes, Charlie Ferry and of course Brendan Bradley. Harps were through to face Bohemian FC in the next round and were also remaining in contention for the league title, along with Cork Celtic and Cork Hibs. Finn Park had become well known as a tough venue for visiting teams and Cork Hibs became painfully aware of this in March 1974.

In a game that saw Harps field a number of walking wounded, it is a wonder that Hibs didn't collect the full two points. Paul McGee and Terry Harkin were playing through the effects of injury and, with Tony O'Doherty also struggling, Harps were reduced to less than their full attacking force, not that this prevented Bradley from nearly stealing a win late in the game. The real arguments came after the game from Hibs who were incensed at having had a penalty appeal turned down, along with a disallowed goal from Martin Heffernan.

Harps ran out on to Dalymount to face a Bohemian FC side that was one of the favourites to lift the cup. In a game that The Gypsies should have won, Harps were thankful for the cool head of Charlie Ferry, who rescued a replay. Hughie Brophy had given Bohs the lead and, despite a number of chances for The Gypsies, they would have to make the long trek to Ballybofey the following Wednesday afternoon.

The replay was a different story for both clubs. Two Charlie Ferry goals kept the cup dream alive for Harps and sent them through to the semi-finals for the first time in the club's history. A goal direct from a corner caught Mick Smyth unawares in the Bohs goal and another set piece did for Bohs when Ferry clipped in a free kick. Harps manager Patsy McGowan was delighted with the performance of his side and admitted after the game that he felt they 'were always on top and I never had a moment's worry'. The stakes were getting higher now for the men from Ballybofey as they became the new FAI Cup favourites.

The semi-final draw saw them pitted against Athlone Town at Oriel Park. This novel pairing was matched in the other semi-final, which saw St Patrick's Athletic take on Drogheda United.

The semi final at Oriel Park will always be remembered as the 'Crossbar Game', despite a sublime performance from Harps, which saw them canter to a 5–0 win and earn a place in the final against St Pats. In goal for Athlone was the genial Mick O'Brien, a great character in League of Ireland goalkeeping folklore. With about twenty minutes left in the game, O'Brien broke the crossbar by swinging from it. Cue carpenter at large Patsy McGowan, who came onto the pitch armed with tools and nails to restore the precarious crossbar. I wonder would his handiwork win him the ever-popular crossbar challenge these days? After a fifteen-minute delay, the game resumed, but soon afterwards, McGowan, who was now obviously concerned for the well-being of his handiwork, flagged the referee's attention. Disaster was just moments away from Mick O'Brien in the goalmouth. O'Brien decided to climb up the goal netting and bounce on the crossbar until the both himself and the goal frame came crashing down. The Harps fans were not amused and nor was the referee, who sent O'Brien off for his antics. O'Brien had form when it came to crossbars as the week before, against the same opposition, he brought the crossbar down at Finn Park while swinging from it after a corner had gone over the goal. Despite all this, Harps kept both their concentration and fluency and roundly dispatched the Midlanders with goals from Ferry, Harkin, McGrory and two from Bradley.

With Harps' title challenge just running out of steam towards the end of the season, all efforts were focused on the cup final. Harps were favourites and 14,000 turned up at Dalymount to see if the team could capture the FAI Cup for the first time. They didn't disappoint and once again their cup talisman Charlie Ferry was on hand to score the opener from a free kick. Ferry had now scored in every round of the cup. Pats did manage to equalise when Sean Byrne was on target to get the Inchicore side level. Pats had chances to take the lead and paid the ultimate price for passing these up with just ten minutes left. Bradley, who had been well marshalled by The Saints defence all day, got onto the end of a cross from Jim Smith and rose to power a header into Pats' net.

The third goal came from a Charlie Ferry breakaway in the middle of the park. He passed the ball out to Peter Hutton and his low cross was driven home by Bradley again to seal the game. The win represented the high point for this exciting Finn Harps side and for manager Patsy McGowan. It was a monumental achievement for all involved at the club, which had become a member of the League of Ireland just five years earlier.

Like Finn Harps, Home Farm were relative newcomers to the League of Ireland, having finally been granted membership in 1972. The club came into being in 1928, when a road league competition set up by Leo Fitzmaurice, brother of the famous aviator, Cornel James Fitzmaurice, brought together two teams. The club website tells the story of how the two teams came to merge over a burst football. The Home Farm Road team, including all five boys from the well known Menton family, were approached by the Richmond Road team, as their football had burst and they had no means of playing without challenging the Home Farm side to a game. The Menton's would go on to become synonymous with Home Farm FC as the amalgamation would form the world-renowned schoolboy club of today.

In 1972, the indebted Drumcondra Football Club was sold by its owner, Sam Prole, to Home Farm and it was as Home Farm Drumcondra that the club started life in the League of Ireland, gaining Tolka Park for their home fixtures. By the following season, the Drumcondra aspect of the team name was gone. They reverted back to being called Home Farm and won the cup in 1975 in their famous blue-and-white hooped shirts.

When Dave Bacuzzi joined Home Farm after his successful period at Flower Lodge with Hibs, he inherited an all-amateur side, in keeping with Home Farm's amateur ethos. Dave was charged with looking after the League of Ireland side, but he was also employed to *'direct the coaching operations of the entire Home Farm complex'*, as Dr Brendan Menton advised on Dave's appointment. While their league position didn't improve greatly, Dave's first season will always be remembered for that exciting run in the FAI Cup which saw Farm account for Dundalk, Cork Celtic, who were league champions, and St Patrick's Athletic.

Their run in the cup began at home against Dundalk and came on the back of some good league results. A single goal from full back Joe Smyth was enough to see off Dundalk at Tolka Park. Dave Bacuzzi's side was beginning to develop, with Jim Grace, Frank Devlin, Dermot Keely and a sixteen-year-old Martin Murray in the line-up. Next up was a boy's own win in the dying seconds to secure a 3–2 victory at Tolka Park against Cork Celtic. Frank Devlin was on hand to head home Joe Keely's cross and send Farm through to the semi-finals for the first time. In a match recorded by *The Irish Times* journalist Derek Jones as containing one of the best second half's of cup football he had ever seen, the only negative point was the low attendance. Home Farm had struggled to garner support, probably given their schoolboy beginnings and their newcomer status to League of Ireland football.

The semi-final brought them up against St Patrick's Athletic and again they prevailed by the odd goal in five. This time though there was no need for last-minute heroics as Farm lead 3–1 before a second Saints goal with fifteen minutes left gave the Inchicore side a brief lifeline, which they couldn't take. The crowd was disappointing, with an attendance of approximately 4,000 turning up at Dalymount. It isn't easy for a new team to build up support in the League of Ireland, but one would have expected more fans from the established St Pats supporters base.

The final was to be an all-Dublin affair for the first time in eight years. Shelbourne would provide Farm's opposition at Dalymount. Shels were desperate to make up for their FAI Cup final defeat to Hibs in 1973 after a replay at Flower Lodge. It would also be club legend Eric Barber's last appearance in a cup final for Shels and so it presented an opportunity to send him off on a high note. Shels manager Gerry Doyle was confident before the game, despite a poor league campaign which had seen Shels having to seek re-election to the league. Despite Gerry's confidence, he was quick to dismiss the notion that Home Farm had reached the final due to luck and the mistakes of their opponents, noting that in each round a different Home Farm player had come to the fore to win the day for the team. He also remarked that footballing style of Home Farm, under Bacuzzi's stewardship, had put pressure on even the very best of teams. For Dave Bacuzzi, the question was whether the fairy tale could continue in the final round. His unfancied team were now just ninety minutes from being FAI Cup winners and capping a magnificent achievement.

The final itself was decided by an early goal from Frank Devlin after just seven minutes, but the difference between the teams on the day could have been much greater. As Shels captain Paddy Dunning remarked after the game, the scoreline had treated Shels kindly. Despite their best efforts, Shels just couldn't seem to get going and when a rare chance fell to Eric Barber, Jim Grace in the Farm goal somehow managed to tip the ball over for the save of the match. For Home Farm and Dave Bacuzzi, it was a victory for teamwork and hard work, as they ran Shels to a stand-still and even though Bacuzzi had a wealth of success with Hibs, he remarked that this had been his finest moment in football: *'I always maintained that my first FAI Cup win with Cork Hibernians gave me some of my best moments in football, but this beats the lot'.*

Fifteen years after the Home Farm amateurs had lifted the trophy, the FAI Cup was set for another fairy tale. Leinster Senior League side St Francis FC, from The Liberties in Dublin, had seen off the challenge of League of Ireland clubs Kilkenny City, Cobh Ramblers and Newcastlewest on their way to a semi-final meeting against Bohemian FC at Tolka Park. The novel pairing attracted a crowd of over 8,000 to witness the event. With ten minutes left to play, the game was still scoreless, despite both sides having had chances. With a replay looking likely, it took a classic Roy of the Rovers moment to break the deadlock.

St Francis captain Martin Kerr had left the confines of his sick bed to play his part on this historic occasion for his club and it was his pass that started off the move which led to the winning goal. Stephen O'Reilly collected Kerr's pass on the right-hand side and took on the Bohs defence. As he slipped a neat pass into Brendan

Toner, it looked like the Bohs defence had any trouble covered. However, instead of clearing the danger, the Bohs players collided with each other and the ball broke to Toner. Quick as a flash, he squared the ball across the face of the goal and, as Bohs looked on, John Murphy nipped in to put the ball in the net. St Francis were 1-0 up, with nine minutes left to play and the dream was still alive. When referee Oliver Cooney blew the final whistle, Bohemian FC were finally convinced of St Francis's cup pedigree. The joy after the game from the happy St Francis fans was akin to them actually winning the trophy itself. Manager Pete Mahon refused to take any of the credit for his side's performance on the day, pointing out that he had only picked the side. It was typical of Mahon to deflect the praise away from himself, but his stamp of commitment, work ethic and belief were evident throughout the side.

St. Francis would now take on another surprise package as Bray Wanderers overcame Derry City in the other semi-final to set up a unique paring in the final. In addition, the FAI had made the decision earlier in the season to move the final from Dalymount Park to Lansdowne Road. Considering the two clubs now set to take part in the final, the FAI may have been rightly concerned about the shrewdness of their decision.

They need not have worried, however, as a crowd of over 29,000 descended on a sunny Lansdowne Road to see whether Francis could complete their unlikely run to cup glory. As the 23,000-seating capacity soon filled, the decision was made to open the terracing to the remainder of the fans, so, in a sea of green and white and on a badly rutted pitch, both sides found themselves ninety minutes away from potential glory.

As with all fairy tales, there is a villain and St Francis's villain came in the guise of Bray Wanderers' John Ryan. While the final will always be remembered for St Francis's participation in it, Ryan played a huge role in how it played out as he scored a cup final hat trick and joined Miah Dennehy from Hibs in the history books. His first goal came after a long free kick was partly cleared. As full back Trevor Coleman attempted to intercept the ball, he misjudged its flight and the ball hit his arm, resulting in a penalty kick for Bray Wanderers being awarded by referee Kevin O'Sullivan. Ryan took the kick and placed the ball past Matthews with ease.

His second goal was far more elegant. He curled a beautiful shot high into the corner of the net from twenty yards, after a good pass inside from McDermott found him in the right place. Two nil to Wanderers and the end of the road for

Francis. Ryan's hat trick goal came from the penalty spot after Nugent was fouled by goalkeeper Matthews. Ryan crisply dispatched the penalty kick to secure the matchball for himself and cap a glorious day for Bray.

For Mahon and his merry bunch, it was time for reflection on the cup run. Even though the final leg didn't go their way, they were happy to have played their part on the big occasion. Mahon remarked after the game, *'What we achieved today is the equivalent to winning the lottery ... We were as professional as we possibly could have been over the last three weeks.'* For Bray Wanderers manager Pat Devlin, talk turned to the fact that Bray would be in the European Cup Winners' Cup competition the following season. *'It's frightening to think we'll be in Europe.'* he quipped. Perhaps Europe was thankful that Bray had done them a favour.

Domination Provençale
Keeping it Country, 1975 to 1984

The late sixties and early seventies had seen a blue wave from Waterford dominate the league and, although Rovers still dominated the FAI Cup during this period, Waterford's success was empirical evidence that Irish football did not revolve around the clubs from the capital. Despite Bohemian FC's best attempts, the league would continue to be dominated by provincial clubs. However, while it had been mainly one club before, the period from 1975 to 1983 would see more clubs achieve success and a greater distribution of silverware around the country.

The late seventies and early eighties was a time of great characters and talent in League of Ireland management. Billy Young was making up for lost time by welcoming professionals and trophies to Bohemian FC. Amby Fogarty was bringing European football and his own brand of positive motivation to Athlone Town. Sean Thomas was back in football and back at Milltown, winning one more trophy with The Hoops, before making way for John Giles in 1977 with an unfulfilled vision of making Rovers a European force. Eoin Hand brought great success to Limerick and put Markets Field back on the map as a place where the visiting side got nothing. In the Midlands, Turlough O'Connor cast a spell of success and conjured up silverware for his home town club, Athlone Town. There was one man, however, that would bring unprecedented success to his club over this period. Others came and went, but this genial man from Derry revolutionised League of Ireland club management.

When Jim McLaughlin arrived at Oriel Park in late 1974, no one could have predicted how he would change the fortunes of this great club. Jim had spent most of his playing career in England with Shrewsbury Town and Swansea City, having started out in the game with his home-town club, Derry City. Playing as a striker, he scored over 100 league goals in England and managed to score on his international debut for Northern Ireland against Scotland at Windsor Park, Belfast. He spent twenty-five years in management in the League of Ireland, sandwiching his time at Rovers, Derry City and Drogheda United, with stints at Dundalk. And it was at Dundalk that the legend began.

Everything could have been so different for both Jim and Dundalk. In November 1974, Dundalk were not the only club trying to entice Jim to the League of Ireland. Sligo Rovers were also hot on the trail of the Derryman following the departure of Johnny Crossan. Dundalk were looking to replace John Smith and had initially tried to lure Paddy Mulligan back home from Crystal Palace. This idea floundered, however, because of the possibility that Palace would claim compensation for releasing Mulligan from his contract. Sligo had also inquired about the services of former Linfield manager Billy Sinclair, who was in Sydney at the time. In the end, Sligo went with Billy and Dundalk got their man.

Jim took over at Oriel in a player-manager capacity, with his first run out for The Lilywhites taking place at Tolka Park against Home Farm. His new club won 2–0, but the ease of their win was in stark contrast to the difficulty their new player-manager endured trying to get to the game. Living in Swansea and unable to get a flight to Dublin from Cardiff airport, Jim got in his car and drove to London. He managed to get a flight and arrived just in time for kick-off, nearly nine hours after leaving Swansea. As Peter Byrne pointed out in his match report, if McLaughlin showed this level of commitment in getting to the game, then Dundalk were in good hands.

Jim set to work at Oriel. As he noted himself, there were the makings of a good side in place, but in that first season, there would be a few bumps and setbacks along the way. The most notable of these was the club's exit from the FAI Cup in round two, after losing to Home Farm. Future Dundalk legend Dermot Keely played a significant role in helping Farm to overcome their more illustrious opponents that day in Tolka Park. Despite this, a finish of fifth in the league during Jim's first season in charge represented progress, even if it was just a one-place improvement on the previous season.

Jim set about adding to the squad for the new 1975–76 season. His additions saw a familiar face return to Oriel Park. Back in Lilywhite was Tommy McConville. Tommy had been transfer-listed by his club Shamrock Rovers the previous September, with a restrictive price tag of £6,000. Dundalk had made enquiries about Tommy's availability earlier in the year, but discussions with Rovers' Louis Kilcoyne had failed to yield a positive result for Dundalk. Now, nearly a year after that transfer listing, Tommy was coming home to Dundalk for a third spell at the club, having served time at Bangor, Waterford, Shamrock Rovers and a spell in the United States with the Washington Diplomats.

Tommy started out with local junior club Rangers and made his first team debut for Dundalk in 1964 against Cork Celtic. He spent most of the rest of that season in the reserves, but had the pleasure of picking up a Castrol Cup winners medal and playing in the company of his older brother Brian. Another McConville – his youngest brother Wally – was lining out for the Dundalk youth side during this time.

Tommy's first senior medal came for Dundalk in the Dublin City Cup final in 1968, when Rovers were defeated thanks to a Ben Hannigan goal. Liam Tuohy was a shrewd judge of a player and under his management at Dundalk Tommy became one of the league's best defenders, earning a senior international appearance for Ireland in 1971 during a tough assignment against Austria in Vienna, where Ireland were routed by six goals to nil.

A financial crisis at Dundalk in 1972 resulted in the sale of a number of their star players and Tommy found himself heading to Waterford, where a clutch of medals and five further senior international appearances followed. His displays for The Blues attracted attention from Manchester United, but a move never came about due to a dispute over transfer fees. This dispute led to Tommy moving to Rovers, where he was again under the management of Liam Tuohy, but it seemed that no matter where Tommy travelled, he was always destined to come back to Oriel Park.

Jim McLaughlin's excitement at securing Tommy for Dundalk was obvious: 'It isn't often a player of this class comes on the market. Together I think we can go places.' It was a big step for the Dundalk board as their recent financial woes would have still been fresh in the mind and although the final sum was considerably less than Rovers initial asking price of £6,000, the £2,000 paid represented a lot of belief in both McConville's ability and McLaughlin's talent as a manager.

Jim was starting to have an effect on the side and by the time Rovers were soundly beaten 5-2 at Oriel, thanks to four goals from Seamus McDowell, The Lilywhites were riding high in the league, second, just a point behind Finn Harps. Jim had recruited well. The Derry connection (himself and McDowell) was strengthened when he brought in Seanie McLoughlin. McLoughlin and McDowell in midfield made an immense contribution towards securing the title in 1975–76. Dundalk fans only caught a brief glimpse of Seanie McLoughlin's ability as he was tragically killed in a motor accident just a few months after picking up a league winners medal. Benefiting from the midfield engine room were Terry Flanagan and Sean Sheehy, both league winners with Bohs the previous season, Tony Cavanagh and Jimmy Dainty, while at the back, keeping goal, was the brilliant Richie Blackmore.

With five games to go, the title race appeared to be between Finn Harps and Dundalk. Harps had a comfortable north-west derby win at the Showgrounds against Sligo Rovers by four goals to two. Dundalk welcomed Waterford to Oriel and managed only a 1–1 draw. The pressure was beginning to show for the team, who were attempting to win their first league title in nearly a decade. Chance after chance was squandered against a Blues side with nothing to play for except pride. Facing into a County Louth Derby against Drogheda United the following week, the Waterford draw seemed, to the Dundalk fans, like a vital point that had been needlessly dropped.

Thankfully for the Dundalk faithful, a 4–1 win at Oriel the following Sunday settled their nerves and this, coupled with Finn Harps shock 2–1 defeat at home to Athlone Town, as good as guaranteed The Lilywhites the title. A 3–0 win at Milltown against a beleaguered Rovers moved Dundalk four points clear, while Harps' implosion continued at Tolka Park, where they drew 1–1 with Home Farm. Harps' season finally disintegrated when they were knocked out of the Cup in the semi-final the following weekend by the other County Louth team, Drogheda United.

There was a carnival atmosphere at Oriel as a huge crowd came out to see if Dundalk could secure the title. Amid bands playing and presentations of player-of-the-year awards, the Hibs team was intent on spoiling the party. In fact, Jim McLaughlin nearly spoiled the party for himself when the player-manager was shown a red card for a tackle on Hibs's Dave Kirby towards the end. In what was a tense match for the hosts, it took Terry Flanagan to settle the nerves and deliver the title with a sixty-fifth-minute winner. The board's faith in Jim McLaughlin had been rewarded, but for Jim this was just the beginning.

Over at the Showgrounds in Sligo, things had been tough for many seasons. Sligo's one and only league championship had been secured back in 1937. Although they had failed to secure Jim McLaughlin as manager, they had succeeded in convincing former Linfield manager Billy Sinclair to leave Sydney for Sligo. Billy signed for the Bit O' Red as player-manager, after numerous spells at other clubs since joining Greenock Morton as a sixteen-year-old, including Chelsea, Glentoran, Kilmarnock and Linfield. After a short spell as manager at Linfield, where he won three trophies but not the league or Irish Cup, he moved to the Marconi club in Sydney. The pressure to win at Linfield had been intense and he recalled years later that managing Linfield was easy, as long as you kept winning. An Irish Cup final defeat to deadly rivals Glentoran in 1973 didn't improve Billy's case at Windsor Park.

Sligo Rovers' first outing at the Showgrounds under Billy's management didn't seem to signal any great change in fortunes. They went down 3–1 to north-west rivals Finn Harps. Billy's first season saw Sligo finish at the bottom, winning just seven league matches that season. There were, however, the foundations of a team to build on, with Tony Stenson, Mick Leonard, Paul McGee and Tony Fagan all at the club. Billy's first full season would see a slight improvement, with a tenth-place finish, but they won a game less, triumphing just six times in league competition.

The turnaround during the 1976–77 season was truly seismic. Sligo travelled to the Cup holders, Bohemian FC, in late October to play their fourth league match. The early league table showed Drogheda United with a 100 per cent record and nothing of note separating Sligo in second place and St Pats in tenth. Sligo went on to record their biggest win at Dalymount in five years, beating The Gypsies by three goals to nil.

Sean Pender in *The Irish Times* noted that while there wasn't any standout individual performance from Rovers, it was the balance of the side, coupled with their flair and penchant for attacking football, that would see Rovers enjoy a good season and win friends and admirers across the league. Billy Sinclair wasn't interested in winning admirers – he wanted to win trophies – but this admiration would help build confidence amongst the players and fans alike.

Two successive league defeats checked the Rovers fans enthusiasm. Even the return from retirement of David Pugh in defence could not prevent a home defeat to Pats. It was going to be a rollercoaster season for the Bit O' Red. Following that defeat against Pats, Rovers found their groove and went on a goal spree, beating

Home Farm and Athlone Town on successive weeks by five goals to nil. The defeat of Athlone was noted by the knowledgeable Mels crowd as one of the best performances by a visiting club in many years.

Next there was a top-of-the-table clash against surprise leaders Drogheda United. Willie Roche, the Drogheda player, was in confident form before the game at the Showgrounds. 'This is a nightmare for the critics', he commented, knowing that not many would have counted on these two clubs leading the race for the title at that stage of the season. Roche felt that if they could achieve some good results over the following few weeks, then United would be thereabouts at the finish line. This sentiment was qualified by Peter Byrne in *The Irish Times*, who pointed out that while Drogheda had done well to date, they had trickier fixtures left to negotiate, whereas Sligo had encountered some tough fixtures in the early rounds of the championship. Michael O'Boyle, Sligo's club secretary was effusive in his praise of Billy Sinclair and how he had turned the club into real title contenders: *'We have acquired maturity ... I am satisfied there will be no collapse'.* Billy was used to pressure, but perhaps a club official could have kept this kind of remark for the committee room and not a newspaper.

The game itself was decided on a moment of controversy, as a hotly disputed penalty was awarded to Rovers with the scores level at a goal each. The huge home crowd's excitement had been dampened a little as Drogheda took the lead through Cathal Muckian, despite setting out their tactics to defend from the start. Graham Fox was on hand to score from a Paul McGee corner and bring the sides level. McGee was also involved in the controversial second goal. He took a short corner to Paul Fielding, whose shot was trapped between Ian Hines's hip and the post on the goal line. Referee John Carpenter pointed to the spot. Up stepped Paul McGee to take the kick, which was saved by Leo Byrne, but the rebound was knocked into the net by the onrushing McGee to give Rovers the lead. Mick Leonard was on hand to make it 3–1 with twenty minutes left and secure the two points for Sligo.

Jimmy McAlinden, Drogheda's manager, was rueful after the game: 'This was the second game we have lost away from home in the championship and on each occasion we were beaten by a doubtful penalty'. Chris Rutherford and Tony Stenson came in for praise for their defensive duties and it was said that their ability and form were the backbone of the Sligo Rovers team in their march onwards in the championship. Added to this were the thirty goals which Sligo had scored. Bass, who were the league's sponsors, had offered an incentive of £500 to the club who could score thirty goals by Christmas. The honour of achieving this feat fell to Mick Leonard in a 1–0 win against Albert Rovers at the Showgrounds. Leonard was described as 'practically kicking himself over the line in his willingness to score'.

Dundalk, who were well off the pace this season in the title race, decided to remind everyone of their ability when Rovers came to Oriel Park after Christmas. The Lilywhites sent the Bit O' Red home with a flea in their ears after a three one demolition secured two points for the home team. The weather was next to take issue with Rovers title credentials. In a Rovers home fixture against Waterford, the match was abandoned with thirteen minutes left to play due to bad light. The match had been put back by fifteen minutes on a day described as 'one of the vilest days of the decade', on which the Showgrounds was hit by lightning, hailstorms and icy rain. The match was scoreless at the time, despite the best attempts of Paul McGee.

McGee was awarded a penalty after being fouled in the box and decided to take the spot kick himself. In goal for Waterford, facing the penalty, was Peter Thomas. Thomas decided to take up the role of groundsman and walked from his goal line to clear the ball of any hail, snow or dust that would hinder McGee from giving Rovers the lead.

Thomas was booked for his good Samaritan efforts, but his antics seemed to do the trick for Waterford. McGee seemed to be enraged by Thomas's gamesmanship and in an attempt to fire both Thomas and the ball in to the net, cracked the penalty kick off the upright. The ball flew twenty yards away, leaving a smug Thomas in goal, a red-faced McGee and a freezing crowd who were no doubt wondering what all the fuss was about.

A 4–1 cup exit at the hands of Limerick came as a shock considering the game was at the Showgrounds and may have served to re-focus minds on the championship. A vital 1–0 league win at Inchicore and then at home against their cup slayers, Limerick, kept Rovers on top of the championship table, with five games to go.

Finally, in mid-April, the day of reckoning arrived for the Bit O' Red. Shamrock Rovers stood in the way of the League Championship. It was not a vintage Shamrock Rovers team but for every nervous Sligo fan those green and white hooped shirts probably seemed filled by world beaters. Fans flooded into the Showgrounds from early that afternoon, entertained by the Sligo Pipe Band and eager to see the return of the league championship pennant for the first time in forty years.

Despite an early goal lead, it seemed that Sligo were intent on inflicting more mental torture on their fans as they forgot to play the kind of football that had brought them to this point in the competition. The Hoops sensed the unease in the crowd and their football was rewarded with an equalising goal. It was time for Billy Sinclair and his men to show their mettle. Again, the man to take charge was Paul McGee. His corner was headed home by another man who never shirked hard work, Chris Rutherford. The score was now two one, cue scenes of delirium. McGee scored a third goal towards the end and the pressure was off. The dream had been realised and a turnabout of epic proportions had been achieved by Billy Sinclair and Sligo Rovers in just three years.

After the game, Sinclair acknowledged that the pressure had affected the way Sligo had played: 'When you are out in front for so long, the pressure becomes nail-biting'. However, he was also quick to praise the character of the team, which, he felt, had seen them over the line: *'When you break it down, successful football is all about character and courage. This team showed that they had both assets in abundance'.* They also had some wonderful footballers, like Rutherford and Stenson at the heart of the defence. Up front, Mick Leonard and Gary Hulmes grabbed twenty-four goals and were ably assisted by local hero Paul 'Ski' McGee.

However, for one man, that league-winning season meant so much more. Tony Fagan had experienced the hard times with Sligo. He had made his debut ten years before, against Shamrock Rovers, as a sixteen-year-old local boy. Tony stood by Sligo during dismal campaigns, re-election to the league and FAI Cup humiliation to non-league opposition. In a career that would see him play over 590 times for Sligo, it was fitting that he should win a league winners medal for all the courage, heart and determination shown throughout his career in red. He would have one more big day out with Sligo, but for now a league winners medal washed all the previous disappointments away.

The FAI Cup final win in 1977 saw another trophy return to Dundalk's Oriel Park, but the club fell away in that season's league race, finishing ten points behind eventual champions Sligo Rovers. A Synan Badish goal in a replayed semi-final against St Pats would be enough to see Dundalk through to the showpiece against Limerick at Dalymount Park. Dundalk's hero in the final was Terry Flanagan, who scored twice to seal a 2-0 win. The first goal came from a low McLaughlin cross into the box, which was swept home by Flanagan. Despite Limerick's best attempts to get back on terms, they finally succumbed to defeat with three minutes left to play. Flanagan won a corner and the delivery from Seamus McDowell was bravely met by Flanagan, who headed the ball almost out of Limerick goalkeeper Kevin Fitzpatrick's hands and into the net. Jim McLaughlin was pleased with the outcome, if not the performance, remarking after the game that, *'I would like Dundalk to have won in a more positive fashion but after losing so many games we ought to have won in the Championship it was great to get this one'.*

The Dublin clubs managed to regain some pride in 1977–78, when Billy Young's Bohemian FC took the title to Dalymount for the second time in four seasons. Bohs great rivals, Shamrock Rovers, won the cup final thanks to a Steve Lynex goal, which helped them see off Sligo Rovers. This cup win was the only silverware to head to Milltown during John Giles' reign.

While Louis Kilcoyne's aspiration of turning Rovers into a full-time team with an academy of excellence for young, upcoming footballers was commendable, it would prove difficult to put into practice. The legendary Giles came back to Dublin, bringing with him former internationals Ray Treacy, Paddy Mulligan and Eamon Dunphy, but the success the idea promised never came to fruition over the six years that Giles was at the club. Giles had also taken up a role at Vancouver Whitecaps during his spell at Rovers and it was felt that it had become difficult for him to concentrate on both clubs, given that their seasons began to overlap. Giles left Milltown in February 1983, with Noel Campbell taking over team selection.

The tragedy of this period is that one of our greatest footballers and the country's most successful club could not make the full-time football project a sustainable reality in the League of Ireland. It would be nearly twenty-five years later before anyone would try full-time football again at home. However, given the protagonists involved in 1976 at Rovers, it was hard to see how anyone else could succeed where these luminaries had failed.

Jim McLaughlin had led his team to win two trophies in his first two seasons at Oriel, but 1978-79 would eclipse all that had gone before. New faces were now at the club: Dermot Keely, Paddy Dunning and Martin Lawlor joined Tommy McConville in the defence, earning themselves the tag, 'The Mean Machine'. Leo Flanagan, Sean Byrne, Hilary Carlyle and Cathal Muckian were all added to refresh the attacking set-up, spearheaded by Mick Lawlor, as Jim planned another raid on the League championship.

Jim's description of Dermot Keely took some working out: *'He couldn't kick, couldn't head or couldn't pass'*, Jim commented, but one thing Dermot Keely could do was pick up winners' medals. Five league championships, five FAI Cup wins – and this was just as a player. There could be no doubt that Jim's remark was definitely tongue in cheek. Dermot won a FAI Cup winners medal with Home Farm before moving on to play for St Pats. After three unsuccessful seasons at Inchicore, he joined former Saints Leo Flanagan and Sean Byrne at Oriel Park. While at Oriel, he would be a key part of the infamous back line, which included Dunning, Lawlor and McConville in front of Blackmore in goal. The 'Mean Machine' conceded just thirteen league goals in his second season, but fell agonisingly short of the championship as Limerick beat them to glory by a point. The real highlight of Dermot's three-season spell came during the club's European Cup adventure in 1979, where once again Dermot's commitment and dedication showed as Dundalk fell just a goal short of the European Cup quarter-finals.

Dermot went on to have great success with Jim McLoughlin when the two met up again some years later at Shamrock Rovers. In addition to his playing success, Dermot became known as a manager of hard-working teams that delivered league titles. Rovers, Dundalk and Shelbourne would all taste league-title success under Keely's guidance.

Dundalk opened their 1978-79 league campaign by remaining undefeated for the first twelve games, until a loss by two goals to one was incurred at Ballybofey. They bounced back the following week, with a 2-0 win over Cork Celtic at Oriel, but some commentators were questioning this Dundalk side's ability, despite their league position as joint leaders with Bohemian FC. However, the mettle of this Dundalk side shone during a mid-January visit to the Showgrounds, where they came from behind to beat Sligo Rovers by two goals to one. A tough home win on a snow-covered Oriel pitch against Cork Alberts further dispelled any concerns about the teams appetite for hard work.

Pats were dispatched in the FAI Cup in February a week before the top two met at Oriel. Bohemian FC were taken apart by a wonderfully efficient Dundalk team and although they had just Paddy Dunning's goal to show for their efforts, it was the team's performance rather than the scoreline which had people talking. Jim McLaughlin had once again been proved right as his mix of players was finally gelling together into one of the most formidable sides in League of Ireland history.

By St Patrick's Day, Dundalk were just four points from the title, after a 3-0 hammering of Shelbourne at Tolka Park. They were still in the FAI Cup, too, after avenging their earlier league defeat against Finn Harps with a 2-0 win at Oriel in the quarter-final. The semi-final win against Cork Alberts kept them on course for an historic double. The league title was secured at Flower Lodge in what would be Cork Celtic's last match in the League of Ireland. Amby Fogarty was back at Celtic, answering the call of his former club, which had come on hard times. The financial situation was perilous for Celtic and the juxtaposition between them and Dundalk was illustrated by the empty terracing at Flower Lodge that Sunday afternoon. Celtic's fans had stayed away and by July of that year Cork Celtic had been expelled from the league.

Jim McLaughlin enjoyed a second league title in four years with Dundalk. The first leg of a unique club double was secured and Waterford was now all that stood between Dundalk and history. McLaughlin commented that Dundalk's success had been a reward for the board, *'who did not hesitate to spend when necessary and players who did not shirk their work'*. These words must have been hard for Amby Fogarty to hear. Hard work, enthusiasm, commitment were all bywords for Fogarty's teams and football beliefs, but as he looked around Flower Lodge during his last League of Ireland appearance, it must have seemed to him that sometimes the obstacles are too high to overcome.

Dundalk was rapidly gaining a reputation as a club to be reckoned with and their place in the history books was secured when they overcame Waterford by two goals to nil in the FAI Cup final at Dalymount Park. The first goal was somewhat controversial as a linesman's flag initially indicated that Dundalk forward Cathal Muckian was offside. This decision was overruled by the referee, Paddy Daly, and the resulting passage of play finished with Sean Byrne firing past Peter Thomas in the Waterford goal to give The Lilywhites the lead. It was typical of the luck that Waterford had in the competition at this time and a rueful Peter Thomas said after the game, *'I still blame myself for the goal. I saw the shot all the way and I ought to have stopped it'*. The game and the double was put beyond all doubt in injury time, when Hilary Carlyle ran onto a Keely clearance and beat Thomas for Dundalk's second. It was a season of glory for the Oriel men and it seemed like Dundalk could go on to dominate for a long time to come. Jim had put together a cracking outfit and the team would get another chance to test their mettle in Europe the following season.

Until Shamrock Rovers qualified for the Europa Cup group stage in 2011, it was Dundalk who held the domestic bragging rights for European adventures. One particular season would define that claim. It came in 1979 in a series of games in the European Cup against Linfield, Hibernians of Malta and Celtic.

The date 29 August 1979 will live long in the memory of anyone who was in Oriel Park or Dundalk town itself that day. A European Cup game between the League of Ireland champions and the Irish League champions would always be tense. However, in the wake of the Mountbatten murder and Warrenpoint bombing, the match had been turned into a tinderbox. Linfield were the visitors and the behaviour of some of their so-called fans on that autumn evening must surely rank amongst the worst acts of hooliganism, thuggery and wanton vandalism ever seen on the day of a football match. Flag-burning, provocative songs and stone-throwing were the order of the day.

The game itself was almost incidental. Warren Feeny gave Linfield the lead just after half-time, the start of which had been delayed due to the ongoing running battle on the terrace between the Gardaí and Linfield hooligans. The Linfield players and their manager Roy Coyle eventually had to come out and appeal to their fans to behave before the game could restart. The fighting resulted in dozens of injuries, with Peter Byrne describing the dressing rooms as looking more like a field hospital than a changing area.

Commentating for RTÉ Radio, Philip Greene was more like a war correspondent than a football reporter, describing the scene as one hooligan tries to scale a flag pole to avoid six Gardaí trying to arrest him. Later during the game, while a number of hooligans are being carried away, one of them catches Greens's eye, *'by jove it takes four guys to carry him off. He is bucking there and he has no intention of going...he is some tough guy, he is. He is gone and half his scarf is gone with him'*. As the fear and commotion raged all round Greene still managed another classic turn of phrase when remarking that 'the cocky bravado of the stone trowing hooligans' had been quelled by Gardaí, 'neck and crop and out they go'.

While Greene is describing the scene of people standing up in front of him and moving about, there is suddenly a big cheer in the background. Cue vintage Philip Greene: *'A goal, a goal ... somebody says the ball is in the net ... But what has happened, I don't know. Liam Devine has scored apparently and I couldn't tell you, because I couldn't see it'*. The confusion went on for a few minutes because Greene could still not see the game due to the celebrations of the Dundalk fans and was unsure whether the match had been restarted from the centre circle.

This led to another gem from the voice of the League of Ireland: 'that was about the only time in my life that I myself couldn't feel satisfied with the scoreline'. While the words and phrases may not have passed into sporting history, like those of many of his contemporaries, the ability he had to convey a scene is still in evidence.

The game finished 1–1, but the battle was far from over. Outside the ground, riots popped up between some local youths and Linfield hooligans. The Linfield hooligans also decided that local houses and shops were now 'fair game' for their rampage and set about destroying whatever lay in their path. The situation remained tense in the town for a number of hours after the final whistle and over a dozen Linfield hooligans were arrested and detained by Gardaí. The atmosphere was summed up by Dundalk captain Mick Lawlor, who described the game 'the most frightening experience of my life ... With so much passion on the terraces it was impossible to concentrate on playing football'. 'Passion' was a generous way of putting it, but from a gentleman like Mick Lawlor, it was probably the strongest word he could bring himself to use.

UEFA took a dim view of the situation. In addition to the heavy fine levied on Linfield, the club was ordered to play the return game, which had been intended for Windsor Park, away from home and outside the UK. Haarlem in The Netherlands was to be the scene of one of Dundalk's best European performances. They beat Linfield 2–0 on the night, thanks to a brace of goals from Cathal Muckian.

Mick Lawlor tells a story about the team having nothing to do in Haarlem the night before the game. The players were feeling a bit cooped up and a delegation went to see Mick about getting out for a bit of relaxation. Jim McLaughlin was approached and he agreed that the team should head into Amsterdam with two provisos: firstly, that Mick Lawlor go along with them and, secondly, that their curfew would be one o'clock. So there it was: on the night before a big game, the lads went out in Amsterdam to let off a bit of steam. This was classic McLaughlin: ahead of his time and still with his finger on the pulse of the players. I wonder what could be learned from these tactics in today's micromanaged world of football.

Hibernians of Malta were next up for Dundalk. Hillary Carlyle and Liam Devine gave The Lilywhites a 2–0 advantage after the first leg at Oriel, but it was a game that Dundalk probably felt they should have won by a greater margin. Chances for Keely, Flanagan and Dunning were all missed and a goal for Muckian disallowed. The return leg was a little more difficult for Dundalk, but they managed to scrape through, losing 1-0 on the night, but winning 2-1 on aggregate. There was a brilliant line in the *Dundalk Democrat* about that return game in Malta: 'It was like playing marbles in the grass against a grasshopper, because the grasshopper would have been playing at home and who else could play marbles in the grass'.

Next on Dundalk's European odyssey was Celtic. The first leg in Parkhead was one of the most memorable nights in League of Ireland history as a cobbled-together team managed to trade blows with Celtic, just losing out 3-2. McCluskey and McDonald had put The Bhoys two up and it looked like it would be a long night for Dundalk until Cathal Muckian got one back from a header before Tommy Burns restored the two-goal advantage. A turning point came after an hour when, thanks to good work by Dermot Keely and Leo Flanagan, Mick Lawlor got through one on one with Peter Latchford in the Celtic goal. As Latchford came out, Mick nonchalantly clipped the ball over his head and into the net from thirty odd yards.

Back to Oriel for the return, which proved to be a night of drama. A crowd of 17,000 crammed into Oriel to see early chances for Celtic before a Mick Lawlor header went just wide. However, the night would be remembered for one moment which fell to Tommy McConville. Pop Flanagan's free kick came into the area and was flicked on. The ball came to Tommy, but with the goal at his mercy, he just could not manage to connect with the ball and turn it in to the net . That was the chance and it slipped past Dundalk. A trip to the Bernabeu would have been their reward, but it was a European adventure like no other before and was probably the highlight of Jim McLaughlin's tenure at Oriel Park. Tommy summed up the spirit and belief of that Dundalk side when he said, ' I was never afraid of anybody when playing in Europe for Dundalk. Apart from Keely!' While Dundalk had good forwards, it was clearly the team's strong defence that made a major contribution to their success during this period. With a goalkeeper and back four of Richie Blackmore, Martin Lawlor, Paddy Dunning, Dermot Keely and Tommy McConville, it was probably one of the best defences ever seen in League of Ireland history.

It had been twenty years since Limerick had won their only league title under manager Sonny Price. Since then, a sole FAI Cup win against Drogheda United and a name change to Limerick United in 1977 had been the extent of the excitement at Markets Field. Limerick chairman Michael Webb had great ambition for the club and, after achieving a record points total the 1978-79 season, probably felt that the appointment of the experienced Eoin Hand would help Limerick bridge the gap with Dundalk, Drogheda United and Bohemian FC.

Hand had made his name with Drumcondra in the late sixties before securing a move to Portsmouth, where he would play over 250 times for the club. Eoin also represented Ireland at senior level on twenty occasions.

Hand's impact as player-manager was felt immediately and it was Cork United that were on the receiving end in an early league fixture at Markets Field, when Hand scored all four goals in the 4–1 victory. The victory meant it was three wins from three and a good start to the campaign for The Blues. It was a good start for Hand too, who went on to pick up the player-of-the-month award for September.

A big crowd turned out at Markets Filed to see this rejuvenated Limerick United side take on their first real test of the season when Bohemian FC came to visit. Once again, Hand was the main man as he scored the only goal to win the game in injury time for Limerick, maintaining their 100 per cent start to the new season. In fact, in their first seven league games, Limerick United dropped just one point in a 3–3 draw against Thurles Town.

By mid-November, there were no signs of the Limerick challenge fading away and the interest in the club's fortunes was such that their top-of-the-table clash against Dundalk at Markets Field was an all-ticket affair. Hand was leading the charge and also leading the goalscorers' charts, with seven goals all from his midfield position. In conjunction with six goals from Tony Morris, the pair had accounted for thirteen of the twenty goals Limerick had scored to date. The league champions were put away by two goals to nil and now there was a clear gap of two points at the top of the table, with Limerick looking down on those below. Limerick again grabbed victory late, with both goals against Dundalk coming in the last six minutes.

This, coupled with late wins against Bohemian FC and Finn Harps, led *Irish Times* writer Peter Byrne to label Limerick the 'Harry Wragg' of football teams. Wragg had been a successful jockey in Britain and Ireland, with a noted style of holding back or preserving his horses for a late challenge towards the end of races. For Hand and Limerick, it didn't matter when they scored, as long as they were in the lead at the final whistle and so far this had generally been the case for Limerick United.

By December, the title was looking like a real possibility and Hand thought it best to take out what could be described as an insurance policy against any derailment of Limerick's plans to bring the title back to Markets Field. In an unusual move, Hand contacted officials from his previous club, Portsmouth, and managed to secure a reserve of players from Portsmouth, if the need should arise for Limerick on their title quest. 'At the moment, I am happy enough with our resources, but any team with designs on the championship must be prepared for any contingency', he said. Hand was already showing the attention to detail and preparation skills which would land him the Ireland manager's job in a few short years.

Halfway through the league programme, Limerick were three points clear and things were looking good for The Blues. Players like Kevin Fitzpatrick, Des Kennedy, Pat Nolan and Ger Duggan were all playing vital roles alongside Hand.

Kevin Fitzpatrick played in goal for Limerick for twenty-two seasons, earning himself a reputation as one of the best keepers in the league and one of the longest serving. Making over 670 appearances for the club, he also won one international cap for Ireland against Czechosolvakia in Prague in 1969.

While Kevin was keeping them out, Des Kennedy was putting them in at the other end, with help from Tony Morris and Gerry Duggan. Des will forever be linked with the two goals he scored in both legs of Limerick's 1980–81 European Cup against Real Madrid. His goal at Lansdowne Road gave Limerick a shock lead. A Gerry Duggan header came to Des and he coolly slipped the ball under the Real keeper and in to the net. The delight was written all over Des's face as he wheeled off to towards the West Stand blowing kisses to the crowd. His goal at Estadio Bernabeu came as consolation with Limerick crashing to a 5-1 defeat.

When former Limerick manager Ewan Fenton signed Pat Nolan from junior club Wembley Rovers in 1974, it was a dream come through for the local lad. Pat played a vital role in Limerick's success and holds the distinction of having scored the only goal in European competition for Limerick at Markets Field, against AZ67 Alkmaar of the Netherlands. The strength of the Limerick team was being felt across the league and it was clear that Hand's appointment had been a fantastic move for Limerick United.

A trip to Oriel in the FAI Cup resulted in a 1-0 victory for Limerick and left The Lilywhites to focus on the championship race. There was talk of a double on Shannonside and despite having been troubled by St Pats, who took three league points off Limerick that season, it seemed that there was little by way of opposition to Limerick's march towards domestic silverware. Dundalk kept up the chase to the end and, with just five games to go in the campaign, the sides met again at

Oriel Park. Revenge was sweet for Jim McLaughlin as Dundalk secured a 1–0 victory thanks to the recently returned Brian Duff from Liverpool.

Waterford United proved to be the double-dream destroyers when they defeated Limerick in the semi-final of the cup after a replay at Milltown. Waterford were 3–0 up at half-time and despite a spirited comeback from Eoin Hand's team, the final score was 3–2 and Waterford progressed to play St Pats in the final. That final finally saw Waterford bring the cup back to Kilcohan Park and rewarded veteran goalkeeper Peter Thomas a cup winners medal at last.

The penultimate league match for Limerick would be their last at home as they crushed Home Farm by four goals to nil. This left them just one point away from claiming the title. Dundalk kept up their slim hopes by beating Sligo Rovers 3–2 at Oriel, but it was all in Limerick's hands now. However, Eoin Hand spoke a word of caution before their trip to St Mel's for the final game: *'There is no way we will approach the Athlone game in the hope of salvaging a draw, for that would be to court disaster'.* While the scoreline against the Farm had been emphatic, it had also been obvious that an element of fear and nervousness had crept into Limerick's play and this was having an effect on even the most experienced of players.

At Mels, it fell to Tony Meany to secure the title. He scored from the penalty spot to level the game after Michael O'Connor had given Athlone the lead. It was Athlone who won a lot admirers on the day for their style of play and their manager, Turlough O'Connor, was pleased with what he saw and how his side managed to contain and even outplay Limerick. It was a hint of things to come at Mels. For now, though, all the glory belonged to Limerick as the title was secured in front of an enormous travelling support, decked out in blue and white and waving flags and banners. 'Our Eoin League', proclaimed one of the slogans.

Hand was absolute delighted by the achievement of his side: 'This is the most satisfying moment in my entire career. I won a few medals as a schoolboy with Stella Maris but this league one becomes the most important I ever won'. Hand also commented on the team's belief and spirit when it came to digging in and getting over the line when trailing to O'Connor's goal for Athlone. Summing up the exhaustion of winning the league, he finished by saying, *'Now that it is all over, we are going to take a complete break from the game, but not until after we have had a few drinks in Limerick tonight'.*

Limerick United and Eoin Hand would have one more big day out when they secured the FAI Cup in 1982 against Bohemian FC, thanks to a Brendan Storan goal. For Bohs manager Billy Young, it was hard to take as his young side had fought valiantly on all fronts that season, only to end up empty-handed at the finish line. For Kevin Fitzpatrick, though, in goal for the last time for Limerick, it was a fitting end to a long career with Limerick. Hand was already combining the role of Limerick player-manager with that of Ireland team coach.

The strain of trying to combine both roles began to tell and in February 1983, Hand resigned his position as Limerick manager to concentrate on Ireland alone. It had been a wonderful period for football in Limerick and resulted in a league title, the FAI Cup and memorable European nights against Real Madrid, Southampton and AZ67 Alkmaar.

Finally in this period of league domination, there was one more club ready to put up its hand and keep it country as far as the silverware was concerned. Turlough O'Connor had done it all as a player with Dundalk and Bohemian FC and now he was back in his home town of Athlone as manager. What he had seen towards the end of the 1979–80 season convinced him that he had a side with the capability of challenging for honours. Things were about to get interesting again for football in the Midlands.

It was a cracking Athlone Town side that included players such as veteran goalkeeper Mick Smyth, Turlough's brothers Michael and Padraig, Larry Wyse, Denis Clarke, Frank Devlin, Stefan Feniuk, Noel Larkin and Eugene 'Pooch' Davis. They weren't short on flair either and, with Turlough in charge, they were always going to be pleasing to the eye. As well as winning the league championship that season, they also broke some league records, including a record number of points accumulated and a record number of goals scored. Athlone dropped just nine points in thirty matches and ran out winners in twenty-three league games. They scored sixty-seven league goals, of which Davis got twenty-three to finish top scorer in the league and Michael O'Connor got sixteen.

The crowds flocked to Mels to see this entertaining and freescoring side. One such crowd witnessed those perennial challengers Dundalk put to the sword with goals from Clarke and Davis. It said a lot for Dundalk and Jim McLaughlin that The Lilywhites were showing no signs of becoming one of those clubs that pops up for two or three seasons and then disappears; last year's runners-up still needed to be reckoned with. But The Lilywhite's efforts were not good enough that day at Mels and Athlone rolled on to face the champions , Limerick United, in their next game at Mels - or so they thought.

Athlone were all set for their biggest crowd of the season. The fixture between the sides at the end of the last campaign had seen Limerick crowned champions at Mels, but both sides were seeing things differently by December 1980. Limerick had appealed to the League Committee for the fixture to be postponed as they were enduring an unprecedented bout of injury and illness at the club. The committee were of the view that the fixture should proceed as scheduled and at 2.30pm on Sunday, both the Athlone Town team and the referee reported for duty, but alas Limerick United did not appear. The committee called an emergency meeting in Dublin the following day. In an ironic twist and in typical League of Ireland administrative fashion, the meeting had to be called off as the provincial board members had not had enough notice to travel to Dublin. The meeting was rescheduled for eight days later.

With speculation growing about the outcome of any meeting, Athlone Town official Seamus O'Brien let it be known that Athlone would not seek to have the points awarded for the fixture, but would look for compensation. 'There is only one way of winning a Championship - on the field. And to that extent, we will welcome the chance of beating Limerick at St Mel's Park', he said. Tough talk - and probably an indication of the confidence there was in this Athlone Town team. As it turned out, the committee decided that a six-week ban for Limerick United manager Eoin Hand, accompanied by a fine of £1,000 was in order, and the fixture was re-arranged for St Stephen's Day. The game itself, when it was played, ended in a scoreless draw, but the scoreline didn't do justice to the efforts of both sides. The game lived up to the billing, even though it was short on goals.

Wins over Thurles Town, UCD and Galway Rovers came either side of an FAI Cup exit to Finn Harps at Ballybofey. By the start of March, a 1-0 league win against Harps at Finn Park put Athlone in the record books for twenty-two unbeaten league games and broke the record which had been held by Dundalk. The two sides met at the end of March in a fixture which would have a huge influence on the destination of the league title. For all Athlone's style and verve, Jim McLaughlin's Dundalk were still hanging in there, but there could be no doubt at the final whistle just who now was assuming the mantle of best in the league. A 3-0 demolition of Dundalk in front of the Oriel Park faithful was laid on by Athlone. While the game was marred by some crowd trouble, which was quickly sorted out by Gardaí, there was no such animosity at the end of the game, as Jim McLaughlin was on hand to welcome the Athlone Town players back to their dressing room and offer his congratulations on a fine victory. The game was won on the back of goals from Davis, Michael O'Connor and Conway, with Davis's goal bringing him to twenty-one for the season, just one short of the *Soccer Reporter's* prize of £1,500 for the player who scored twenty-two.

Now needing just two points to secure the title, Athlone welcomed Shamrock Rovers to Mels in front of a huge crowd, fully expecting a victory. Much to the crowd's disappointment, Mick Savage stepped up to equalise for Rovers and the game ended in a draw. It seemed that the football gods wanted one more piece of drama. Athlone would go to Markets Field and Limerick United to try win the title.

It turned out to be a great day for Athlone Town as the team secured the title by two goals to nil. Both goals were scored by Eugene Davis, securing him the *Soccer Reporter* prize money. Turlough O'Connor was rightly proud of his team and their achievement, noting it was a great day for the Midlands.

The title had been won with a game to spare and the last fixture at home to Waterford extended Athlone's unbeaten run to twenty-seven league games. All that was left was for Padraig O'Connor to accept the league trophy amid great scenes at the final whistle. It was an historic moment for Athlone Town, who had been playing league football for just twelve years, since 1969.

More success was to follow for O'Connor and Athlone Town as they won the League Cup the following season and retained that trophy in 1983. Dundalk and Jim McLaughlin were to have their revenge in 1981–82, when they beat a revitalised Shamrock Rovers side to the title by four points. However, Athlone came back with a bang in 1982–83 and, with just one league defeat in twenty-four league games, coming against Shelbourne, they had the title wrapped up by the end of March. Typical of a side coached by Turlough O'Connor, their emphasis was on attacking play; they scored over sixty league goals that season. O'Connor was quick to rubbish suggestions that his side were defensive and pointed to this statistic.

At the end of the season, the only statistic which mattered was the league table and that showed that Athlone were far and away the best team, finishing sixteen points ahead of Drogheda United, who were in second place. Added to the league medals for the Athlone players was a nice windfall as the side had backed themselves to win the championship at the start of the season, at odds of 20/1. *'We just could not let those sort of odds go by without having a flutter'*, O'Connor said, with a smile.

Sligo Rovers would bring an end to this period of provincial dominance when they won the FAI Cup at last against Bohemian FC, in the rain at Dalymount Park. Barry Murphy put Bohs ahead. Tony Stenson scored a cracking goal to equalise for the Bit O' Red, connecting first time with a low ball into the penalty box to give Dermot O'Neill no chance on his near post. The winner was equally spectacular: a long ball out of defence came to Harry McLoughlin, who got on the ball and cut inside to the edge of the box. After a quick glance up, he curled a beautiful effort over the head of O'Neill and into the far right-hand corner of the net for one of the best FAI Cup final goals seen at Dalymount. It was Sligo Rovers legend Tony Fagan who was presented with the trophy to bring back to the Showgrounds for the first time in the club's history.

This period was an exciting time for League of Ireland football and although Dundalk were the dominant team of the era, those other clubs that rose to the challenge brought with them a distinctive style and a freshness which the league had badly needed. Titles for clubs like Sligo Rovers and Limerick United helped to encourage support at these venues, which had for too long been starved of success. Athlone Town brought delight to the Midlands and although clubs like Drogheda United and Finn Harps failed to collect silverware, they certainly contributed to the countrywide aspect of League of Ireland football.

Four in a Row-vers Say Farewell to Milltown Rovers All Over, 1984 to 1987

When the gates closed for the last time on 12 April 1987, no one could have foreseen the monumental impact that the decision to sell Glenmalure Park would have on Shamrock Rovers. The Hoops had been playing football at the Milltown venue for over sixty years and the decision to sell the ground to developers came quickly and was a huge shock to Hoops fans who had regularly made pilgrimages to the venue to see some cracking sides over the years.

Anger, disbelief and a feeling of abandonment were the overriding emotions on that sunny April afternoon, as Sligo Rovers became the last visitors to the famous ground. A 1–1 draw in a cup semi-final hardly seemed a fitting send-off for a ground where the likes of Liam Tuohy, Frank O'Neill, and Johnny Fullam *et al* had thrilled thousands. A half-time pitch invasion marked the beginning of the fans' protest and resistance, which was ultimately in vain.

The future should have been bright, as Rovers were dominating Irish football once again after a period in the wilderness. The Hoops had just secured their fourth consecutive league title and their third consecutive double. It seemed that Rovers' new period of domination would have no end.

This new-found success and the recent haul of silverware were a welcome change for Hoops fans. The previous decade – the 1970s – had been a tough one for Rovers. After competing in a play-off match against Cork Hibs to decide the league title in the 1970–71 season, the club fell away from being a regular challenger for honours. The Cunningham family, who had been in control of the club since the mid-thirties, decided to sell the club to three brothers, Paddy, Barton and Louis Kilcoyne, in 1972. Louis Kilcoyne took over as managing director of the club. The aim was to bring Rovers back to the forefront of Irish football. Louis was a successful businessman from Dublin and had been involved in football circles in recent times. He had accompanied the national team on a trip to Brazil and had managed to organise for Brazilian club Santos to visit Dublin to play a friendly at Dalymount Park. He was also involved in bringing Leeds United to Dublin to play UCD in a game to celebrate UCD's seventy-fifth anniversary.

A number of managers came and went at Rovers during the seventies – Liam Tuohy, Mick Meagan and Sean Thomas – all without having brought the glory days back to The Hoops. However, in 1977, Rovers pulled off something of a coup when John Giles agreed to come to Milltown.

Giles, who had been player-manager at West Bromwich Albion the previous season, had taken over at Rovers to great interest from the football public at home. It was perhaps a final throw of the dice for Rovers, who had experienced a huge decline in attendances at Milltown over recent years. If the novelty of Giles managing Ireland's most popular club could not convince the Dublin football public to come out and watch The Hoops, then nothing would.

An ambitious plan was also to be put in place under Louis Kilcoyne. The ambition was for Rovers to become a centre of football excellence in Ireland, the country's premier club, with an academy to prove it. Both the footballing and educational needs of the trainees would be catered for and it was hoped that this would breed the success which would see Rovers not only regain their top spot in Ireland, but also present a challenge on the European front. This might have seemed fanciful in 1977, but a glance at any of the world's leading football clubs will reveal that this is the model in place: the clubs seek to cater for footballers' needs from the moment they walk into the club until the day they leave. Ajax, Barcelona and Arsenal have all shown the way with this academy set-up as the backbone of their clubs. Rovers were not fanciful, just a little ahead of their time.

Fewer than 2,000 people turned up at Iveagh Grounds in Crumlin to witness Rovers' first competitive game under Giles against St James's Gate. However, the crowd that turned up at Milltown would be the real test for the Rovers board. In an era when belligerence and self-preservation were the watchwords for sporting bodies in Ireland, Rovers took the unsurprising step of playing their first home league fixture, against Waterford, in direct competition with the All-Ireland hurling final. In a decision which seems crazy today, Rovers ploughed on, determined to cling to the historic appeal of their brand. Luckily for Rovers, a reasonable crowd turned up to 'trample the grass', which had been growing steadily on the Milltown terraces in recent seasons. However, with the Dublin Gaelic footballers in the football final some weeks later, Rovers didn't want to tempt fate twice and moved their game to Saturday.

To aid Rovers' attempts to return to the top, Giles brought Irish internationals Eamon Dunphy, Ray Tracey and Paddy Mulligan to mix with the young players and contribute in a training and coaching capacity. It turned out to be a good season for The Hoops, they finished just four points behind eventual champions Bohemian FC and negotiated their way through to the FAI Cup final against Sligo Rovers.

On a day of slate grey skies and pouring rain, a crowd of 15,000 turned up at Dalymount to witness referee John Carpenter award a penalty to Rovers for a foul on winger Steve Lynex. The penalty occurred in injury time at the end of the first half and where those additional three minutes allocated came from is still disputed to this day. When asked after the game about the additional time, referee Mr Carpenter remarked, *'As far as I am concerned, the half lasts forty-five minutes. That's how long it lasted on my watch, allowing for the fact that some players were time-wasting'*. Time-wasting during the first half of a cup final when the score is 0–0 seems a little unusual and, given the weather conditions, it would be surprising if anyone was dawdling at any stage. Nonetheless, Ray Tracey stepped up to take the penalty and bring the trophy back to Rovers for the first time in nine seasons.

If anyone thought this was going to be the beginning of a trophy-laden spell for The Hoops, then they were sadly mistaken. Despite the best intentions and efforts of Giles and Kilcoyne, the new dawn at Milltown just couldn't seem to get going and the full-time set-up was eventually pared back to a part-time professional structure. Rovers never really got into a position to challenge for league honours under Giles either, with a number of fans criticising his team's style and approach as being too conservative.

The nearest Rovers did come was in 1981–82, when that uniquely League of Ireland idea of having a '4-3-2-1' points system was in place. This system awarded four points for an away win, three points for a home win, two for an away draw and one for a home draw. Only in the League of Ireland could a draw be worth different amounts of points for both teams. Giles had also undertaken an appointment in

Canada with Vancouver Whitecaps and it was becoming difficult for him to do both jobs. Giles left Rovers in February 1983. The dream had been unfulfilled and a chance had been lost to take a giant step forwards in League of Ireland football. Noel Campbell took over until the end of the season. Kilcoyne would produce another rabbit from the hat later on in the year, with the arrival of Jim McLaughlin. The Derry man would be the one to lead The Hoops back to glory.

For a brief period in the summer of 1983, it seemed that Jim McLaughlin would remain in his position at Dundalk. McLaughlin had indicated to the Dundalk board his desire to move on and find a new challenge and both Rovers and Irish League side Newry Town had been linked with the Derry man. At the start of June, Dundalk issued a statement, declaring that McLaughlin had changed his mind about leaving and would be at the helm in Oriel Park for the new season. A fortnight later, McLaughlin changed his mind again and resigned for the second time in two weeks. Citing the goodwill and encouragement of so many people at Dundalk, McLaughlin said that he had allowed himself to be dissuaded from resigning and that with hindsight this was a mistake. He felt that his relationship with the Dundalk board remained healthy and that they parted on good terms. 'It was simply a matter of feeling that I had achieved all I was going to do at Dundalk and that I needed a new challenge to become motivated again'. Nine days later he was unveiled as the new Hoops boss.

McLaughlin wasted no time in setting about rebuilding Rovers' pedigree as a winning club. Rovers' fans were placing a lot of faith in Jim's amazing success at Oriel Park and hoped that he would be able to sprinkle some of that same magic dust at Milltown.

McLaughlin brought in a number of new faces to freshen things up. Goalkeeper Jody Byrne was brought in from Dundalk, which meant that Alan O'Neill moved on to UCD. Mick Neville from Drogheda United and Terry Eviston from Bohemian FC were two other new additions. Anto Whelan came back home from Manchester United to play for Rovers and McLaughlin also managed to sign Harry McCue, who returned from San Diego. These signings added to the likes of Jacko McDonagh, Alan Campbell and Liam Buckley, quickly had Rovers looking like a formidable outfit.

One other signing would, for many Hoops fans, prove to be the real key to their success. Pat Byrne had been playing football with Heart of Midlothian in Edinburgh. Pat had signed with the Scottish club after spells with Leicester City,

A Fan For All Seasons

Philadelphia Fury and Bohemian FC, where he had achieved League of Ireland and FAI Cup success. Upon his arrival at Milltown, McLaughlin made him club captain and it was hoped that his experience would be put to good use in guiding Rovers towards success.

After appearing in a pre-season friendly for Rovers against Oxford United, it transpired that Hearts were now looking for a fee as they insisted that Pat was still under contract to the club. Hearts had just won promotion back to the top tier of football in Scotland and Hearts' assistant manager Sandy Jardine outlined their case for compensation: *'Pat is an exceptionally good player and but for the fact that he was unable to settle in Scotland, would now figure prominently in our programme for the new season'*. Jardine went on to say that given Hearts were a 'professional club', they 'must insist on compensation'. The news of this claim came as something of a shock to Rovers, especially when Hearts floated a compensation fee of around £10,000. Pat had signed for Rovers under the impression that he was a free agent and citied a verbal agreement he had reached with Hearts when he had originally signed from Leicester City in 1981. His understanding was that he would be released on completion of his contract.

Given that the fee demanded by Hearts was now a serious impediment to him playing for Rovers, Pat sought the assistance of both the Scottish Football Association and the Scottish Professional Footballers Association to resolve the matter. Rovers insisted that they had signed the player in good faith and were happy to leave the matter to Pat and Hearts to resolve; however, The Hoops did enter into discussions with Hearts and the matter was resolved, allowing Byrne to play unimpeded.

Byrne had an immense impact on driving The Hoops forward and although they didn't always get the results that their play deserved, it was evident to all that Rovers were heading in the right direction and would prove a serious challenger for the league title. The McLaughlin magic was again at work and an old partnership was to be renewed: Dermot Keely, who had taken over at UCD as player-manager, made the move to Rovers and teamed up with his old Dundalk manager.

Rovers travelled to St Mels in November to take on League champions Athlone Town and again it was Pat Byrne who was instrumental in all Rovers' good work. But it was by no means a one-man show and the front pairing of Alan Campbell and goalscorer on the day, Liam Buckley, ensured that things up front went well. They had scored eleven of Rovers seventeen league goals to date.

The attendance for this game between the champions and league leaders was disappointingly low. Rovers were experiencing something of a resurgence and Athlone were experiencing their most successful period ever, which emphasises how far behind the league had fallen in popularity. Derek Jones, in his match report for *The Irish Times*, asked a question which is still being asked today: *'Is it television or simply lack of interest or finance in domestic soccer affairs that is keeping the crowds away?'* It was probably a combination of all three, which has resulted in a lost generation of League of Ireland fans and the marginalization of the competition in the sporting public's mind.

To ensure that the rest of the league was aware of the new-found confidence at Milltown, Rovers went on a scoring spree at Lourdes Stadium against a hapless Drogheda United side that saw seven goals go unanswered. Rovers were now clear of the chasing pack by four points and the league table saw Rovers, Bohs and Shels in the top three positions. It was something of a renaissance for Dublin football after years of domination by the country cousins.

Athlone's visit to Milltown presented one of the last obstacles to Rovers in their quest to end the long wait for the league title. The outgoing champions had no answer to McLaughlin's well oiled Rovers team. The Hoops fans were treated to a wonderful display by a Rovers team now high on confidence, with the league title within their grasp. Athlone Town, who had delighted in victories over Rovers during their recent period of league championships, were swept aside by four unanswered goals from Noel King, Alan Campbell and Liam O'Brien, who scored twice.

The nineteen-year gap was finally bridged at Milltown on April Fools Day against old rivals Shelbourne in front of another disappointing crowd. Those that were there witnessed Alan Campbell score two goals in a 3-1 win. This resulted in Campbell being the leading league goalscorer that season with twenty-four goals.

The turn around in Rovers fortunes had been mesmeric. Rovers, who had seemed to have left their best days behind, were now back in the vanguard of player recruitment and footballing success. Key to their success was McLaughlin's ability to develop a winning mentality so quickly. Louis Kilcoyne also deserved huge credit as he released the finances that enabled McLaughlin to bring in players like Byrne and Keely, who really made the difference and had the experience to bring Rovers over the line to glory. Without these funds and investment, it is questionable whether even a man of McLaughlin's talent could have delivered the league title so quickly. Indeed, it was McLaughlin himself who pointed to the influence of Keely and Byrne during the campaign: *'I am taking no credit for it [the league title]. This was an achievement by the players. Dermot Keely and Pat Byrne were our only players to win medals before, so the others wanted to match them on that one'.*

Rovers were now on course for a league and cup double after overcoming Shels in the FAI Cup semi-final. Standing between them and the double was UCD. The final at Dalymount proved to be a disappointing affair. On a hot day, with a bone-hard pitch, neither side managed to deliver as tension gripped the occasion, which was witnessed by just 7,000 people. In a game that saw just eight shots on goal in total, it was clear that defences were on top. With McDonagh and Keely lining out for Rovers and Paddy Dunning and Ken O'Doherty in the Students' defence, it was always going to prove difficult for Buckley and Campbell and Joe Hanrahan and Frank Devlin to see their way through to goal. A replay the following Friday night at Tolka was necessary to separate the sides.

Thankfully for the 5,000 who turned up at Tolka, the replay proved to be a far more interesting match than the original, with penalties scored and missed, four yellow cards, five minutes of stoppage time and a dramatic winner. It was Joe Hanrahan who put the Students into the lead after forty minutes, when Martin Moran put him clear forty yards out with the Rovers defence in chase. As Hanrahan neared the Rovers goal, he kept his nerve and slid the ball past the oncoming Jody Byrne to put UCD in front. The goal came immediately after Rovers had a good shout for handball turned down after Moran's hand prevented a Noel King pass reaching Neville Steedman. There was a penalty just before the break, after Noel King brought down UCD midfielder John Cullen. Ken O'Doherty came up to take the kick, but his powerful shot was saved by Byrne to keep The Hoops deficit at just one goal.

Rovers did equalise and once again a penalty was to play a part. Paddy Dunning took the legs from under Liam Buckley and referee John Carpenter pointed to the spot. Jacko McDonagh brought The Hoops level and it was all to play for. Just when the fans thought they were in for extra time, drama struck. With the match in its fifth minute of injury time, UCD's Keith Dignam launched a hopeful free kick into the Rovers area and, in a moment of redemption, Ken O'Doherty managed to out-jump The Hoops defence and get his head to the ball, beating Jody Byrne and bringing the FAI Cup to Belfield. All that remained was the restart and within seconds the final whistle had blown, heralding one of the most unlikely FAI Cup final victories in recent years.

The double was gone for The Hoops, but it was their only blemish as three successive doubles followed. Rovers were all over the mid-eighties and it seemed like no one had any answer.

With Alan Campbell and Liam Buckley leaving for Spain and Belgium respectively, it was down to Mick Byrne and former Athlone Town goalscorer Noel Larkin to keep The Hoops goals coming during 1984–85. Noel had started out the season with Athlone, but when a transfer to Galway United seemed to be on the cards, McLaughlin swooped in to bring him to Milltown. Rovers retained their league title at a canter, beating Bohemian FC by six points and losing just three league matches. Larkin had contributed twelve goals in the hooped shirt and, in a twist of fate, his thirteenth goal would be the FAI Cup final winner against Galway United at Dalymount Park. This goal secured the double for The Hoops for the first time in twenty-one years and confirmed to anyone who still harboured doubts that this Rovers team was head and shoulders above the rest of the competition.

The advent of the new Premier Division in 1985, replacing Division A, didn't halt The Hoops' progress. Galway United, under Tony Mannion, put up a spirited chase, but The Hoops claimed their third successive league title. Rovers now boasted the likes of Paul Doolin and Kevin Brady as regular starters and the midfield pairing of Pat Byrne and Liam O'Brien kept Rovers ticking over with guile and flair. The double was secured again against Waterford, with two early goals in the final.

The first came from a Kevin Brady effort that just crossed the line before Waterford goalkeeper David Flavin could get it back into play. The second was an own goal from the unlucky Noel Synnott. Two goals down with less than fifteen minutes played found Waterford facing an uphill battle, which they were never likely to overcome. Rovers made history by becoming the first club to retain the double.

A change in management at Rovers came about when Jim McLaughlin moved back to his native Derry to take up the general manager's role at Derry City. McLaughlin admitted that breaking the bond that had developed between him, the club directors, back room staff and the players was one of the toughest decisions of his career. However, he noted that he was swayed by the potential of Derry City, remarking that 'they can do things which no other club can dream of in this country and I want to be part of that challenge'.

A Fan For All Seasons

Rovers were on course to report a financial deficit and it looked like the sale of players might be necessary to address the shortfall. Despite the money situation, the Rovers job was still an attractive offer. The work McLaughlin had done in his three seasons had left the club in good shape on the pitch and the front-runners for the vacant manager's chair were current Rovers defender Dermot Keely and former Rovers player Mick Lawlor, who was now managing Home Farm. The Rovers board moved quickly. Within twenty-four hours of McLaughlin's departure, Dermot Keely was announced as The Hoops' new player-manager.

The manager may have changed, but the results on the pitch did not. Rovers sealed an unprecedented four in a row, winning the title against Galway United on Keely's thirty-third birthday. An interesting statistic appeared in *The Irish Times* the day after the title was won: in the ninety-seven league games since Jim McLaughlin had taken over and up to the current league win, Rovers had lost on just ten occasions, winning seventy-two games and scoring well over 200 goals.

Their superiority was so apparent that after the match Keely admitted that if his side didn't make it to another cup final this season, he would be bitterly disappointed. Forgoing a birthday party in preparation for the FAI Cup semi-final, Keely said, *'if we are playing in that final, and we win it, as I expect we will without being big-headed, then you can prepare for the party of a lifetime'*. This wasn't bluster from of the manager of the new league champions, but a simple statement of truth; no one could compete with The Hoops. Their league success surely eclipsed that of Waterford's domination of the championship in the late sixties and early seventies. It also eclipsed Rovers' six consecutive cup wins in the sixties. Milltown had never seen a Rovers team as dominant in the league before and Milltown wouldn't see its likes again.

For all The Hoops' domination of the league and cup competitions, their failure to make any impact in European competition remains a spot on the team's obvious talent and ability. McLaughlin could not work the oracle at Milltown in the same way that had done at Oriel Park. Four attempts in the European Cup yielded just three draws and two goals. The opposition encountered during this time was Linfield, Honved, Celtic and Omonia Nicosia. Progression in the competition should have been achieved on at least two occasions, given the players in the Rovers ranks. Soon, though, the fans would have more on their minds than the team's lack of European success.

News of Rovers leaving Milltown broke the day before the FAI Cup semi-final first leg against Sligo Rovers. The Hoops were to move north-side to share Tolka Park with Home Farm. Dr Brendan Menton, president of Home Farm, dismissed any talk of a merger between the two clubs: 'We shall be merely offering Rovers a playing facility at Tolka'. Louis Kilcoyne confirmed that meetings had taken place with Home Farm, but would not comment further on the move, except to say that Rovers would retain their identity.

The Hoops had spent a considerable amount since 1980, including for the installation of floodlights at Glenmalure Park in 1980 and ground redevelopment amounting to nearly £200,000. Add to this the cost of running the club, which amounted to £150,000 for the current season. It was time to put the club back on sound financial ground.

Despite their on-pitch success, attendance figures continued to drop during this period, with the gate receipts amounting to less than a fifth of the cost of running the club. The fans were not impressed by the move and felt that Rovers could have stayed nearer to their traditional home or, at the very least, on the south side of Dublin. Joe Cunningham's son Des echoed these sentiments when asked about the move away from Milltown: *'The obvious place for them to go was Richmond Park … I cannot now see these people making the journey to Tolka Park'*. Cunningham emphasised his concern at the state of the game in Ireland and said that if Rovers could not attract sufficient gates then the game in general was at risk in Ireland.

Crestfallen Hoops fans lining up outside the turnstiles of Glenmalure Park on that April day were angry, bitter and upset and when asked if they would travel to Tolka the following season, few, if any, said they would. Even the editorial in *The Irish Times* remarked that it was the end of an era. Under the sub-heading, 'The Holy Ground', the writer remarked that another piece of 'Old Dublin' was disappearing before our eyes and wondered if Rovers would recreate the golden days of Milltown north of the Liffey. It was the beginning of a period of darkness for the country's most successful football club, with very little light to illuminate the gloom.

The Milltown Saga was to rumble on in the press as Rovers reached the 1987 FAI Cup Final after overcoming Sligo Rovers. It transpired that the Jesuit Order had originally owned the grounds at Glenmalure Park and that an option to purchase the land had been taken up by the owners of Shamrock Rovers in 1986. The Reverend Senan Timoney, Assistant Provincial of the Jesuits, noted that development of the lands hadn't arisen in the discussions to purchase the land and that the order believed it was a case of 'the club buying its own grounds', which in fact it was. Reverend Timoney went on to say that the order would be sad to see the grounds no longer being used in a recreational capacity. Dublin Corporation were also sounded out by Frank McDonald and Peter Byrne of *The Irish Times*, but their only comment was that they would like to see current recreational areas preserved for the public's benefit. In a front-page piece, the Corporation, through an unnamed official, advised that the Corporation *'really can't do anything about it unless the public themselves get a campaign going to make this a political issue'.*

Minister for Sport Sean Barrett raised the point that every effort should be made to make sure Glenmalure Park remained a sporting facility. He advocated ground-sharing with another club or even another sport and voiced the opinion that money might be made available through National Lottery funding.

Over at the Mansion House, the Home Farm and Rovers board were holding a press conference and the issue of money and betrayal came up many times. Questions ranged from the Kilcoyne's family connection with building company Healy Homes to money generated by supporters for the floodlight system. Paddy Kilcoyne emphasised that the Kilcoynes were business people and that when they purchased the ground, the intention was to develop the ground for football. Subsequently the family realised they would not be able to achieve this with their own resources. On the question of betrayal and the floodlights, Paddy Kilcoyne stated that no decision had been made regarding the fate of Glenmalure Park yet, but that the supporters had assisted with the floodlight funding.

However, despite a stream of questions aimed at both Louis and Paddy Kilcoyne about the move to Tolka, the most telling reply came from Paddy Kilcoyne, who said, 'If enough people felt sufficiently passionate about keeping the club at Milltown, they could have pre-empted this move by turning out in reasonable numbers to watch our games'. Therein lay the problem for all concerned: the crowds had deserted the game at home and, despite letters to newspapers and editorials and opinions, it really was the case that not enough of the public cared to save Milltown when they had the opportunity.

On the pitch, the FAI Cup final against Dundalk ended in a 3-0 win for The Hoops. This gave them a treble double, but it was cold comfort for fans. There was also the spectre of crowd trouble at the final as Rovers and Dundalk fans clashed on the terraces, resulting in a series of baton charges by Gardaí. Order was restored quickly but it had been a month of bad news for Irish football.

By early May, a group called KRAM – Keep Rovers at Milltown – had been formed. Under their chairman, Brian Murphy, they held discussions with the directors of Rovers in an attempt to purchase both the club and grounds. A meeting was held at the Mansion House to outline their appeal to raise £250,000. Amongst the attendees were Rovers legends from yesteryear, Paddy Coad, Eamon Darcy, Liam Tuohy, Gerry Mackey, who was the groups spokesman, and Paddy Ambrose. There was also a political flavour, with former Lord Mayor Michael Keating and current Lord Mayor Bertie Ahern in attendance. Brian Murphy outlined that the committee already had £50,000 and that they were confident that they could cover the estimated annual bill of running Rovers, believed to be nearly £120,000.

Despite this optimism, the Rovers directors rejected a bid made within two weeks of the meeting. In a short statement, Louis Kilcoyne outlined that the directors had agreed to meet and listen to the KRAM representatives, as *'they want to make us change our mind': 'We agreed to meet them yesterday to listen to what they had to say. Well, we haven't changed our minds'.* Protests, vigils at the ground and bye-laws could not prevent the move from happening.

The Hoops had run out for the last time at Milltown. In a final act of protest, the Shamrock Rovers supporters club decided to boycott the teams games at Tolka Park the following season. For The Hoops' first game at Tolka Park, against Athlone Town in the League Cup, approximately sixty supporters turned up to protest. Both boycotters and those going in to watch The Hoops threw insults and accusations at each other in an attempt to get their message across. For Louis Kilcoyne sitting in the stand, it was now time to look to the future for Rovers. He pointed out the benefits of Tolka, which had more covered seating, plans for redevelopment and was in a bigger catchment area to draw paying fans; however, home is where the heart is and The Hoops' heart will always be in Milltown.

There was to be no fifth successive league title for Rovers playing out of Tolka and despite all the drama off the pitch, the team did manage a respectable fourth-place finish, just five points behind champions Dundalk. By July 1988, the Kilcoyne brothers had sold Rovers after a successful takeover bid. KRAM and the Shamrock Rovers Supporters Club gave assurances that the boycott of Rovers home matches would be lifted for the 1988-89 season as the team moved from Tolka Park to Dalymount for their home matches. Dermot Keely had resigned as manager and was replaced by Noel King, who would have to plan without the services of Kevin Brady, Paul Doolin and Mick Neville, who all headed north to Jim McLaughlin's Derry City.

The Royal Dublin Society would be Rovers' next port of call in 1990. A crowd of 22,000 fans turned out to welcome The Hoops back to south Dublin when they took on St Patrick's Athletic. A single league championship was secured during their spell at the RDS under Ray Tracey before they were on the move again. Dalymount, Tolka Park, Richmond Park and the Billy Morton Stadium would all host 'home' games for The Hoops over the coming years. For fans, the question remained whether Rovers would ever find a new permanent home and whether the club would ever recover from the Milltown Saga, which had cast a long shadow over this famous club and their most successful period on the pitch.

European Nights, Part II
Nearly, Nearly – Highlights and Hidings

It was apt that the doyen of rugby correspondents, Edmund Van Esbeck, should contribute a piece for The Irish Times prior to Dundalk's visit to Anfield in 1969. He would have been used to the final scoreline being more representative of a somewhat one-sided rugby match, rather than a game of Association Football.

Under the headline 'Dundalk are banking on defence', Van Esbeck set out just how difficult it was going to be for Liam Tuohy's Dundalk team. Not only would they need to contend with a formidable opponent that was second in the top division in England but Liverpool had also gone unbeaten at Anfield all season. Added to this was the 'Kop Factor', something which very few visiting sides overcame. All this was before you even considered Liverpool players such as Emlyn Hughes, Roger Hunt, Tommy Smith and Ian Callaghan – and as for the manager, well, Mr Shankley would have had you believe that his side inhabited a different realm of being altogether.

Although Liam Tuohy had decided that defence was the best strategy, he was under no illusion about how difficult the job would be: 'Being honest about it, we will be very satisfied to get away with even a two- or three-goal deficit'. In a sign of the times, Dundalk flew to Liverpool the day before the game and held a short training session 'in a local park' in Southport. According to the article, the session lasted about twenty minutes, after which the team was named. Despite Tuohy's hope that a respectable scoreline might be achieved, Van Esbeck ensured that we were aware of Dundalk's 'terrifying task': *'They will do very well to keep that to three goals'*. There were certainly no great expectations in sight.

A goal down after less than a minute and five down at the break, Van Esbeck noted that the scoreline could have been worse. Maurice Swan, the Dundalk goalkeeper, came in for special praise. Having been under siege, he pulled off at least five magnificent saves to keep the score at ten. At the other end, there was a debut in goal for Ray Clemence. He would have tougher days. When the mauling was finally over, the last word went, as always, to Shankley: *'We approached it professionally. That's the best compliment I can pay to Dundalk'*. But it was not particularly comforting for Liam Tuohy and his Lilywhites, who still faced the return at Oriel.

It was up to Liam Tuohy to try recover some dignity for Dundalk. He promised that Liverpool would not find things as easy at Oriel: *'I can guarantee that Liverpool will have to work a lot harder for their goals tonight'*. Although the genius of Ian St John and Peter Thompson proved too much for Dundalk, the scoreline was kept under control by the courage and commitment of the Dundalk players, who showed their tremendous spirit in the face of a very competitive Liverpool side, despite losing 4-0 on the night.

At the bell, it was 14-0 on aggregate and without doubt the worst result for the League of Ireland in European competition. Only Drumcondra, in 1958, had anything like this aggregate result when they lost 13-1 to Atletico Madrid.

It must be noted that the Liverpool side of the time was exceptional. It was Dundalk's misfortune to come up against a team of such class. It was also typical of Liverpool and Shankley that they put Dundalk to the sword at Anfield and then sent out an equally formidable team at Oriel when the tie was over. For Shankley, each game that Liverpool played was a chance to emphasise the greatness of, and his belief in, Liverpool FC. He seldom let that opportunity pass by. For Dundalk, however, there would be better days ahead in Europe, but at that time they were still being taught some tough lessons.

While the early days of European competition had thrown up some enjoyable results for Irish clubs, by the mid-seventies, these were becoming a rarity. The days of Rovers, Drums and Shels getting a result at home against one of the European powerhouses were fading memories for fans. A whole generation of potential fans was being lost to defeats – and not against teams of Liverpool's calibre. TJ Gottwaldov from Czechoslovakia, Omonia Lefkosia from Cyprus, Randers from Denmark and Buraspor from Turkey were hardly household names for the fans of Bohemian FC, Waterford, Shamrock Rovers and Finn Harps. It was difficult to encourage new fans when teams were being beaten by this standard of opposition. In just the same way that European football had encouraged so many to come along to games in the late fifties and early sixties, the same competitions had them now turning away in droves.

For fans of the great Waterford side of the sixties and seventies, the disparity between league success and European success was galling. In six attempts at European Cup football, they won just one tie, against Glentoran of Belfast, and on three occasions the aggregate score hit double figures. This was the premier side in Ireland for nearly eight seasons. This raised the question: were we so far behind? The same question would arise again in relation to another legendary side: the Shamrock Rovers team of the mid-eighties. Champions four times in a row, they never made it past the first round in the European Cup. Linfield, Honved, Celtic and Omonia Nicosia all blocked this great Hoops team.

However, it wasn't all doom and gloom on the European front and when surprising results did occur, they created a little bit of folklore and some memorable moments for the fans.

Over at St Mel's Park, Athlone Town were looking to back up their runners-up position in the league in 1974–75. Athlone were taking part in European competition for the first time and had been drawn to play Valerenga of Norway in the first round of the UEFA Cup. Athlone Town and their manager, Amby Fogarty, were taking the tie seriously and had enlisted the help of Amby's former teammate at Sunderland, Alan Brown. Brown had spent a season at the Hamarkameratene club in Norway in 1973. Unfortunately for Amby, the 'Brown Dossier', as it was known, was little use in preparations, given the turnover of players at Norwegian clubs. According to Amby, while Brown's notes couldn't shed any light on the current Valerenga team, they did make it clear that *'like most continental teams, they tend to build their attacks around the short one-two'*.

Whatever other glimpses into Norwegian football were provided, Brown's astute knowledge of the game itself must have done the trick, not that Amby was short on ideas himself: 'Our task today is to destroy and construct. To hit the Norwegians hard at the start and then build on their troubles', he declared in a pre-match interview, while also promising that his side would have a 'real go' at winning the match and scoring goals.

A Fan For All Seasons

This outlook was typical of one of the great motivators in League of Ireland history. Amby Fogarty had made his name with Sunderland, in the company of fellow Irish international Charlie Hurley and the legendary Brian Clough. Amby was never short of a line for the press or short on ideas when it came to football. He made an immediate impact at Cork Hibs as player-manager upon his return from England, where he finished his career there with Hartlepools United. As former Athlone player Paul Martin remarked, *'he instilled great confidence in the side. He was a wonderful motivator and a really great guy'*.

Athlone did what Amby said they would. A goal from Paul Martin and two from Eugene Davis secured a 3-1 win at Mels. Despite having the best of the play, Athlone were wasteful in front of the goal and it took Davis's strike five minutes from time to put breathing space between the sides before the return in Oslo. It was a great result in Athlone's first European game at Mels and sent the 4,000 fans home kindling thoughts of more to come. True to form, Amby sent Athlone out to attack from the off in the second leg and was rewarded for his bravery when Paul Martin put the Midlanders ahead after twenty minutes. Despite an equaliser ten minutes into the second half, Athlone held on for a 4-2 win on aggregate. Their first tie had been negotiated successfully. This European football was easy pickings. Next up for Athlone was some club from Italy…

When the news came through from Zurich that AC Milan were Athlone Town's next opponents, the joy on Amby Fogarty's face could hardly be disguised. 'God drew this one for us', he remarked to reporters. The prospect of playing a club which had won the European Cup twice in the past was daunting, but there was no certainty that the game would take place at Mels. When asked for his opinion on the prospects of AC Milan coming to Mels, Amby reflected that there were two ways of looking at the question: *'The Athlone public who have travelled all over the country with us deserve a home game. But they also deserve facilities'.* Now, nearly forty years after that remark, the same question is still cropping up for League of Ireland teams when they enter European competition. For a club like Athlone Town, who were only in their sixth senior season, the balancing act between revenue and the wishes of fans was a high-wire act.

Mels finally got the nod to hold the game and the club set to work to increase the ground's capacity by 2,000 to 10,000. The main stand in the ground held just 200 and with the level of interest it was going to be a tight squeeze for all concerned. The main question on everyone's lips was not the capacity, however, but rather what the glamorous Italians would make of drab Mels. As Nero Rocco, their manager, put it when addressing scribes over lunch, *'the big worry … was the state of the playing surface. Now that we've seen it, I'm satisfied'.* While this remark would have been expected, given visiting team's deference to their hosts, his next was a little more unexpected: *'Athlone players may only be part-time professionals, but I shall be happy enough to go home with a scoreless draw'.* Perhaps Amby and his ebullient character had convinced Rocco that he needed to cover his bases just in case these characters from the middle of Ireland could play ball after all. As Amby said, *'My boys are going out to play football and enjoy themselves – there will be no wild kicking and I think we can hand them a few surprises'.* What a wonderful way to spend a Wednesday afternoon in Athlone.

If ever a picture painted a thousand words, that well known picture of the AC Milan players disembarking from the team coach after arriving for the game did. The coach came to a stop in what can only be described as a mud bath. The image of the players, all immaculately dressed, stepping down into the mud is beautifully juxtaposed with a young boy with his trousers tucked in to his wellies, wearing a bobble hat and looking like he had just come from the milking parlour to watch the match. The Italians were in for a tough days work.

The AC Milan players thought that the best formula for winning the game was provocation of the Athlone Town players at nearly every opportunity. A bad-tempered match had Amby Fogarty remarking that four of Milan's players could have been dismissed. Nero Rocco took a more balanced view that the tackling was hard, but the game was never really dirty. As for the football, although Athlone Town recorded one of the great days in League of Ireland football with a goalless draw, it remains a case of one that got away.

The teams entered the pitch accompanied by the Athlone Pipe Band and their mascot, a goat, to the acclaim of the near 10,000 fans who packed into St Mels. The game started at a frantic pace and Athlone matched their illustrious opponents from the outset. Despite AC threatening from the start, they gradually fell back into that traditional Italian defensive football and it wasn't until just over twenty minutes into the game that they managed to formulate any kind of effort on goal. For Athlone, though, a golden chance would present itself after just thirty minutes, when they were awarded a penalty for a foul on Terry Daly. Daly was running onto a pass from Eugene Davis when he was brought down from behind. Mr Sorrenson, the referee, pointed to the spot much to the delight of the hoards of home fans.

A Fan For All Seasons

Up stepped John Minnock, a man who hadn't missed a penalty in two years. Unfortunately for him and the Athlone faithful, he struck the ball low, to Albertosi's right-hand side, and the Milan keeper guessed right, saving the penalty and with it went a golden chance for Athlone to take the lead. This is probably the most famous penalty miss in Irish club football history and I'm sure John Minnock wishes that someone would destroy the tape to prevent it from continually being trotted out at regular intervals. In an RTÉ News segment which appeared in 2006 to mark the closure of Mels, the penalty miss was once again replayed to the nation. However, in a light-hearted moment of the report, John Minnock was invited back to Mels to 're-take' the infamous penalty, this time achieving the desired result.

The Sunday before the AC Milan match, Athlone had been awarded a penalty against Hibs in a league fixture. Up stepped John to win the game for Athlone, scoring low to the keeper's right. It was rumoured that there had been an AC Milan spy in Mels that afternoon and that Minnock's penalty technique was duly reported back to Albertosi.

Despite the penalty miss, there was a little glory for Athlone. As an eloquent Amby Fogarty said after the game, *'I was proud of the way my lads played out there … we had players of ability and this, for the doubters, was surely the final irrefutable proof'*.

The second leg in the San Siro would see Milan progress to the quarter-finals with a 3-0 win, but not until Athlone had held out for an hour of play. Noel Larkin, then just nineteen, described the atmosphere as 'a bit scary' and noted that it wasn't so much the players or the tactics that annoyed the Milan fans, but rather that the Athlone kit was identical to Milan's bitter rivals Internazionale.

Despite the defeat, Athlone had managed an eventful first foray into European competition and had done both themselves and the league proud. Again, stories accompanied this European adventure. Before the second leg in Italy, the Athlone team was staying at a hotel just outside Milan. To their surprise, Omar Sharif was also staying there as he was taking part in a bridge tournament at the time. Sharif was once ranked among the world's best fifty players of contract bridge. As the opportunity could not be passed up, the team sought out Sharif for photos and autographs and I would like to think that there is a photograph somewhere of Dr Zhivago wearing an Athlone Town scarf.

The following season, it would be the turn of Finn Harps to see if they could emulate the feats of Athlone Town, although they were drawn against a significantly better outfit: Dave Mackay's Derby County. This would be Harps' third adventure in Europe. They had managed to score in three of their four previous games. While results had still been a little one-sided in their previous two ties, nothing could have prepared them for the storm of goals that rained down on them in the Baseball Ground. Derby were nine up at half-time and ran out 12-0 winners at the whistle, with Kevin Hector getting five and a hat trick each for Charlie George and Leighton James. Bruce Rioch pitched in with the other goal. Afterwards, Harps manager Patsy McGowan commented that they had simply been outclassed, but finished by remarking that if Dave Mackay failed to bring a full-strength team to Ballybofey for the return, *'the football public of Ireland will feel insulted'*.

Things didn't improve in the return at Finn Park, despite 3,000 watching Roy McFarland's own goal giving Harps the lead after less than a minute. Even though there could be no doubt about the ultimate outcome of the tie, there was a chance for Harps to salvage some dignity from the ruins of the Baseball Ground defeat. A chance to prove to themselves and their fans that the character and spirit which had seen them win the cup in 1974 and finish league runners-up just a few months earlier was still alive. Inexplicably, however, Harps failed to show any fight or spark, despite the goal start they were given. Peter Byrne succinctly described the response of a fairly deflated Harps team: 'They accepted defeat pretty meekly and the manner of their capitulation had already been established within half an hour'.

Meekly accepting defeat was never an accusation that could be levelled at a side managed by Jim McLaughlin. Following their third FAI Cup win in five years, Dundalk, under McLaughlin's guidance, entered the 1981–82 Cup Winners' Cup in the autumn of 1981. They were drawn against Icelandic side Fram Reykjavik in the first round and disposed of them by five goals to two on aggregate, turning around a first leg 2-1 deficit in Reykjavik by winning 4-0 at Oriel in the second leg. In the second round, they drew Tottenham Hotspur, with the first leg scheduled for Oriel Park on 22 October. For The Lilywhites, this draw was just another in the recent sequence of top European clubs that they were now playing on a regular basis. PSV Eindhoven, Hajduk Split, Celtic and Porto had all visited Oriel Park in the last number of years, thanks to Dundalk's domestic success in the league and cup, and none of them had managed to get anything better than a draw.

A Fan For All Seasons

As the game drew closer, it was clear that the evening would be a significant event for both the club and the town. Twenty thousand fans were expected to descend on the border town for the big game, generating a significant cash injection for the Oriel Park coffers. Looking back at the democracy of the draw, where the teams were pulled out of a hat for a simple two-legged tie, I feel nostalgia for the days when ties of this kind could actually occur. With today's seedings and groups and losers from the Champions League getting a second chance, it seems that the lustre has gone from the great nights in Europe. European football has become a cash cow for clubs to fuel an ever-increasing wage bill and winning the competition has become secondary to getting into it to begin with. As John Giles said, you can have the money or the glory, but not both.

Dundalk had the gate receipts for the tie, but they were also going to try to achieve the glory as well. Jim McLaughlin noted before the match that given the talent of the Spurs squad, Dundalk should really not be in a position to compete with the FA Cup holders. The Spurs side included the talents of Hoddle, Ardiles, Perryman, Crooks and Archibald, but, as Jim assured Spurs, *they'll know they have been through a game when they come off the pitch*. Spurs boss Keith Burkinshaw wasn't taking the tie lightly either. Spurs had beaten Ajax in the first round and he sought to temper any notions of complacency in his side by pointing to Dundalk's recent home games in European football. 'I for one will deem it a good result if we go home with a scoreless draw', he said.

Burkinshaw may have got the scoreline wrong, but the sentiments expressed before the game certainly rang true after ninety eventful minutes on the Oriel Park pitch. Despite taking the lead when Garth Crooks beat Richie Blackmore for the opener, it was not all one-way traffic and Dundalk matched the English club for most of the game. Tommy McConville, Paddy Dunning, Martin Lawlor and Eamon Gregg all put in an excellent shift at the back and with Leo Flanagan and Sean Byrne in the middle nipping at Hoddle's heels, the Englishman never really seemed to get into his rhythm. Added to this were the efforts of Hillary Carlyle and Mick Fairclough up front, who kept the Spurs defence on their toes and ensured that Ray Clemence did not have as easy a ride as the last time he had faced Dundalk.

Despite their best efforts, Dundalk were 1-0 behind with about ten minutes left in the game when Martin Lawlor picked up the ball. He slipped a pass in to Mick Fairclough, who turned, beating Spurs Paul Miller before slipping the ball coolly under the advancing Ray Clemence for the equaliser. Oriel Park erupted with joy.

There would be one late chance for Sean Byrne to write his name into the Dundalk history books with a winning goal, but his twenty-five yard effort flew agonisingly wide of the right-hand post with Clemence well beaten. One all the final score.

As the crowd stood to applaud the efforts of the home side at the final whistle, McLaughlin summed up the night and the belief in his side: *'My players were a credit to Dundalk and the country in general and I am not in the least intimidated at the prospect of meeting Tottenham again in a fortnight's time'*. Keith Burkinshaw had remarked that he worried more about playing teams like Dundalk than playing sides like Manchester United and said he was 'delighted to be going back to London with a draw'. Despite being disappointed with letting a lead slip, Burkinshaw reminded everyone of the quality test his side had just gone through: *'one must give them due credit for the quality of football they produced'*. Dundalk were still in the race for a spot in the quarter-finals and despite the tough task that lay ahead of them at White Hart Lane, it was by no means impossible that they would make it through.

With the tie still very much alive, the words of praise from both managers for the opposite teams were positively endearing. McLaughlin hit off first, with the sickly sweet line, *'You look at the Tottenham team sheet and in a sense feel privileged to share the same pitch as them'*. This was classic McLaughlin in Europe, putting on the well-worn-underdog act of benevolent Irishman, just delighted to be here and not expecting much. Burkinshaw was also caught up in the love-bombing: *'Much of the football they produced in the first game would have done justice to professional teams over here'*. However, for Burkinshaw, it might have been a case of prudence in the face of a potential banana skin.

The match very nearly did cause Spurs to slip up. Despite having most of the play, they only managed to beat Richie Blackmore once and sneaked through 2-1 on aggregate. Blackmore had pulled off two great saves in either half from Steve Archibald, in what was becoming almost a personal duel between the two. Dundalk, playing in unfamiliar red, did manage to create a chance just before half-time. The opportunity fell to Hillary Carlyle, but just as he was about to shoot, Perryman came in to clear the danger. It may have been a different evening had they taken the lead at that stage. As it turned out, it would fall to Garth Crooks to score again in the tie after just an hour to settle the proceedings. The goal was a little unfortunate from Dundalk's perspective. A corner from Hoddle was headed on in the box and bounced up just as Paddy Dunning was preparing to clear. Crooks nipped in to collect the breaking ball and slotted it into the net, much to the relief of the Spurs fans in the ground.

For all their effort, commitment and courage, Dundalk was out, but for McLaughlin there was no disgrace in defeat. He drew attention to the fact that Dundalk had continued to play football, even when they were under severe pressure. Spurs could be magnanimous now. Burkinshaw commented that they had been given a tough game and were not able to relax at any stage. But, fittingly, the last word went to Jim: *'There were no heads dropping in the last half hour and that was a measure of the character of the players',* he said.

Spurs would be well prepared the next time they came across League of Ireland opposition, this time in the 1983-84 UEFA Cup. In a twist of fate, Spurs took on Dundalk's County Louth rivals, Drogheda United, just two years later. Burkinshaw unleashed the full torrent of Spurs' ability and they swept United away in the first leg at United Park by six goals to nil. Spurs added a further eight in the return a fortnight later, finishing with an aggregate scoreline of 14-0. Spurs would go on to win the competition that season, beating Anderlecht in the final.

It was a case of one step forward and two steps back for the League of Ireland clubs during the early eighties, as good work was undone by Athlone Town, Shamrock Rovers and Sligo Rovers, who all suffered heavy defeats. Coincidentally, on the same day that Drogheda United conceded eight at White Hart Lane, Athlone Town shipped the same amount of goals against Standard Liège, in Belgium. The only positive thing that can be said of Athlone Town is that they did at least score twice in reply to the eight conceded.

Generally, up until 1984, reports of League of Ireland clubs' adventures in Europe had been confined to the sports pages of newspapers and the sports supplements on television programmes such as *Sports Stadium*. The noted exception had been Linfield's visit to Oriel in 1979. The date 18 September 1984 will, however, go down as a night of infamy at Dalymount Park, when Bohemian FC met Rangers in the first round of the UEFA Cup.

The UEFA Cup tie had sparked huge interest and there was a huge Garda operation to ensure that order was maintained. The charmless behaviour of a number of Rangers fans after their European Cup Winners' Cup final win in Barcelona in 1972 remained fresh in the minds of many. Rangers' fans had run on to the pitch in the last few moments of second half injury time to celebrate Rangers 3-2 win against Dynamo Moscow. The pitch invasion meant that captain John Greig received the trophy in a committee room in the Camp Nou rather than in front of the clubs fans.

Bohemian FC had gone to great lengths to secure the perimeter of the pitch at Dalymount Park, with the installation of extra fencing and caging along the Tramway End goal line and Connaught Street terrace. The work took place on the Monday night before the game, when the old ground reverberated with the sound of generators powering drills instead of the trainer's whistle signalling drills of a different type. RTÉ had sent a camera along to view the installation of fencing, which had never before been required in over eighty years of football at the ground. A demonstration of the effectiveness of the new fencing was carried out for the cameras as a young man attempted to scale the cage-like structure. The footage shows a rather unconvincing effort and I wonder if he would have given up so easily if there had been a couple of attack dogs below him.

Bohs seemed happy with the arrangements made for the game. They had been in contact with officials from Rangers FC, Rangers' supporters' clubs, An Garda Síochána and a member of the British Embassy in Dublin had even come out to Dalymount to offer advice and guidance. Rangers manager Jock Wallace was also keen to see the tie pass off peacefully, saying that, 'We have made every effort to ensure that our fans will not give offence in Dublin'. However, in a moment of far-sightedness, he added that 'you cannot legislate for every contingency'.

Over 3,000 Rangers fans descended on Dalymount that Tuesday evening. The vast majority travelled from Scotland and there were also a number of fans from Northern Ireland who travelled down for the game. The scene on Phibsborough Road before the game saw shops with boarded up windows and doors as a preventative measure against any violence or damage that might occur. As for the fencing around the ground, it turned out to be no more an obstacle to the Rangers fans then a small garden wall. Even before kick-off, fans had climbed over the cages and were gleefully sitting atop the fencing, waving their flags and hurling insults. However, not all the insults and taunting came from the blue end of the ground. A group of Celtic fans were in attendance at the School End and took up the mantle of jeering and goading with relish. Flags were set alight at both ends and there was a feeling that it would be a nasty evening ahead.

The start of the game was nasty too for Bohs, who found themselves a goal down after just seven minutes: Davy Cooper crossed the ball into the six-yard box and Ally McCoist was on hand to beat Dermot O'Neill in the Bohs goal and give the Rangers fans cause to celebrate. A mix-up between Nicky Walker, in the Rangers goal, and Craig Patterson, resulting in the latter attempting an ill-judged back pass, allowed Bohs to equalise. David 'Rocky' O'Brien was on hand to take advantage of the error and bring The Gypsies level. It would take just four minutes for Rangers to regain the lead, when a Dave McPherson header seemed to hang in the air and fall gently into Dermot O'Neill's goal. But this Bohemian side was not in the mood for rolling over. Where teams before them would have succumbed to defeat, it was once again Rocky O'Brien who pulled Bohs level, with a header ten minutes before the interval. While it wasn't a game for the football purists, four goals in the first half had certainly been worth the admission.

However, trouble flared up between Gardaí and Rangers fans at half-time. As the Welsh referee blew his whistle for the end of the half, some Rangers fans attempted to encroach onto the pitch. They were met by Gardaí, who were unable to contain the trouble as they came under attack from a hail of bottles and coins from the Rangers fans. As they retreated, two officers lay injured on the terrace. Despite this, the rain of missiles continued to pour down from the visiting fans and it took the appearance of Gardaí in full riot gear from Mountjoy Station to restore order on the terraces and rescue the injured Gardaí. During this period, sectarian chants and songs were being sung from both ends of the grounds and both the Tricolour and Union flags were burned. It took Rangers captain John McClelland pleading with the Rangers fans to behave before the second half could begin.

Despite the trouble on the terrace, Billy Young's team was not shaken and the winning goal, when it came just seven minutes into the second half, would be good enough to decide any match anywhere. The honour would fall to Eugene 'Gino' Lawless, who played a captain's role by striking the winning goal from twenty yards, cutting in from the left wing and unleashing a fierce shot, which flew past Nicky Walker in the Rangers goal, leaving him rooted to the spot. Rangers were not finished yet, but chances for McCoist, Clark and Fraser were all passed up and the best of the remaining opportunities fell to Bohs.

While Gino Lawless got the glory of the goal, there was another man in red and black whose performance shone out like a beacon. His touch, skill and vision, not alone in this game but on a regular basis, earned him the nickname 'The Great Man' at Dalymount. It was, of course, the legendary Jackie Jameson.

There was a moment in the second half of the Rangers game when Bohs were under pressure which showed Jackie at his best. As the ball broke to Jackie, he seemed to have all the time in the world to lay the ball off and then get on the end of a Larry Wyse pass to take on the Rangers defence. Heading towards the penalty area Jackie beat two Rangers defenders by beautifully gliding the ball around both with his left foot. The camera just managed to catch both Rangers players on the ground, looking on as Jackie bore down on Nicky Walker. Luckily for Rangers, Alistair Dawson was on hand to come across and intercept the ball. But Jackie wasn't done. He chased down Dawson in the corner and forced a throw-in for Bohs. Later in the game. Jackie picked the ball up in midfield and surged towards goal, beating three players on the way. The ball got a bad bounce on the Dalymount turf, but this didn't stop Jackie from improvising a shot, which nearly beat Walker again.

These were just little cameos from a player who always had time on the ball and played the game with a leisurely elegance, which is all too rare today. Although he didn't get on the score sheet that night, his contribution to a famous night in League of Ireland football would not go unrecognised.

As Bohs grew in confidence, they would have one last chance to take a two-goal lead to Ibrox Park in the return. Unfortunately for Bohs, Larry Wyse's effort fell just the wrong side of the post and 3–2 was the final score. It was a memorable night for good and bad reasons. Bohs' job was done, but the Gardaí still had work ahead of them. As the Rangers fans filed out of the ground, they were met by several hundred Gardaí in riot gear, ready to shepherd them away from Phibsborough.

There was a brief incident outside the ground that resulted in some shop windows being broken, but this was nothing compared to the trail of destruction left in County Louth and County Meath early the following morning. The towns of Slane, Dunleer, Castlebellingham, Ardee and Dundalk all suffered damage to cars and property as Gardaí convoyed buses of Rangers fans back across the border. Bottles, coins, cans, and rocks were thrown from passing buses as they sped through the towns.

For Rangers manager Jock Wallace, there was no denying the shame brought on his club by these hooligans. Commending Bohemian FC officials and Gardaí for their handling of 'extremely hazardous circumstances', he was moved to reflect that 'what we saw here tonight was a disgrace to football and a sad reflection on Rangers club'.

In terms of the football, which had been overshadowed somewhat by events, Wallace had no complaints: *'I don't think anybody can argue about the merits of the scoreline'*. Billy Young, as well as voicing his disgust at events on the terrace, was keen to have his team's efforts acknowledged: 'In terms of courage and commitment, this was a famous victory', he said, before adding that he felt 'Bohemians did League of Ireland football proud with this performance'.

In the return leg, Billy Young was in full voice, assuring all that his Bohemian side was not travelling to make up the numbers at Ibrox and for eighty-four minutes they held the hosts scoreless. It took headers from Craig Patterson and Ian Redford to eventually break down Bohs' resistance, much to the relief of the anxious home crowd. As was to be expected, a low number of away fans travelled and just thirty souls in red and black were to be found in the away fans' section of Ibrox. Jackie Jameson treated those who did travel to a vintage display as he turned the Rangers captain on the night, Craig Patterson, inside out with a demonstration of skill and close control. It could have been different for Bohs, who had chances through Rocky O'Brien and Paul Doolin, before Rangers scored, but it wasn't to be. Two late Rangers goals put an end to Bohs' dreams of achieving a huge upset.

From then on, good results became a rare commodity for League of Ireland teams. In the late eighties and early nineties, a 0-0 draw was considered a noteworthy achievement at home. Long gone were the days of Drums beating Bayern, Shels beating Belenenses and Rovers beating Schalke 0-4. League of Ireland fans were getting used to a new world, where European games inspired only dread and trepidation for the clubs, but there would be one last European experience that would bring a smile to fans' faces.

The UEFA Cup fixture between Cork City and Bayern Munich in 1991 wasn't so much a great Irish football night, as a great Irish football afternoon. The game was played in Dolphin RFC's ground, Musgrave Park, which had no floodlights at the time, necessitating a late afternoon kick-off.

The quality of the opposition facing City was not lost on the team management. Noel O'Mahony, club manager, commented before the game: 'You draw a club like Bayern Munich and you quickly realise that it will take a little miracle to beat them'. Noel acknowledged that miracles don't come along very often and recalled a sobering day when playing for Hibs in the European Cup in 1971 at Flower Lodge. Borussia Mönchengladbach was the visitor to Leeside and they took the home side apart to the tune of five goals. Noel was determined that his City side would not suffer the same fate.

On that day, a true Cork sporting legend wrote his name into the history books. Dave Barry had won two All-Ireland Football titles with Cork in 1989 and 1990. As well as playing for Cork City, he was lining out for his GAA club, St Finbarr's from Togher. Dave was a man of action as a midfielder for City and as a half forward for the county footballers. On that sunny afternoon in Cork's main rugby ground, Musgrave Park, he displayed all the enthusiasm and drive that had been so often witnessed at Paírc Uí Caoimh and Turners Cross.

Peter Byrne, writing in **The Irish Times**, described Dave's performance as *'quite simply stunning'* and suggested that in all his sporting career he had never put in a performance as good as the one he gave against Bayern. He helped out in attack with Pat Morley, covered in defence and tested the goalkeeper with his free kicks. When the chance arose, it was Dave Barry who was on hand to shoot City into the lead.

Bayern lost the ball in the middle of the park, under pressure from Mike Conroy, who slipped the ball left into the path of Dave, who was breaking from midfield. Dave was now moving like a train towards the Bayern penalty box. The sight of this speeding Corkonian was enough to convince Bayern defender Roland Grahammer that attempting a tackle would be dangerous for both Bayern's defensive fidelity and his own health. As Dave neared the goal, Grahammer did something that most German defenders never do: he pulled out of a tackle and in doing so performed a half-jump in the air, almost a pirouette. Dave feinted left and then drew the ball onto his right foot as Grahammer danced out of his way. With a delicious blast of his right foot, he fired the ball towards the goal. Gerry Hillringhaus in the Bayern goal was caught by the quickness of the shot and only managed to get a hand to the ball, but not enough to prevent it bouncing once and into the net. Cork had the lead and Musgrave Park went wild.

But City could not maintain their lead to the break. Stefan Effenberg struck with a cracking shot from the edge of the box that gave Phil Mooney in the City goal had no chance. The attendance on the day was disappointingly low for such a big game in such a sports-crazy city. Just 4,000 fans were there to witness a titanic effort from the local side in a game full of excitement and with two superb goals. The poor attendance was blamed on the admission prices, which started at £8 for the terrace, but surely the glamour of the opposition would have warranted splashing out on this occasion.

However, for those inside the ground, it was a day of great joy and for Dave Barry it constituted another highlight of his sporting career: *'I have rarely felt so shattered after a game,'* he said, remarking that every blade of grass had been covered on the pitch by the Cork City side, in an attempt to keep Bayern at bay. *'I felt as fulfilled as the afternoon I won the first of my two All-Ireland medals with Cork's Gaelic football team'*, he added.

Both managers seemed satisfied with their teams' efforts. Noel O'Mahony was delighted with the defensive ability and the discipline of his players, who stuck to the instructions given to them before the match. Jupp Heynckes was also satisfied, noting that City had pushed his side all the way: *'On balance I think the scoreline was a fair one'*, he said.

City made another great effort during the return leg at the Olympic Stadium two weeks later, where they held out against the hosts until the seventy-fifth minute, when Bruno Labbadia managed to nose the home side into the lead. More heroics from City had seen both Pat Morely and John Caulfield miss chances to grab an away goal and put real pressure on the home side. How many times in the future would that deadly duo come to the rescue of Cork City? Unfortunately, on that occasion, their efforts, along with the efforts of the rest of the City side, were not enough and a late penalty awarded to Bayern sealed the side's victory.

To Cork's credit, although they had not won the match, they did win the admiration of the German fans, who applauded them off the pitch in recognition of their tremendous effort.

The games described revealed a lot about League of Ireland football at the time. They gave a valid and fair reflection of the standard of both the players and the way we thought about the game. It is no coincidence that some of the best results were achieved through the genius of the great men of League of Ireland football, those who relished pitting their skill and wits against the best in Europe. Admittedly, they did not always get it right, but on those nights when a top European side was humbled at Dalymount, Oriel, St Mel's or Milltown, they were the equals of any player or manager in Europe.

Our Friends in the North
Derry City Come Out to Play

The defeat of a Portadown FC motion, advocating for the return of Derry City home matches to Brandywell, before the Irish League Committee was the final straw for this proud club. After forty-three years in senior football in Northern Ireland and membership of the Irish League, Derry City resigned their membership of the Irish League in 1972. The club had won the Irish Cup on three occasions, beating Glentoran each time and they were also league champions in 1964–65.

The club was founded in 1928. In an attempt to be inclusive, they rejected the official name of the city at the time, Londonderry, and also that of Derry Celtic, which had been the city's previous club. Settling on Derry City FC as the club name, it was successful in gaining admission to the Irish League the following year and began their league campaign in the 1929–30 season at home against Glentoran.

For forty years, Derry played their home games at the city's municipal ground, Brandywell Stadium. The stadium had been let to the club by Londonderry Corporation, now Derry City Council, under the constraints of the Honourable Irish Society, which stated that the stadium must be at the disposal of the community for recreation purposes.

In January 1969, the first signs of difficulty with Derry City fulfilling their home fixtures at Brandywell began to appear. An end-of-season league fixture between The Candystripes and Linfield was marred by crowd trouble. Police had to shepherd visiting fans to and from the ground and during the game, rocks and stones were thrown, sectarian songs were sung and articles were burned. Given the political situation and the civil unrest that was gripping Northern Ireland at the time, and the fact that Derry had seen some of the worst of the unrest, Linfield decided that they would not travel to Brandywell for any future fixtures. It was 2005 before The Blues ran out onto the Brandywell pitch again. By 1970, Derry City were playing their home fixtures against Linfield at Windsor Park in Belfast, which necessitated a 150-mile round trip for a 'home' fixture. A number of other league clubs also took Linfield's position, stating that they also would not travel to Brandywell for safety reasons.

Following another incident which involved Ballymena United's bus being burnt out during a visit to Derry, the Irish League Committee decided that all of Derry City's home games would now be played at the Showgrounds in Coleraine for safety and security reasons. This was a disaster for The Candystripes as Coleraine was 30 miles from Derry and the move would have a serious impact on attendances and the financial well-being of the club. Derry City had enquired about using Finn Park in Ballybofey, but this was rejected by the Irish League as the ground was not in their jurisdiction. Permission to use a ground in the town of Limavady was also refused, so City had no choice but to travel along the north coast to Coleraine for their home games.

The Irish League stated that the arrangement of Derry's home games in Coleraine would continue for the new 1972–73 season and officially designated Derry's home ground as the Showgrounds. The club began a 'Back to Brandywell' campaign and refused to play 'home' fixtures against Bangor and Coleraine. Derry had received clearance from security authorities to resume their home games at Brandywell and for a brief period it seemed that this assurance would sway the Irish League and Derry would be granted their wish to return to home. Despite putting this clearance before the Irish League committee they were refused permission to return to Brandywell after a vote of Irish League club members.

Portadown FC's motion failed by just one vote and, on 13 October 1972, Derry City said goodbye to senior football in the Irish League. Upon receipt of Derry's resignation, IFA President Harry Cavan was asked to comment: 'I sincerely regret this move, but it is not a decision of the making of the Irish League, and in fact has been forced on Derry through the very circumstances of their surroundings'. Cavan went on to remark that he would certainly support any move by Derry City to return to the league, but it was difficult to see how this could come about without the support of all the league clubs, the Irish League and the IFA.

In 1974, the city had been without senior football for two seasons and it was hoped that perhaps in another few years the atmosphere would have improved enough to try to register Brandywell as a home venue again and rejoin the Irish League. That hope went unfulfilled and it would be another eleven years before a senior league match would be payed by Derry City.

The process of trying to rejoin the Irish League was getting nowhere fast. Ten applications had been rejected by the Irish League on the grounds of security concerns at Brandywell. It was time for Derry City to look elsewhere for a chance to play senior football and so they turned their attention to joining the League of Ireland. In March 1984, led by Tony O'Doherty, Terry Harkin, Eddie Mahon and Eamonn McLoughlin, City made a formal application to be considered for League of Ireland membership for the following season. However, all league applications for the following season had to be received by 1 February and therefore they could not be considered. This was just one of the problems that they faced, as FIFA rules dictated that teams were restricted by political and national boundaries. Derry City would probably have to seek a special dispensation from FIFA to play League of Ireland football. To counter this border argument, Derry City cited the case of Berwick Rangers, a club based in England but that played in the Scottish league, as a precedent. There was also the possibility of basing the club in Buncrana, County Donegal, but this was quickly dismissed by Derry City officials, who were determined to register Brandywell as their home ground and bring football back to the city.

Shamrock Rovers, never a club to take a step backwards, gave the Derry City case a timely boost when they agreed to travel to Brandywell to play a friendly match a few weeks after City's league membership application. Although the application had been rejected because it had been submitted too late, the fact that it had not been rejected out of hand was encouraging for Terry Harkin: 'while they have not accepted us yet, at least they have not thrown out our application. That is great news for us'. In an interview at the time of the Rovers visit, Harkin told *The Irish Times* that he was tired of seeing local youths playing football with no prospect of being able to go on to play senior football in their home town. He remarked that when teenagers returned from unsuccessful trials with English clubs, they had nowhere to turn to at home for senior football. Harkin also took a swipe at the IFA and the Irish League over their refusal to grant Derry City Irish League membership over the last number of years, remarking that GAA matches were being played in Northern Ireland without any trouble.

A Fan For All Seasons

As the FAI and the League of Ireland prepared for their AGM in 1984, Derry City made the trip to Dublin to explain their case for membership of the League of Ireland. They were met by the city's Lord Mayor, Michael Keating, and Fianna Fáil TD, David Andrews. The Lord Mayor was keen to support Derry City's application and remarked at a press conference that both the FAI and the IFA were obliged to do something to remedy the plight of The Candystripes. The meeting with Andrews, however, would have been more significant, given his patronage of the FAI. Although not speaking on behalf of the FAI or in any FAI capacity, Andrews remarked that 'there is surely a legitimate right for Derry to become a member of the League of Ireland', a remark which must have been seen by the Derry City delegation as good news for their membership application.

Andrews and Keating were not the only political figures to take an interest in Derry City's plight. MP for the Foyle constituency, John Hume was also keen to see the situation resolved and senior football brought back to Derry. Derry City had also take their case to both FIFA and UEFA, but typical of the bureaucratic style of these two governing bodies, they decided to defer any decision back to the national associations. Given that both the FAI and the IFA were involved, it was left to whichever association felt like taking up the issue. Although they knew that there was no chance of being able to play in the League of Ireland for the 1984–85 season, this didn't do anything to diminish the efforts of the Derry City committee.

In September 1984, Derry City got the boost to their campaign that they needed when the Irish League and Irish Football Association declared that they would not object to Derry City's League of Ireland membership application. One major sticking point had been cleared, which took any potential repercussions from FIFA and UEFA out of the equation for both Derry City and the FAI. The FAI had also rubber-stamped the creation of a new League of Ireland First Division at their AGM in Bundoran and this also gave Derry City hope as the League of Ireland would need teams to fill this new league and compete with the four teams who would be relegated from the A Division that season.

Eamonn Morris, the secretary of the League of Ireland, advised in November that the management committee hoped to give a decision on the applications received from clubs to join the new First Division by Christmas. There were six places available for the ten-team league and they had received eight applications for those six places. Derry City was one of those applicants, but the same issue which had dogged their membership applications for the Irish League now began to emerge amongst the Dublin clubs, in particular. Just how safe was Brandywell? The League Committee meeting at Merrion Square on Friday, 23 November, proved to be a tumultuous affair. The meeting to allocate the six new places turned into a discussion of the merits of Derry City's application alone. It pitted league president Fran Fields against Noel Murphy, the Limerick City delegate, in what reports described as resembling almost a personal duel. Fran Fields was from Donegal and it was clear that he would welcome another club in the north-west, along with Finn Harps and Sligo Rovers.

The meeting was addressed by the league's executive, who assured delegates present that they need have no concerns regarding the safety of Brandywell. Noel Murphy needed further convincing of this and raised a number of questions with Fields directly. Security, player insurance and that players would 'miss work on Monday morning' due to the distance were all issues of concern for Murphy. In response to these questions, Fields replied that the League of Ireland had been advised that the Royal Ulster Constabulary would have *'no objection to Derry City entering the League of Ireland'*. On the insurance issue, Dundalk delegate Enda McGuill advised that there would be no concern regarding insurance cover for players travelling to Derry. McGuill was an insurance broker himself and so he could speak with authority. McGuill, Eamonn Reid of Waterford and Paddy Kilcoyne of Shamrock Rovers expressed the opinion that the general impression from clubs, even prior to the meeting, was that Derry City would be very welcome in the League of Ireland.

Despite Noel Murphy's concerns, Derry City was eventually approved for membership of the League of Ireland First Division for the following season. But Murphy had not been alone in voicing concerns. Along with his Limerick City club, neither St Patrick's Athletic nor Shelbourne were in favour of Derry City's application.

This didn't matter a jot to the Derry City committee. They had finally made a breakthrough and achieved their goal of bringing senior football back to Derry and back to Brandywell. It had been a long road, with numerous setbacks since 1972, but at last they could make plans and prepare for a new era. All that was left for The Candystripes was to make sure they made the most of this new opportunity.

As luck would have it, both Sligo Rovers and Finn Harps joined Derry City in the new First Division. This insured six north-west derbies that season and the prospect of these fixtures, especially the Finn Harps game, was not lost on Terry Harkin, who boasted that a Finn Harps fixture at Brandywell could attract 10,000 fans to the ground.

A Fan For All Seasons

Joining the three north-west clubs were EMFA, Bray Wanderers, Monaghan United, Drogheda United, Longford Town, Newcastle United and Cobh Ramblers. The inaugural First Division Championship would be a quick-fire eighteen games, with the top two gaining promotion to the Premier Division.

As the start of the season drew closer, excitement about Derry City's debut in the League of Ireland was building. For the other nine clubs, it may have seemed that Derry City was the only show in town. A substantial amount of newspaper articles were devoted to The Candystripes, all outlining the club's twelve-year absence from senior football, their rift with the Irish League in Belfast and how the city was being re-awakened by the thoughts of seeing those famous jerseys running out onto the Brandywell pitch for competitive football again.

Those League of Ireland clubs that had been so quick to welcome Derry City were now troubling themselves about security and safety concerns at Brandywell. However, Derry City had come to a unique agreement with the RUC. It was agreed that Derry City officials would provide their own match day security at home fixtures and that the RUC would operate outside the ground and would be called on only if needed. As City's secretary, Seamus Hegarty advised, anyone who had concerns, 'in this new situation with teams travelling from the South on Sundays, we don't see that [trouble] happening'.

In front of a crowd of 8,000 fans, Derry City began life as a member of the League of Ireland against Home Farm in a League Cup game at Brandywell. With a queue of fans still outside at kick-off and the club's souvenir match programme sold out, it turned out to be a great day for The Candystripes. Any concerns about safety or possible trouble were allayed and Home Farm also played their role by being beaten by three goals to one. It was Derry City centre forward Barney McCreadie who got the show on the road, with the opening goal following good work from former Sunderland, Manchester City and England player Denis Tueart. Tueart was also involved in the other two City goals, following Mick Moody's forced equaliser for Home Farm. Tueart showed all his ability and experience in setting up former Bolton Wanderers striker Garry Jones to seal a memorable win and return for Derry City. The other teams competing in their League Cup group were Monaghan United and UCD.

After a six-week period after the League Cup group games were concluded, Derry City could look back and survey the scene. They had won two, drawn one and lost three. It wasn't a bad start to their new campaign, but City manager Jim Crossan felt that City needed to improve their results and competitiveness. Crossan handed in his resignation, stating that he believed 'the team needs a player-manager out there on the pitch with them'. He went on to say that 'the team would be better with a man out there with them, for until now we have been blundering our way through and not really knowing where we are. It's not fair to our fantastic supporters who deserve better than what we are giving them'. It was a strong, frank and heartfelt statement from a man who was totally committed to the good of Derry City FC. It also went to show that no matter how romantic a story your club has, football is still a results business and there is little room for sentiment.

The opening game of the First Division for Derry would see them travel to Buckley Park in Kilkenny to take on fellow newcomers EMFA. A 1-1 draw secured a first league point for The Candystripes, but attention was definitely focused on the probable new manager, especially when the name hotly linked with the job was none other than the manager of the league champions Shamrock Rovers, Jim McLaughlin. However, McLaughlin turned the role down, but he did recommend player-coach at Rovers, Noel King ,who took up the job in mid-November.

By the fifth round of league matches, it was Sligo Rovers who were leading the way in a bid to gain promotion back to the top flight. For Derry City, the days of excitement and expectation were replaced by slow hand clapping at Brandywell as Noel King's team were defeated 2-0 by Sligo Rovers and were still seeking their first league win. That first win did arrive in the seventh round of matches, away at Monaghand United, but by then it was too late for Derry City to make a real charge for promotion, given the eighteen-game format of the league. They would have to wait a while longer to play with the big boys in the League of Ireland.

For the other new clubs in the First Division, they had to learn as they went, especially those new to League of Ireland football. Newcastle United, from Limerick, managed their first win at home in Newcastle West when they beat EMFA 4-2. The club would change its name to Newcastlewest the following season and play for a total of five seasons in League of Ireland football. Despite not really challenging for promotion during their tenure in the league, they did reach the quarter-finals of the FAI Cup on two occasions, both of which were noteworthy.

The first time they reached the quarter-finals, in 1988, was controversial as they defeated Cobh Ramblers at home after a replay. Cobh lodged a complaint that

A Fan For All Seasons

Newcastlewest had fielded an ineligible player, Billy Daly. Daly had just been transferred to Newcastlewest from Cobh, but the objection was based on the belief that Daly was signed too late to play and was therefore ineligible. The FAI agreed with Cobh and awarded them the tie. In a fit of pique, Newcastlewest decided to pull out of the First Division. It took a two-hour meeting of the League Committee to resolve the situation, with Newcastlewest agreeing to fulfil their league fixtures. The cup tie itself was replayed and, in an ironic twist, it was Billy Daly who scored the only goal of the game for Newcastlewest.

They reached the quarter-finals again two seasons later, having produced a major shock by beating Sligo Rovers at the Showgrounds. They were next drawn against intermediate side St Francis in what would have been seen as an easy tie; however, Newcastlewest were to fall to the might of the part-timers in their historic march to the FAI Cup final that year.

EMFA, from Kilkenny City and under the guidance of club secretary Jim Rhatigan, would go on to participate in the League of Ireland for twenty-one years, gaining promotion to the Premier Division twice. They won two pieces of League of Ireland silverware by winning the First Division as Kilkenny City in 1996–97 and the First Division Shield in 1986–87 as EMFA, beating Finn Harps in the final at Oriel Park. Despite a number of notable managers throughout the years, including Eamonn Gregg, Joe McGrath, Alfie Hale, Pat Byrne and Pat Scully, the club could never really secure a substantial support base. This difficulty was unsurprising in a county famed for its hugely successful hurling culture. There is no longer any senior football team in Kilkenny and any prospect of a club from that part of the country making an application to join the League of Ireland looks decidedly remote at present.

Monaghan United had been playing League of Ireland B Division football since 1983 and joined the new First Division directly from this league. The club spent the vast majority of its League of Ireland spell in the First Division, winning promotion on three occasions. However, during the 2012 season, when they were members of the Premier Division, they withdrew from the league, citing financial difficulties. The Premier Division was left with just eleven teams and results of other clubs against Monaghan United for that season were not included in the allocation of league points.

For Cobh Ramblers, it was always a case of living in the shadow of whichever Cork city club was present at the time. The Ramblers, however, had a strong and successful tradition as a Munster Senior League club. Cobh started out as a hockey club, but founded a football club in 1922 and won their first Munster Senior Cup just three years later. They have won just one piece of league silverware, when they secured the First Division title in 2007.

Completing the roll call of new clubs to the League of Ireland was Bray Wanderers. It would be a memorable season for The Seagulls, who won the First Division title under the management of Pat Devlin. A 0–0 draw at home to Finn Harps on the last day of the season gave Bray the point they needed and was enough to see off Sligo Rovers, who had to settle for a runners-up spot. It was a great achievement for a club that had no previous experience at that level and had competed against four teams that had been in the top division just a season earlier.

The first outing of the First Division had been a success and despite their poor start to the league season, Derry City managed to finish in fourth place and won the first League of Ireland First Division Shield, beating Longford Town 6–1 in a home and away final. The smaller clubs had all played their part and there were no casualties for the following season.

City swept to the First Division title the following season, winning sixteen of their eighteen games, losing one and drawing one. Powered by the eighteen goals of Yugoslavian Alex Krstic, they secured promotion, along with runners-up and previously relegated Shelbourne. City were now firmly established as a main player in the League of Ireland and had one of the league's all-time greatest managers at the club.

Jim McLaughlin had joined in June 1986, leaving the league champions Shamrock Rovers, for a general manager position at his home-town club. Noel King stayed on as player-manager during the successful First Division championship season, but with a man of McLaughlin's presence at the club, it was difficult to see how King could last in his role as player-manager. By March 1987, there was already speculation about King's future with The Candystripes, but club officials seemed happy to tell the media that the final year of King's contract would be honoured.

It also looked like striker Krstic would also be leaving Brandywell with King. Krstic had caught the eye of Dundee United manager Jim McClean and travelled to Tannadice Park for a meeting with McClean. The £75,000 deal fell through, however when Krstic said that he felt unhappy with particular aspects of the deal. Krstic did leave Derry City in September 1987 and joined West German club Saarbrucken for £50,000. Although the deal was worth considerably less to Derry City, the salary on offer for Krstic at the German club was significantly better than that offered by Dundee United or Manchester City, who had also expressed an interest in signing the Yugoslavian.

King's time at Derry City came to an end in October 1987, when his resignation was announced at a press conference. King was adamant about his loyalty to Derry City and said he had no grievance with the club, although he did say that *'Derry City as a club is not being run properly because of the different factions involved'*.

An indifferent league campaign saw Derry City finish in eighth place in McLaughlin's first season in charge. The club did, however, reach that year's FAI Cup Final for the first time, overcoming Longford Town in the semi-final. Their final opponents would be McLaughlin's old club, Dundalk. Despite bringing over 15,000 fans to Dalymount to roar them on to victory, it wasn't enough, as a John Cleary penalty decided the match and secured the cup for Dundalk, who had also just won the league title. The City fans won huge credit for their colourful and boisterous support of The Candystripes and although they were defeated, Derry City had European football to look forward to the following season.

Those enthusiastic Candystripes fans had a lot more to get excited about during the 1988-89 season, as the McLaughlin magic started to produce results. City went on to complete a clean sweep of domestic trophies, achieving the first ever treble, after winning the league championship, the FAI Cup and the League of Ireland Cup.

The haul began in October, with a superb 4-0 revenge win over Dundalk at Oriel Park in the final of the League Cup. The quality of the play by both sides merited a standing ovation at the final whistle. McLaughlin had gone back to his former club Shamrock Rovers and brought in the experienced defending expertise of Mick Neville and Kevin Brady, who teamed up with team captain and local man Paul Curran. There was also the French flair of Pascal Vaudequin at full back, giving the back four a solid look. Former Hoops midfielder Paul Doolin also arrived at Brandywell and, along with veteran Noel Larkin, former Northern Ireland international Felix Healy, a youthful Liam Coyle and the goal instincts Jonathan Speak, they formed a formidable line-up, capable of beating all comers.

The Candystripes would battle with Dundalk for the league championship, but as the title race neared its end, it was Derry City who proved to have the nerve needed to get over the line. Shamrock Rovers' visit to Brandywell at the beginning of April should have provided the single point necessary for City to claim the title. The Hoops were having a bad season and were over twenty points behind Derry City in the league standings.

How ironic it was that this Rovers team, managed by Noel King, should force a postponement to the title celebrations, as David Kealy scored the only goal to give Rovers the points. King was warmly welcomed back to Brandywell by the Derry City fans and received a special ovation when he shook hands with Jim McLaughlin. The respect and affection that King still held for Derry City was evident in his post-match comments: *'I hope in all sincerity that this defeat does not cost them the championship. They richly deserve it on their form this season'*.

For City, the champagne was on ice and there was still the small matter of an FAI Cup semi-final in their quest for the treble. Rovers once again provided the opposition, but this time the result went with form and Derry City secured a 3–0 first leg lead, thanks to two goals from Johnathan Speak and one from Liam Coyle. A 1–1 draw at Dalymount in the second leg ensured a safe passage to the final.

It was back to finishing the job at hand in the league, as Cobh Ramblers made the long journey north for the final game of the season. This time, City did not disappoint and a 2–0 win was more than enough to claim a first League of Ireland Premier Division title for The Candystripes, twenty-four years after their only other senior league title win in the Irish League. With this win, they joined Austrian club Rapid Vienna to become one of only two clubs to have won league titles in two different football jurisdictions.

Not that any of this mattered to the thousands of fans that crammed into Brandywell with their flags, banners, klaxons and air horns. The scene resembled an Argentinian club match more than a scene from the north-west of Ireland. All that was missing was the ticker tape but the showers of sleet and snow that hit Brandywell provided an admirable substitute. Two goals in the first thirty minutes, both from Paul Doolin, set any nerves to rest. As the crowd saluted the players and management at the final whistle, Jim McLaughlin was visibly moved to tears: *'I have known no such emotion on the terraces of any football ground. They simply willed us to victory and the players responded in kind'*. McLaughlin acknowledged that although his success at Dundalk and Rovers had been immense, this league win was, *'as a Derryman ... something extra special'.*

The last leg of this epic season would be the FAI Cup final against Cork City. The first game in front of over 20,000 fans at Dalymount turned out to be a damp squib as the game petered out in a 0-0 draw. The replay attracted just over 10,000 fans, who saw a Felix Healy goal win the final and the treble and confirm Derry City as a team without equal that season.

Derry's football journey had been a tough one, marked by numerous setbacks both on and off the pitch over the previous fifteen years. The treble success of 1988-89 was a testament to all those who ensured that the club remained functioning throughout what Derry City fans refer to as the 'Wilderness Years'. Derry City was now very much a League of Ireland club.

Saints March Back
Kerr, Dolan and Buckley - Cup Winners at Last

By November 1986, it had been a long time since there had been anything to celebrate in Inchicore. The Saints' golden period of success was a faded memory best left to the oldies on the Richmond Park terrace to remember. The time of the greats in red - Gibbons, Whelan, Peyton, Lowry and Dunne - seemed to be an epoch ago and despite valiant attempts to try bring the FAI Cup back to Inchicore, the trophy cabinet had been conspicuously bare for decades.

Many good men had tried and failed to revive the club's fortunes: Peter Farrell, John Colrain, Charlie Walker and Jimmy Jackson to name a few, all determined football men but they were unable to weave that magic spell which would result in a trophy being collected by the St Patrick's Athletic captain.

Despite the team's lack of success, The Saints did manage to unearth two stars, who would go on to have excellent careers abroad. Firstly, there was Noel Campbell, who would become the club's top goalscorer for two consecutive seasons from 1968 to 1970. Noel would also become the first Irishman to play in the Bundesliga when he joined SC Fortuna Köln in 1971 and be the first Irishman to represent and play for Ireland while playing for a mainland European club. The second star needs no introduction. Charlie Walker signed Paul McGrath from Dalkey United and his class was evident from the beginning. In his sole season with The Saints, Paul won the PFAI Player of the Year award and earned himself a move to Manchester United.

While at Manchester United, he won an FA Cup winners medal in 1985 and after a move to Aston Villa, he collected two League Cup winners medals in 1994 and

A Fan For All Seasons

1996. Paul won eighty-three caps for Ireland in a lengthy International career and was the cornerstone of many of the national team's success at the time, playing in two World Cup tournaments and the European Championships.

Sadly for The Saints fans, these highlights were just fleeting bright spots during a prolonged period of grey anonymity that seemed to be permanently resident at the club. However, a significant change was to take place on 1 December 1986 upon the appointment of a man who would become for many the very embodiment of Saint Patrick's Athletic Football Club.

Having seen off other prospective managers such as Willie Roche and Fran Gavin, Brian Kerr was appointed as Saints' boss, leaving his previous role as assistant manager to Mick Lawlor at Drogheda United. Kerr took over a club, which was short on resources, and demonstrated his ability to find players and to mould a winning team. Within weeks of joining the club, he led them to their first trophy in eleven years: they beat Bohemian FC 1–0 in the final of the Leinster Senior Cup.

While this trophy was a welcome addition to the success-starved fans, it was just a taster of what was to come in a rollercoaster of ups and downs the following season.

At the start of January 1988, just four points separated the top four teams in the league championship race and St Pats were amongst those top four, with Dundalk, Bohemian FC and Rovers. It was a remarkable upturn in fortunes for The Saints and their good form had seen the return of some long-lost fans to Richmond Park. The team had improved considerably and now contained a mix of players who were putting it up to the best. Players like Dave Henderson in goal, along with Damien Byrne and rising star Curtis Fleming, were ensuring that little was getting through to trouble the Pats goal. In the middle were Maurice O'Driscoll and Paul Byrne, ready to supply Paddy Dillon up front. Emboldened by Kerr's belief in them and their success to date, they took on league leaders Dundalk at Richmond at the end of January in a top-of-the-table clash.

The Saints raced into a two-goal league in front of a packed ground and it seemed like they would be going to the heady heights of pole position. The Lilywhites, who had been runners-up the previous year and were determined to go one better this time around, had other ideas and fought back to claim a 2–2 draw. There was late drama in the game when three minutes from time, The Saints had the ball back in the net for three two, but the referee disallowed the goal and the points were shared.

Despite losing the extra point, Pats maintained their unlikely charge towards the championship and cemented their credentials with a convincing 2-0 win over the reigning champions, Shamrock Rovers. A lot of attention was being focused on this young side, the average age of which was just twenty-two and who had come out of nowhere to become viable title contenders. By mid-March and with four games to go, Pats were still there, joint leaders with Dundalk and Bohemian FC, all on thirty-nine points. Pats dropped a precious point when they drew at home with Bray Wanderers, while both Bohs and Dundalk capitalised with away wins.

It was looking like The Saints' run in the title race was coming to an end as there was a two-point gap and just three games left to play; however, it was Bohemian FC who folded first when they drew with Waterford United at Kilcohan Park. This result left The Gypsies needing results to fall in their favour fast as the last round of fixtures pitted Dundalk against St Pats at Oriel in a potential winner-takes-all climax. Both Dundalk and Pats won their penultimate matches to ensure that the title would go to one of the sides running out at Oriel.

During the title race, both Dundalk and Pats had been drawn against each other in the semi-final of the cup. At this time, the cup semi-final was a two-legged affair. Dundalk won the first leg at Oriel by a goal to nil and such was the interest generated by this young Pats side in Inchicore that the second leg was an all-ticket event. Despite the best efforts of a bumper crowd, The Saints could not overturn the deficit and fell to a heavy 3-0 defeat, thereby ensuring their wait for FAI Cup glory was prolonged for another year.

As the league decider drew nearer, Kerr was asked to reflect on his first full season in charge and on the remarkable progress of his young side. He told *The Irish Times*: *'when I took up the job I hoped to have the ability to knock the club into shape. But to be honest I didn't think it would happen so quickly'*. He also noted the rocky start to the campaign when they collected just four points from their first five matches, but remarked that the injection of youth had come good for the club: *'the developments of our youth policy did the trick'*.

With the coaches and cars packed full of fans, The Saints travelled to Dundalk, hopeful that they might secure their first league title since 1956. In their way was

A Fan For All Seasons

Turlough O'Connor's highly experienced Dundalk team, which contained players such as Alan O'Neill, Gino Lawless, Martin Lawlor, Terry Eviston and Dessie Gorman. On paper, the experience of these players should have been enough to see off the pretenders from Inchicore.

In front of a crowd of over 6,000 an early penalty from Pat Fenlon, after a Gino Lawless handball, put The Saints ahead and within touching distance of the title. However, a Dessie Gorman header midway through the first half brought Dundalk back on level terms and despite efforts from Paddy Dillon and full back Pat Kelch, The Saints could not fashion a winner and a point was good enough to bring the title back to Oriel.

Given the years of under-achievement that had gone before, the season could be seen as something of a success for The Saints. They had made a real challenge for the title and had developed a young squad of resourceful and willing players. By finishing runners-up, they also qualified for the UEFA Cup and they could harbour the hope that an attractive tie would provide much-needed resources to the club.

For Brian Kerr, turning the club around had been a remarkable achievement, but he was only getting started. Despite a move away from their spiritual home of Inchicore to Harold's Cross for what was hoped to be a short time, Kerr would deliver the title to The Saints faithful on Easter Monday 1990.

Having added to their young squad with players of the calibre of Paul Osam and Tony O'Connor, The Saints had a perfect blend of experience and youth. Damien Byrne, team captain and in the game since 1973, was on hand to collect his first winners medal as a senior player amid joyous scenes at Drogheda United's United Park. The Saints clinched the title with a 2-0 win and relegated United in the process. There were winners medals for John McDonnell, Pat Kelch, Pat Fenlon and Dave Henderson, to name just some of those who had come so close at Oriel Park two seasons earlier. For Kerr, it was a special day. He remarked that *'to manage the club you followed as a boy is a privilege. To lead it to the championship after all those years is the stuff of fantasy'*. And fantasy it was for all the fans who had travelled again to see if they could get over the line on this occasion. He noted, with a sense of pride, that the victory had been three years in the making and that a lot of heartache and character-building had been endured along the road. Also, in a nod to the limited resources of the club, he remarked that *'success is not the preserve of the monied clubs'*.

Given the strength of the side, it was conceivable that Pats might go on to enjoy a spell of domination in much the same way as their successful 1950s side. Unfortunately for The Saints and for Kerr, they were never given the opportunity as issues regarding the financial well-being and ownership of the club, in summer 1992, forced the sale of many of those players who had made success possible. An exodus to Bohemian FC, Derry City and Shamrock Rovers followed, with many of the players continuing their success with their new clubs.

A nadir was reached in June 1992, when the League of Ireland executive committee issued The Saints with an ultimatum to sort out the issues at the club and secure new owners or else the league would take over the club and the players' contracts. Much to The Saints' relief, a group of supporters came up with approximately £75,000 needed to save the club from expulsion from the league.

During this time, the club was still playing their home matches at Harold's Cross and it would be nearly another eighteen months before they finally returned to Richmond Park. The three years from 1991 to 1994 would be fallow years for The Saints and given the necessity to sell on any rising stars, it was hardly surprising that Kerr found himself almost back where he began in 1986, building a new squad of players, to try take on the best on a shoestring.

The 1994–95 season hinted that things might at last be coming right for The Saints when they finished just six points behind the eventual champions Dundalk. They also boasted the least amount of defeats, being beaten on just six occasions. However, the fourteen draws during this campaign proved the real obstacle to mounting a more meaningful title challenge.

The following season saw The Saints' rebirth as they duelled it out with Bohemian FC, Shelbourne and Sligo Rovers in the title race. The clubs were toe to toe for most of the season. Despite a setback in December, when The Saints were soundly beaten five goals to one by Derry City, they then managed to go on a run of twenty-two unbeaten games in both the league and cup. Towards the end of the season, a series of games in the league and cup against Bohemian FC demonstrated the mental toughness and physical fitness of this well-coached Pats team. Having drawn with Bohs at Dalymount in the FAI Cup semi-final, Pats managed to follow this up by collecting three points with a win at home to Galway United. They travelled back to Dalymount for a league fixture. A dull 0-0 draw led Gerry Thornley in *The Irish Times* to muse that it might be best if Bohs versus Pats games be played 'in private', such was the ordinary standard of the fare on offer. Thornley further remarked that *'much more of this [standard] and they probably will be'*. However, the way in which this league point had been earned was of little consequence to the Pats fans on the Connaught Street side of Dalymount as it took them that much closer to the title and left Bohs needing a small miracle to claim the championship. The replay of the FAI Cup semi-final at Inchicore also finished in a draw meaning the teams would have to face each other for the forth time in less than a month. By the time Ricky O'Flaherty's two goals had settled the semi-final in St Pats favour both players, fans and the media had seen enough of this fixture to last a very long time.

In an ironic twist of fate for Brian Kerr and his Super Saints, they travelled to Oriel Park to face Dundalk in an opportunity to claim the league title with a match to spare. I wonder whether thoughts of their journey some eight years earlier flashed through the minds of Kerr and the fans. Unlike that day though, it was Dundalk who took the lead, when Peter Withnell connected with a John Coady cross and as the ball broke, Stephen Napier was on hand to volley The Lilywhites into the lead.

This was after the home side had been reduced to ten men, with Richie Purdy dismissed for a foul on Brian Morrisroe. The lead was short-lived as from the restart, the ball was worked to Peter Carpenter and his cross was met with a looping header from Ricky O'Flaherty to draw The Saints level. The ball left O'Flaherty's head and followed a gravity and physics-defying trajectory over John Connolly's head and into the far corner of the net. True to the tradition of their fine club, Dundalk set about trying to upset Pats as much as possible and, despite being a man down, created a number of chances in the second half to keep The Saints fans on edge. A chance for Joe Gallen was followed later by a disallowed goal for Brian Byrne. However, The Saints fought back, with Liam Buckley hitting the post with a header and good chances for O'Flaherty, John McDonnell and Johnny Glynn all going begging.

With five minutes left in the game, it was *déjà vu* for Kerr, with the scoreline showing 1-1. There would be another chance the following week, but how fitting it would be to become champions at Oriel Park. Step forward Paul Campbell.

Dundalk midfielder Brian Byrne lost control of the ball on the edge of his own penalty box and in the process fouled Pats midfielder Noel Mernagh. Normally, this was Eddie Gormley territory, but with Eddie not around, up stepped 'Soupy' Campbell to curl a beautiful left-footed shot beyond the reach of John Connolly.

Eddie would have been hard pushed to finish better himself. As Soupy tore off to celebrate with the pitch-invading fans, the realisation that they were just four minutes from the title dawned on The Saints bench of Brian Kerr and legendary assistant Noel O'Reilly.

The remaining four minutes must have felt like a lifetime for The Saints management and fans, but at the final whistle, joy and relief were evident everywhere. Brian Kerr's jig on the touchline summed up what the achievement meant to him; he had carved out another title-winning team from a club on the brink of an abyss. However, Kerr was quick to acknowledge the hard work put in by all the team and noted that former players from his previous league-winning side had made the journey to Oriel to share in the club's success: *'There was a lot of goodwill towards Pats this week. I think we're popular winners',* he remarked afterwards. Indeed they were. Even RTÉ broadcasting legend Jim Sheridan was quick to congratulate The Saints, when summing up the title win on **Sunday Sport**, noting that *'this must be the most popular title win in many a year'*. It was success too for the new management of the club in chairman Tim O'Flaherty and chief executive Pat Dolan.

A chance to cap off a remarkable season came in the FAI Cup final against Shelbourne at Lansdowne Road. Pats were favourites to achieve the double for the first time in the club's history. Despite a lead goal from Dave Campbell, Shels grabbed a late draw when Tony Sheridan produced a piece of cup final magic to volley the ball over Gareth Byrne's head minutes from time to send the game to a replay at Dalymount.

Again, the following Sunday, Dave Campbell repeated the trick to give The Saints the lead and they were presented with a golden opportunity from the penalty spot to seal the cup. However, Eddie Gormley couldn't convert the spot kick and minutes later Tony Sheridan had the ball in the net to equalise for Shels. The momentum was now with The Reds and as Stephen Geoghegan poked the ball over Byrne's head to give Shels the lead, the double for Pats evaporated. Once again, the FAI Cup proved to be beyond the reach of The Saints.

After ten years at Richmond, Brian Kerr celebrated a decade in charge with a 5-0 rout of old rivals Bohemian FC. It was a fitting way to bring down the curtain on a colourful chapter in The Saints history. Within three weeks, Kerr departed to become manager of the Republic of Ireland under-sixteen and under-eighteen teams. Kerr expressed his disappointment at not being allowed to combine his job at Inchicore with that of his new role by the FAI. However, it would only be a matter of time before he brought his own unique stamp to the international underage scene, along with a huge degree of success, winning the European Championships at both age levels. Brian eventually got the top job in Irish football, when he was appointed senior team manager in January 2003. It capped an amazing journey from his first management role with Crumlin United nearly forty years earlier. He was a winner there also, guiding his team, captained by my father Gerard, to league success.

When Kerr left, it was widely believed that Liam Buckley would take charge. However, Chairman Tim O'Flaherty decided that twenty-eight-year-old Pat Dolan should take the reigns. Pat is one of the most charismatic characters ever seen in the League of Ireland and had been making a name for himself as chief executive. His programme notes were required reading and his crusade to gather respect for the League of Ireland was always heartfelt and well-intentioned. Dolan knew his football too and wasn't afraid to subscribe to an attack-minded philosophy, which appealed not only to The Saints faithful but to many League of Ireland fans around the country.

The side that Dolan created played to a different tune when compared with Kerr's league champions of two seasons previous. Dolan's team combined seasoned, quality players with the buzzing, youthful exuberance of three stars of the Ireland under-twenty side that finished third in the 1997 FIFA World Youth Championships. This side, ironically managed by Brian Kerr, contained Colin Hawkins, Thomas Morgan and Trevor Molloy, who would each go on to win successive championships with The Saints. These three players brought a new dynamic to Richmond Park and created a connection with a younger fan base, who were attracted by their skill and enthusiasm and encouraged by their recent exploits against the best underage teams in the world.

The side was slow to get going, but did manage to gain some momentum during their early series of matches. However, if one signing can be pointed to as having a fundamental impact, it was the capture of Ian Gilzean. Son of the Dundee and Spurs legend Alan, Ian would go on to become a cult hero at Inchicore and made an immediate impact, with a hat trick during his debut against a former club, Sligo Rovers. In a fixture that tested this new team's credentials, it was Gilzean's hat trick which saw The Saints home with a 4–3 victory. Ian also struck up an immediate understanding with Saints' new striker Trevor Molloy, forming a classic little-and-large combination, which was served well by attacking wing backs Trevor Crolly and Keith Doyle. Add to this the clever midfield play of Gormley, Osam and Morgan and it is clear that Dolan had created a wonderfully balanced attacking team.

It would be nip and tuck all the way between Pats and north-side Dublin rivals Shelbourne in their race for the championship. Shels, under the guidance of Damien Richardson, had an equally star-studded team, including the legendary Alan Gough in goal, along with Pat Scully, Pat Fenlon, Tony Sheridan, Dessie Baker and goal machine Stephen Geoghegan.

A home win against Dundalk at Richmond in their penultimate match ensured that Pats went into the final round of matches two points behind Shels and with an inferior goal difference. Both sides finished their campaign away from home, Pats travelling to Kilkenny City and Shels traveling to the graveyard of champions, Oriel Park. As Shels realistically required just a point, RTÉ decided to send their cameras up the M1 and televise the Oriel Park game live. At half-time, both matches were level. Pats, having taken an early lead, surrendered a soft goal midway through the first half to leave the score 1–1 at half-time in Buckley Park. It was 0–0 at Oriel and the pressure and tension were beginning to show at both venues. Damien Richardson, a man of immaculate appearance at all times, appeared from the Oriel Park dressing rooms for the second half without his necktie and looking slightly concerned by his side's inability to break down a determined Dundalk defence.

As the second half rumbled on at Oriel, a cross into the Shels box from David Crawley came to David Ward, who controlled it beautifully on his chest and nearly took the net off when firing it past Alan Gough. It was game on as news filtered through to Buckley Park, where Pats were huffing and puffing and failing to blow Kilkenny's door in. Behind the goal Pats were attacking, a sizeable crowd of Saints fans was desperately trying to suck the ball into the net. News came through on the radio that Dundalk had scored again after a through ball to Brian Byrne, who had scooped a shot over the oncoming Gough. Dundalk was doing everything possible to assist The Saints and presenting Shels with a mountain to climb.

Chances came and went for Pats, but finally a breakthrough came. In what can be best described as a classic penalty-box scramble, with legs flying everywhere and deflections aplenty, the ball broke to Eddie Gormley just on the corner of the six-yard box. Eddie shaped to pass the ball with his right foot into the corner of the goal, but as the ball left his foot, it hit the legs of a Kilkenny City defender, catching goalkeeper John Walsh square and rolling gently into the net, giving The Saints a

2-1 lead. There was a millisecond when everyone seemed to stand still and you could almost sense Gormley's anxiety as he watched his shot to see where it is going to go. Thankfully for him, it went into the back of the net and as Eddie ran to the corner flag, throwing himself to the ground, the pitch was invaded by delirious Pats fans unable to contain their joy. They had travelled in hope, but now they were beginning to believe.

The belief was fading fast at Oriel, however, for The Reds and despite pulling a late goal back from Tony Sheridan, it wasn't enough. The championship was heading back to Inchicore. The following September saw a sea change in the structure of the club, with Pat Dolan moving into the managing director role, while also holding the Director of Football title. Dolan announced that he was taking a stake in the club and would concentrate on the club's business development. This included an audacious plan to build a new 20,000-seater stadium at St Michael's Estate, on the opposite side of Richmond Park on Emmet Road. Dolan felt that the cost would run to approximately £20 million and he felt that the club would be able to fund half the cost involved. He stated that *'This is an opportunity to do something for Inchicore … and will not come along again'*.

This expanded role left no time for the day-to-day management of team affairs and, in a surprise choice, Liam Buckley was invited to take on the running of the first team. Buckley had left Richmond Park over a year and a half previously, having been overlooked for the manager's job when Brian Kerr left. Buckley had moved on to Athlone Town and had managed to guide the Division One club to the FAI Cup semi-final in his first year.

Joining Liam Buckley at Richmond that season was a midfielder of some class. Martin Russell arrived from Irish League side Portadown and, along with Gormley and Osam, completed one of the most gifted midfield trios seen in the League of Ireland. Russell's arrival brought a new dynamic to The Saints and added an additional spark of creativity in their defence of the title.

The championship quickly developed into a two-horse race between The Saints and Cork City, under the guidance of that Leeside legend Dave Barry. The sides met in October in Richmond Park and two early Trevor Molloy goals for Pats settled the tie in a comfortable performance from the champions. The sides were next due to meet at Turners Cross towards the end of January and the match proved to be one of the most memorable in recent League of Ireland history.

The kick-off was fixed for Saturday afternoon and was broadcast live on RTÉ. On that crisp winter day, over 10,000 fans packed into Turners Cross to see the best two teams in the league go head to head. City held a single-point advantage at the top of the table and were by far the better side in the first half. The break saw most of the fans scratching their heads and wondering how City were just one goal ahead. The goal that gave them the lead had been scored by Pat Morley at the Shed End of the Cross and sent the home fans into raptures. City had swamped Pats with wave after wave of attacks and had hit the post twice before taking the lead.

The subtlety of Buckley's management shone through at half-time, when a substitution in the form of Leon Braithwaite, who replaced Ian Gilzean, paid dividends for The Saints. This, along with a masterful display from Martin Russell, ensured that the game was turned on its head with two goals in four minutes. Firstly, Braithwaite drew Pats level and then it was centre back Stephen McGuinness who grabbed the winner in front of a now crestfallen Shed. The Saints had come away with three points when possibly just one was deserved. It was also two wins from two for Pats in the league meetings of the sides.

In the final instalment of the trilogy of fixtures, a Paul Osam headed goal decided the game and probably the title. Again, a huge crowd packed in to see these two sides, but was left a little underwhelmed by the fare on offer. Not that The Saints minded one bit as the three points gained, added to subsequent wins against Shamrock Rovers and Bray Wanderers, ensured the title was retained and stayed in the Richmond Park trophy cabinet.

For some fans and journalists, there was talk that this side could possibly emulate the great Rovers four-in-a-row side of the mid-eighties. However, this was not to be and a humbling defeat in a Champions League qualifier the following season began to reveal some cracks. The Saints were destroyed by five goals to nil in each leg by Zimbru Chisinau of Moldova. It was a massive disappointment to the club and its fans, given the heroics of achieving a 0-0 draw in a Champions League qualifier at Parkhead against Celtic twelve months previously.

Results started to go against the team and a scrappy loss to Derry City at home during the opening weekend of the league season raised doubts in fans' minds, with some calling for a change in management. A run of twelve undefeated matches was followed by three successive defeats and in January 2000, less than two seasons into the job, Buckley was sacked and Pat Dolan resumed his role as first team manager.

A Fan For All Seasons

The Saints didn't reach the heights of championship glory again for another fourteen years. A points deduction for failing to register players correctly cost a good side a league title in 2002, despite the club's continued instance that they were rightfully league champions. By 2003, Dolan had left the club. A proposed merger of Pats with St Francis FC was greeted with hostility by the fans and never materialised.

It would take the coming-together of a new, young and exciting side under the guidance of Liam Buckley, back for a second spell, to see the glory days return. Twelve years after being sacked, Buckley achieved another League title in 2013. However, what the Pats fans really wanted was the FAI Cup, which they hadn't won since 1961 despite appearing in eight finals since.

It might seem that for the majority of clubs, success in any season is probably easiest or best achieved through the FAI Cup. Not for St Patrick's Athletic FC. This club was the king of failure when it came to the cup. There are so many hard-luck stories from which you can choose: Brian Flood, a substitute goalkeeper for Shels in the 1996 final, walked into his goal with the ball under his arm to remove some paper draped around the net, but no goal was given as the referee didn't see the incident. In the 1996 replay, Eddie Gormley missed a penalty to secure the game for Pats. Shels then went the length of pitch and scored. While pressing for an equaliser in the 2003 final against Longford Town, Pats conceded a second goal with no goalkeeper. The goal was offside as only one Pats defender was between the goal and Longford striker Sean Barrett. The Saints playmaker Charles Imbabzi Livingstone had also retired from football due to illness a few weeks before. They were beaten in seven-goal thriller after extra time against Derry City in 2006. They were then beaten by Derry City again after extra time in 2012. Some fans genuinely thought they would never see the big cup at Inchicore, but then, one day in November 2014 …

The emotional release felt by everyone at Pats when they finally beat Derry City 2–0 to win the Cup in 2014 was like a dam bursting. At Lansdowne Road, wearing what their fans called their 'Patselona' kit, The Saints finally put to bed one of the longest-running cup droughts ever. Fifty-three years of heartache were brought to an end by two Christy Fagan goals. With that monkey off their back, there has been hopeful talk amongst the fans when the cup comes around each year. No longer can it be said that anyone can win the cup except Pats.

The Price of Success
Clubs Count the Cost of Financial Folly

At the turn of the new century, the football focus moved from St Pats in Inchicore over the river to those two north-side giants Shelbourne and Bohemian FC. It was to be a decade of dramatic highs and lows for both clubs, during which the League of Ireland as a whole would be plunged into financial issues, which bordered on the disastrous for some and spelled the end for others.

Shels had been threatening to win the title for a number of seasons under the guidance of Damien Richardson. Richardson had brought together a team with flair and ability, but it seemed they just could not make it over the line when it came to the championship. Back-to-back FAI Cups were secured, preventing a St Pats double in 1996 and then retaining the cup against Derry City twelve months later.

Bohemian FC had not tasted league success since Billy Young's side won the title in 1978. The club had been runners-up on six occasions since then. The FAI Cup had also been absent from the Dalymount trophy cabinet since 1992, when Dave Tilson's goal beat Cork City.

Shelbourne got the ball rolling with the appointment of Dermot Keely and although his first season in 1998-99 proved to be unspectacular, he went on to guide the club to their first league and Cup double the following season. This was an historic moment for the club as it was their first double in their 105-year history. They won the league by eleven points from Cork City, who finished runners-up for the second consecutive season. The league title was as good as secured at Richmond Park against the defending champions on St Patrick's Day when Shels ran out 2-1 winners. Pats had failed to mount a realistic challenge to achieve three consecutive titles and had parted company with their manager Liam Buckley during the season. Confirmation of the league title came in a 2-0 victory at the RSC against Waterford United in early April. Shels had also overcome Galway United at Terryland Park in a replay of their FAI Cup semi-final and now looked forward to completing the double against their neighbours, Bohemian FC. The first match provided much in the way of entertainment and good football in the brilliant sunshine of Tolka Park, with just a goal missing from the occasion. The replay the following Friday night at Dalymount was settled when Pat Fenlon capitalised on a loose ball in the penalty box, and slipped the ball past Michael Dempsey in the Bohs goal. The double had been achieved and it was delight for everyone at Tolka Park.

At stages during the following season, it seemed that it was only a matter of time before it would be confirmed that the title was staying at Tolka. Both Pats and Bohs had mounted a challenge, but it seemed that the gap was just too great to bridge and with six games remaining Shels were six points ahead of Pats and eight ahead of Bohs. Roddy Collins had already overseen the miracle comeback for Bohs when they recovered from 4-1 down at half-time against Rovers to win 6-4 at the Morton Stadium. Would a comeback in the league race be too much?

He took his side to Tolka knowing that a win was imperative if they were to have any chance of reeling in The Reds. With the score level at one all at half-time, it seemed that Shels' nerve would hold and they would at worst grab a point from the derby. With twenty minutes left, Shels found themselves 4-1 down thanks to goals from Trevor Molloy, Alex Nesovic and Glen Crowe, adding to Dave Hill's opener for The Gypsies. Perhaps the title race wasn't over just yet.

Bohs seemed to be hitting form at just the right time and boosted their confidence a week later by beating Shamrock Rovers by a single goal in the FAI Cup semi-final. Wins against Bray Wanderers and an important three points against St Pats, coupled with Shels' inability to beat Galway United, left The Gypsies as the only realistic challengers to Shels with just three games left. Finn Harps were humbled at Dalymount by five goals to one while Shels staged a great comeback at Brandywell to salvage a 3-3 draw and reclaim the title lead by a point. Shels held that point lead going into the last day of the season.

As Emmet Malone pointed out in *The Irish Times*, one thing in Shels' favour was that they were not going to Oriel Park, which had in recent seasons become the venue of doom for champions elect. Not that the visit of Cork City to Tolka Park was an easy game. Bohs were off to Kilkenny City, who once again found themselves with a part to play in last-day championship drama.

Kilkenny's role in the drama proved to be fleeting as Bohs steamrolled them with five unanswered goals. Things were not so straightforward at Tolka, however, and City's Ollie Cahill was cast in the role of villain in Shels' fans eyes. Cahill's goal just before half-time proved enough for all three points. It also ensured that Shels had let an almost guaranteed title slip through their hands. Dermot Keely was straight to the point after the game and refused to argue that the best team had failed to win the title: *'The best team wins the league. Bohemians won it and they are the best team so I congratulate them on what they have achieved'*.

At Buckley Park in Kilkenny, a delighted Roddy Collins relayed his joy at bringing the title to Dalymount. Collins recalled that two years earlier, Bohs had been involved in a fight for Premier Division survival. It took a play-off game against Cobh Ramblers to secure their top-flight status. He stated that Bohs were back were they belonged, winning titles. Always one for a story, Collins then told of how he had a premonition that the title would be won by The Gypsies.

Roddy had been given a set of rosary beads and a card a few months earlier by a woman from The Liberties area of Dublin. As he stood in a hotel before Bohs first cup game that season he was struck by *'a strong premonition that I would be sitting on the sofa in that same hotel having a pint after we won the league'*. However, the rosary beads were not enough comfort for Roddy towards the end of the game and he left the dugout for the dressing room. *'My stomach was churning so much'*, he said, *'I just couldn't take it'*.

As the Bohs game finished first, the players gathered around a mobile phone to hear the last minutes of the match at Tolka Park relayed by one of the Bohs player's friends. The sense of unease was replaced by euphoria as the final whistle at Tolka sealed an unlikely championship for The Gypsies. Bohs had won seven of their last eight games, which truly showed title-winning form.

There was also the small matter of a double at stake as the FAI Cup Final at Tolka saw Bohs take on first-time finalists Longford Town. Bohs veteran Tony O'Connor grabbed the winner after an hour and completed a fairy-tale season for the Dalymount club, who achieved the double for the first time in seventy-three years. However, Roddy Collins would not have the chance to perform such miracles twice at the club as within a few weeks of those glorious days, he was no longer Bohs manager. Collins disputed that he was no longer in charge as both he, and Bohemian FC president, Phelim O'Reilly, clashed on an RTÉ Radio programme discussing the issue. Bohemian FC held the view that Collins had failed to turn up for a scheduled meeting to discuss a new contract in May and Collins insisted that he still had a year left on his contract. The discussion descended into farce, but one thing was clear at the end: as far as Bohemian FC was concerned, Roddy Collins was longer the manager. Collins's former assistant Pete Mahon took over in June, but only lasted until December that year, when both and the club parted company.

Mahon cited abuse from fans, directed at him and his family, as the reason for the decision. Mahon thankfully returned to League of Ireland management and enjoyed spells at UCD and St Pats before taking over at Drogheda United, where he is currently still managing with the same commitment and passion at seventy years of age.

Stephen Kenny arrived from Longford Town to replace Pete Mahon at Dalymount. In a twist of fate Bohs were due to play Longford Town in an FAI Cup match shortly after his appointment. Longford obtained a High Court injunction preventing Kenny taking charge of Bohs for that match. When Kenny arrived at Flancare Park, just before kick-off, without having had any contact with his new team, he was greeted by a standing ovation from the Longford Town fans as a mark of their gratitude for his efforts at the club. Bohs ran out 4-1 winners on the night and the Kenny era was underway at Dalymount.

The 2001–02 season saw Shels win their tenth championship; however, the League of Ireland came to national prominence for all the wrong reasons as a points-deduction case involving title chasers St Patrick's Athletic rumbled on for the duration of the season. The Inchicore club had fielded Paul Marney for the first three league games of the season. However, it transpired that he had not been registered correctly and the league deducted nine points from The Saints. The points were reinstated on appeal, but it then emerged that Pats had failed to register another player, Charles Mbabazi Livingstone. Livingstone had played in the first five league games and Pats were now hit with a fifteen-point deduction.

Pats went through an FAI arbitration hearing in an attempt to have the points reinstated, but the deduction remained and Shels were crowned champions. The Saints continue to count the 2001–02 season as a championship-winning season for the club, despite official records showing The Reds as winners. At the end of a trying season, Dermot Keely stepped down, feeling that he had taken the club as far as he could. Pat Fenlon was given the task of continuing the work and securing Shels' credentials at the top of the League of Ireland.

The 2002–03 season heralded the first season of summer football and a truncated league championship of just twenty-seven league matches. The Premier Division had been reduced to just ten teams and it was decided that the season would run from mid-July to mid-January. Irrespective of when the season ran, it seemed that Bohs and Shels were engaged in their own annual see-saw battle for the championship, as the title made its way back to Dalymount under Stephen Kenny. Bohs had lost the previous year's FAI Cup final to relegated Dundalk and the return of the league championship made up for this defeat. It also underlined Stephen Kenny's ability as a manager as Bohs had led the league table from start to finish that season.

The League of Ireland scene was about to change again, with one club taking up a dominant position and leaving the rest scrambling to keep up. For many league of Ireland fans in 2003, it looked like Shelbourne would go on to dominate the League of Ireland and perhaps in time make an impact on European competition in a way not yet seen by a League of Ireland club. At the very least, it was felt that Shels represented the best chance of a League of Ireland club possibly making the Champions League group stages or UEFA Cup/Europa League group stages. The calibre of player at Tolka Park was frightening to the rest of the league clubs, with the likes of, Wes Hoolahan, Jason Byrne, Stuart Byrne, Jim Crawford, Steve Williams and Owen Heary all available to manager Pat Fenlon.

Back-to-back championships were secured under Pat Fenlon in 2003 and 2004. With this success came perhaps the proudest moment for the club as they set out on a European adventure, which supporters of the domestic game had dared to believe possible. The adventure began in July, with a visit to Iceland, in the preliminary rounds of the Champions League. The opposition was KR Reykjavik and Shels found themselves 2–0 down with just over six minutes left to play. Alan Moore grabbed a goal back for Shels and just two minutes later Kristjan Sigurdsson's own goal brought Shels level. Back at Tolka, a 0–0 draw secured Shels' passage to the next round and a meeting with Hadjuk Split.

A Fan For All Seasons

At the Stadion Poljud in Spilt, Glen Fitzpatrick gave The Reds an early lead after just five minutes and an away goal. However, it seemed that the well-worn tale of League of Ireland clubs in Europe was about to repeat itself as Split recovered to hold a 3–1 lead with just minutes remaining. It looked like The Reds' European campaign was going to come to an end in much the same way as their previous attempts against Hibernians, Olimpija Ljubljana and Brondby. Shels had played well and had created chances, with Jason Byrne hitting the crossbar and Stuart Byrne going close with a header. However, for all their success at home, there seemed to be no way through in Europe – until Alan Moore once again came up with a late goal to keep the tie alive and give The Reds a real target to aim for in Tolka Park the following week. In order to progress though, Shels would not only have to overcome a Hadjuk Split side who now knew a lot more about what to expect, but also their dreadful record in European games at Tolka. It had been twelve games and twelve years since Tolka had seen a home win in European competition for The Reds.

On a balmy August evening, in front of 10,000 at Tolka Park, Shels finally bridged that twelve-year gap – and in some style. It looked like fans of every League of Ireland club had made the journey to Tolka to roar on The Reds. For the evening, old differences and loyalties were put to one side in the hope of seeing a little piece of history. Fans wearing Derry City, Waterford United and Galway United shirts joined ranks with locals sporting Pats, Bohs and Rovers shirts and it seemed that Hadjuk Split were not only taking on Shels, but the entire League of Ireland. Perhaps only in Ireland can this kind of situation take place, when the sporting common good comes to the fore and inevitably this is led by the fans, those real sports people who love the spectacle of live entertainment.

Pat Fenlon had set Shels up well for the game and with Alan Moore and Stuart Byrne directing operations, Shels had a number of early chances, including one from Glen Fitzpatrick that produced the save of the game as the Hadjuk keeper saved spectacularly with his foot, having initially gone the other way. Despite the encouragement from the crowd, the tension was building as Shels, for all their play, still needed to score. It was twelve minutes from time when the unlikely Dave Rogers stepped up with a screamer. A Shels corner kick had been cleared, but the ball made its way to Ollie Cahill, who passed it back out right to Alan Moore. Moore lobbed a high ball back into the Hadjuk penalty area and as a Hadjuk defender made a mess of his clearance, the ball came down to Dave Rogers on the edge of the box. Rogers, keeping his eye on the ball, struck a beautiful left-foot volley into the top corner of the goal at the Ballybough end of the ground.

The stands erupted with joy and surprise as the big centre back from Liverpool wheeled away in celebration and was mobbed by his teammates. It brought the tie level on aggregate scores, but Shels weren't done. After a close call when Hadjuk nearly equalised, Shels got a second goal from who else but Alan Moore. Joseph Ndo worked some magic in the penalty area and rolled the ball across the face of goal for Moore to tap in, securing Shels a date with Deportivo la Coruna in the next round.

Shels had made the breakthrough and life was sweet in Drumcondra. Approximately 24,000 fans turned out at Lansdowne Road for the next tie against Deportivo and Shels managed a creditable 0-0 draw. The match was still scoreless at half-time in the second leg, but two goals for Victor and one from Pandiani sent the Galician side through to a group that included Monaco, Liverpool and Olympiacos.

Shels still had the consolation of the UEFA Cup to look forward to and once again put on a dramatic show as two late Glen Fitzpatrick goals rescued a 2-2 draw for Shels against Lille at Lansdowne Road. The journey came to an end a fortnight later when Lille confirmed their progress to the next round, winning 2-0 on the night and 4-2 on aggregate.

Although Shels were out, it was far from failure as they had brought the profile of the club to a new level and a new audience. Shels represented a new confidence in League of Ireland football. It was a club that had put its money where its mouth was and was beginning to see signs of success and some growth on the European front. Summer football was hailed as the panacea to all the league's travails and the question was asked, why we hadn't done it sooner. There was just one small cloud on the horizon: would the crowds keep coming after the European show was over?

As Shels basked in the glow of having retained their league title, the club signalled its intent to keep on growing and bringing the best to Tolka. Five major signings were brought in at the end of 2004: Bobby Ryan, Colin Hawkins, Richie Baker, Gary O'Neill and, most significantly, Glen Crowe from a cash-strapped Bohemian FC. This meant that the country's two most prolific strikers over the last six seasons were now wearing the red of Shelbourne.

Despite the marquee players and the spending, Shels continued to be a club with far fewer supporters than their team and ambition deserved. During this time, the crowds turned up for the European games, but a regular League of Ireland fixture drew just over 2,000 fans to Tolka on any given Friday night. Shels were banking big on a European breakthrough and having come so close against Deportivo, it might have been felt that just a little extra push would see them over the line and into the promised land of Champions League group games. Was it a punt worth taking? With the new signings adding to an already impressive squad and the experience of Europe that season, it may have seemed worth the risk at the time. However, Shels were walking a tightrope and the stakes were huge.

As Shels aimed to make it three league titles in a row, their main contenders turned out to be Cork City and Derry City. Bohemian FC had seen a number of prominent team members leave the club as money became tight at Dalymount and the effects of trying to provide a full-time set-up for football in Ireland began to be felt. There were warning signs of financial trouble everywhere for Shels, including at their old rivals Shamrock Rovers. An eight-point deduction for The Hoops followed in mid-May when the FAI's licencing committee penalised Rovers for providing incorrect financial accounts during their licencing application. Relegation followed for Rovers. The one-time giants of Irish football were now enduring desperately hard times.

Shels faced Northern Ireland club Glentoran in the Champions League qualifiers in July, already six points behind the leaders Cork City, as the league championship was proving a tough test for The Reds. Glentoran were easily dismissed by six goals to two on aggregate, but the draw for the next round was not kind to Shels as they were pitted against Steaua Bucharest. Still, a full house was achieved at Tolka and Shels gave a good account of themselves in a 0-0 draw. In the return leg, the early sending-off of Dave Rogers forced Shels to readjust and the concession of three preventable goals put paid to any chance The Reds had of progression. They did manage to grab a goal back when they were 2-0 down, courtesy of Jason Byrne, but it wasn't enough as Steaua ran out 4–1 winners. In addition to the loss on the pitch, the loss of revenue caused by missing out on another two guaranteed home matches was huge for the club.

Shels missed out on the title too as they finished seven points behind City in third place. This meant no Champions League or UEFA Cup games at Tolka the following season. Shels had to settle for the unloved Intertoto Cup and two rounds in this competition against FK Vetra of Lithuania and OB Odense of Denmark hardly had the sold-out signs up at the Tolka ticket office.

The title was regained in 2006, making it three titles in four years for Shels, but winning back the championship was dogged all season by financial worries at the club, including problems with the payments of players' salaries. The issue of salary payments arose midway through the season and the players had undertaken to secure a written guarantee that if there were any further issues with payments, they would become free agents at the end of the season. Shelbourne chief executive Ollie Byrne had conceded that there had been issues, but that 'less than €10,000' was still due to players in mid-November, however ten players would be out of contract by season's end.

Shels had proposed a move to Santry and there was also talk of a ground-sharing deal with Bohemian FC, who had sold Dalymount Park to developers, but all this hinged on the sale of Tolka Park. It also transpired that there had been significant financial shortfalls at Shels over the last three seasons, despite their on-field success. By the end of November 2006, Revenue filed a petition to have Shelbourne wound up. Shels were now on a downward spiral that would spin drastically and tragically out of control.

In December, Pat Fenlon walked away and there was talk of a mass exodus from Tolka. By January 2007, Joseph Ndo, Stuart Byrne, Ollie Cahill and Sean Dillon had left, along with Gary O'Neill. Club captain Owen Heary followed suit. Pete Mahon was approached to take over the vacant manager's job, but declined, preferring to stay at UCD. The league's leading goalscorer Jason Byrne was next to leave and the FAI finally signalled to the remainder of the squad that they could leave the club.

Just when it seemed that the worst of the nightmare was over for Shelbourne, the saga took a new twist as Ollie Byrne was hospitalised, complaining of chest pains. It had seemed as though former Shels favourite Stephen Geoghegan was in line to take up the vacant manager's post, but this was put on hold when Byrne fell ill.

As the issue of player payments arose again, even for a remarkably cut-back squad, the management committee at Shels approached Finbarr Flood to take over the reigns until Byrne was well enough to return. It wasn't until Byrne was absent from the club that it became evident how much things at Shels revolved around him. As Stephen McGuinnes, PFAI chairman, remarked when trying to resolve the player payment issue with little success, 'the current situation only seems to highlight the extent to which everything at Shelbourne depends on him'.

A Fan For All Seasons

In January, Shels pulled out of the cross-border competition, the Setanta Cup, citing concerns about whether they would be ready to compete and stating that they didn't want to cause any embarrassment to either themselves or the competition's backers. Finbarr Flood resigned less than two weeks later, having completed his work on a survival plan for the club and citing other business and personal commitments. Shels asked for more time to provide the FAI's licencing committee with details regarding their financial affairs for the upcoming season. However, the licencing committee decided to relegate Shels to Division One, despite assurances from the club that any outstanding payments due to players or Revenue would be addressed. The club did consider an appeal, but decided against this and accepted their relegation to Divison One.

A familiar face returned to Tolka: Dermot Keely came back as manager. Never one to shirk a challenge, Keely was tasked with trying to cobble together a team and in some way enable the club to survive and attempt to compete in Division One that coming season.

After all the drama that Shels had encountered over a four-month period since winning the Premier Division, the episode ended on a tragic note, putting football matters into stark perspective. Ollie Byrne passed away in August 2007.

The onset of the financial crisis would scupper plans involving Tolka Park and it was 2016 before any prospect of Shels moving from Tolka Park seemed likely. In 2016, Shelbourne FC Limited came to an agreement with Dublin City Council that would see them surrender their interest as leaseholders in Tolka Park to Dublin City Council and relocate to Dalymount Park as co-tenants with Bohemian FC.

How quickly Shels' success had faded from view, but they were not the only club to fall victim to financial woes. Their north-side neighbours Bohemian FC were also caught up in a series of troubles relating to their home at Dalymount. With the ground in urgent need of repair, and given the house price boom in the naughties, the Phibsborough venue was a prime location for development. Ideas were floated about the club moving from Phibsborough to a new purpose-built site. Locations at Castleknock and Harristown were proposed and with the projected value of the land at Dalymount, it seemed that Bohs' future was secure. However, difficulties arose over the ownership of some of the land included in the redevelopment plans and the project was delayed. This delay also meant that desperately needed funding for the club was on hold.

At the beginning of the 2008 season, Bohemian FC had invested heavily in securing the services of a number of top-quality players and had brought in Pat Fenlon as manager, hoping that he could recreate the success he had enjoyed at Tolka Park. Bohs cantered to the title by nineteen points and won the FAI Cup that season, but posted a significant loss in the process. The debts began to mount and although they won the title again in 2009, the writing was on the wall for Bohs. Bohemian FC PRO Brian Trench remarked that the club was working hard to address the revenue issue and noted that the annual wage bill had been reduced from €1.95 million to €1.2 million. This was a staggering figure for a League of Ireland club. Bohs also failed to make the breakthrough in Europe, failing abjectly in each of their attempts to progress. Both Red Bull Salzburg from Austria and the New Saints from Wales proved too much for The Gypsies to overcome in Champions League qualifying rounds.

Bohs lost out on a third successive title on goal difference to Shamrock Rovers, but in August 2010, they found themselves issuing a plea to fans to assist with funding to see them through to the end of the season. Bohs stated that players' wages could no longer be guaranteed. The club was nearly €6 million in debt and the sale of players was the only viable option in the face of severe cashflow problems. It was obvious that no lessons had been learned from the Shelbourne saga and another appeal to fans to raise €300,000 was issued in November in order to get Bohs through the licencing process and ensure League of Ireland football would be played at Dalymount the following season. Another deal to move from Dalymount Park failed to materialise as the financial crisis hit home.

Bohs slashed their budget for 2011 to €250,000 as Pat Fenlon tried to put together a team capable of competing in the Premier Division. They finished a respectable fifth, but the days of title challenges were over at Dalymount. It was another four years before the fate of Dalymount was decided. Dublin City Council stepped in to purchase the ground in 2015 and set up the deal to redevelop the iconic venue and groundshare with Shels. A brief stay in Tolka is planned until redevelopment is finished in 2020. It will be the start of a new chapter for two clubs who achieved great success during the first decade of this century, but found themselves perilously closer to trouble than at any other point in their long and shared histories.

Financial concerns were not confined to Dublin. The other two clubs that won the league during this decade, Drogheda United and Cork City, also went into examinership. United went into examinership in 2008, just a few months after winning the League Championship. The club had been having one of its most successful periods, after winning the FAI Cup in 2005, having beaten Cork City. They had also enjoyed their European adventures, which saw them progress through a round in both the 2008 UEFA Cup and 2009 Champions League qualification stages.

Paul Doolin's team clinched the club's first title by beating their title rivals, Cork City, at United Park. A last-minute winner from Guy Bates sealed a 2-1 win over City and United went on to finish seven points ahead of St Pats, who had got off to a good start in the league. Like Bohs and Shels before them, Drogheda United boasted a team of excellent players, the calibre of which hadn't been seen at United Park in many years. Brian Shelley, Graham Gartland, Paul Keegan, Shane Robinson, Ollie Cahill and Eamon Zayed all made vital contributions to the club's new-found success.

Their championship reward was a crack at Champions League qualification. United Park failed to meet UEFA regulations, so United moved south to Dalymount, where they faced Estonian side Levadia Tallin. A 2-1 win meant that there was still work to do on the return leg, but Graham Gartland's goal just after half-time eased any fraying nerves and saw Drogehda through to meet Dynamo Kiev.

The first leg at Dalymount left Drogheda captain Stuart Byrne perplexed about how easily they had given away two goals to the Ukrainians. An Adam Hughes header had brought United back level just before an hour's play, but a goal four minutes from time saw Kiev come out on top in an open and entertaining game. It looked like the way was clear for a comfortable passage through to the next round for Dynamo. However, in a game that would rank alongside Dundalk's efforts against Celtic in 1979, the second leg was yet another chance that got away. An early goal for Dynamo seemed to guarantee that there would be no surprises, but then Shane Robinson equalised from a penalty before the break after Richie Baker was fouled. United had an away goal in the bag. Dynamo sneaked ahead again with twenty minutes left before the real drama began.

With two minutes left in normal time, Graham Gartland got on the end of a Paul Keegan free kick to bring the Louth men level again. With the score now 3-2 on aggregate, one more United goal would see them through on the away-goals rule. In games like this teams usually get one chance to score, Drogheda United got two but couldn't take either of them. Firstly, Adam Hughes shot over the bar from six yards with the goal at his mercy and then a minute into stoppage time a pass from Fahrudin Kuduzovic put Shane Robinson away. His low cross struck the base of the near post, rolled under the keeper and across the goal line to safety. It was the narrowest of margins that denied Drogheda a place in the history books and a shot against Spartak Moscow. Paul Doolin was reflective after the game and summed up United's efforts: *'Why say, "so close yet so far"? We should have won. It's simple: we had two chances at the end that should have won the game'*.

By October, those heady days of European football were a distant memory as the High Court appointed an examiner to the club. The club owed significant debts to Revenue. In January 2009, the High Court approved a scheme devised by the court-appointed examiner, which saw United saved from extinction. The scheme signalled the end of full-time professional contracts for players and going forward part-time professional contracts would be offered. This greatly reduced the wage bill, which had been in the region of €2.5 million a year, to €300,000 a year. In addition, there had been considerable support from the fans and local community in Drogheda and from club chairman Vincent Hoey to prevent the club from going under . It was a happy outcome for Drogheda, but the cost was the loss of their league-winning squad and manager. They did manage to survive the following season in the Premier Division under new boss Alan Matthews after beating Bray Wanderers in a play-off. Once again, the price of success was proving costly.

The other club to win the title in this era was Cork City. Damian Richardson finally saw one of his sides reach the promised land of league champions in 2005. Richardson had taken over from Pat Dolan as boss at Turners Cross and delivered the title in his first season. However, the club were also confronted with examinership in 2008, when they sought the protection of the High Court in the face of significant debts, including a debt to Revenue. A scheme was approved by the High Court in October 2008, with club owners Cork City Investment FC Limited. However, by July 2009, the High Court was involved again and a winding-up order was issued against Cork City Investments FC Limited. The High Court acknowledged that the club was insolvent and that there was no other option but to grant the order sought by Revenue.

The club was set to lose its players, who were all told that they were free to leave at the end of July 2009. The players had agreed to defer for a week payments that were due to them in order to help the club meet its obligation to Revenue. With time running out for the club and a return to the High Court pending, both Revenue and Cork City came to a deal on 31 July 2009, which seemed to have saved City. However, the club was landed with another bill, as they were obliged to pay the costs of both sides for the four-month legal proceedings.

Despite the reprieve at the High Court for the club, another problem surfaced after a local radio interview with one of the Cork City players. The Cork City supporters group known as Foras Group felt that the interview amounted to a plea for funding for a bus to bring the team to fulfil a fixture in Dublin. The Foras Group planned to show their anger at the situation, with protests at Turners Cross during a televised match against Bohemian FC.

Manager Paul Doolin left the club and it seemed that things were unravelling fast. The Foras Group had applied to the league for a club licence, just in case they needed to step in to save League of Ireland football in Cork city.

Efforts were made to bring a takeover deal to completion, but time eventually ran out and Cork City FC was wound up in February 2010. A new Cork city club was founded and began life in Division One under the banner of Cork City Foras Co-op, eventually buying the rights to the Cork City name from the Cork City Investments FC liquidator in June 2010. It had been a tough number of years for the Southern Capital's sole league representatives, but thanks to the football fans of Cork, they still have their team playing at Turners Cross today and they remain a hugely valuable asset to the league.

The decade had been marked by a litany of crises at clubs the length and breadth of the country. Perhaps clubs thought that they could bank on future revenue or bury their head in the sand when faced with financial problems. It also seems that clubs felt that the worst would never come to their door and failed to heed the mistakes of others, in both the near and distant past. This laissez-faire attitude proved to be more dangerous to the future of League of Ireland football than any other impediment encountered in nearly one hundred years.

Rovers Return with Partizan Support
A Home at last for The Hoops

In the annals of Shamrock Rovers, there have been many heroes, many gifted footballers and many dedicated players whose talent brought glory to the famous hooped shirt at Glenmalure Park and numerous other venues besides. The name of full back Pat Sullivan will always be recalled when great games and achievements are discussed. Rightly too, as his most wonderful goal in 2011 changed the course of a club and brought the League of Ireland into the spotlight for the right reasons after a decade of bad news stories.

You can never tire of Sullivan's strike from twenty-five yards against Partizan Belgrade in a Europa League qualification play-off at the Partizan Stadion. The goal brought The Hoops level on the night and on aggregate. The goal itself was the sweetest volley Sullivan will ever strike in his life. A Rovers corner was cleared from the box high into the air. The nearest player to Sullivan was about twenty yards away as the Partizan defence came out following the clearance. Sullivan had his head arched upwards and shaped to strike the ball as it came down towards him. Giving it everything he had, he connected sweetly with the ball, which flew like a rocket over the onrushing players and dipped at the end, nestling in the side netting of the goal. The keeper never stood a chance.

While the goal itself didn't win the game, it gave The Hoops the confidence to believe that a result was possible. How many times in the past had we seen League of Ireland teams come so close only to fluff their lines when the chance presented itself? Not this time. At last, the ball went into the net instead of hitting a divot or taking a deflection or in some cases being put out of the ground. Bravery was still needed though and the question was: now that Rovers were in a position to make history, could they take the golden chance that had been presented to them?

Back in March 2009, no one could have envisaged Rovers being on the brink of European history in two years' time. Back then, Rovers were just wakening up to the realisation that at last, after twenty-two years of wandering around various venues in Dublin, they had a ground to call home. Tallaght Stadium was ready to host its first League of Ireland match. With beautiful symmetry, Sligo Rovers, Glemalure's last visitors, would be the first visitors to Tallaght. For so many people, it was a day they had felt would never arrive. Former players turned up to witness the event for themselves and found that they were now able to reminisce about hard times past, safe in the knowledge that those nomadic days were over. For the fans, it would be their first real home game in twenty-two seasons. It may not have been Milltown, but perhaps it was best to leave those ghosts behind and embrace the chance to make new memories for a new generation. A significant lack of recent success had made Hoops fans hungry for new heroes as the glory-day tales of yesteryear were beginning to wear thin.

It had been a long journey for The Hoops and their arrival at Tallaght Stadium had been littered with pitfalls, false starts, objections and the customary legal wrangling, which accompany building stadia in Ireland. In March 2000, when former Taoiseach Bertie Ahern, TD, turned the ceremonial sod at Tallaght, a small group of protesters turned up from Old Bawn Community School. The protesters felt that the land at Sean Walsh Memorial Park should have been retained for the use of its pupils. Although the demonstration was peaceful, things would become more serious over the next eight years.

Work began on the stadium and a pitch was laid. A new stand was taking shape and the concrete structure was in place when work ceased. The site became derelict and wouldn't see any further development until 2008. Rovers entered into examinership in 2005 and also entered Division One as the mighty Hoops were relegated for the first time, following an eight-point deduction for financial irregularities.

A public consultation then took place to discuss ways of finishing the stadium. Local GAA club Thomas Davis took part in the process and proposed that the ground be used as a multi-sports facility. South Dublin County Council adopted the submission and presented a report that provided for the facility to accommodate senior GAA games at the venue. The most significant changes necessary would be an increase in the size of the playing pitch and an increase in the length of the stand. After submitting the report to the Department of Arts, Sports and Tourism, funding from the department was declined. One reason given was that the stand had been partially built with a curved end and it was felt that to remedy this would incur significant additional costs. South Dublin County Council decided to proceed with the original plans for the stadium, meaning that no senior GAA matches could now take place at the ground.

Thomas Davis sought a judicial review of the decision of the council to proceed with the original plans, but was ultimately unsuccessful in their appeal, with the High Court rejecting Thomas Davis challenge to the council's decision. The judgement noted that government funding had been a precondition of making the stadium a multi-sports facility and since that was not forthcoming, the council should not be held to unbudgeted expenditure or any further delay in implementing their plans. The way was now clear to finish the ground and give The Hoops a home.

Rovers won Divison One on their first attempt and had consolidated their Premier Division position by the time Michael O'Neill was appointed as manager in December 2008. O'Neill, who was a former Northern Ireland international with thirty-one caps, left his position at Brechin City FC in the Scottish League to take up the job at Tallaght. As a player, he had started out with Coleraine in the Irish League and went on to have spells at Newcastle United, Dundee United, Hibernian and Wigan, to name just four of his clubs in Britain, before returning to the Irish League with Glentoran. At The Oval, he picked up three winners medals, a League Championship, the Irish League Cup and the County Antrim Shield with the east Belfast club.

His appointment at Rovers was something of a coup for the club and O'Neill saw the job as the right challenge at the right time. At his first press conference, he said, 'There is an expectation that the job will involve taking the club forward in the new stadium and the wider area where they have located themselves. That was a big factor in me taking the job. It's not something I fear'. He also pulled no punches about what he would expect from his new players, citing hard work and high-tempo football as cornerstones of his playing philosophy. Players would be expected to express themselves and play without fear.

While all this was music to The Hoops fans' ears, the only thing that mattered on Friday, 13 March 2009, was The Hoops running out at Tallaght in their first home game when 3,500 fans turned up to see Rovers christen their new home with a 2–1 win. Indeed, Rovers fought well in the title chase against Bohemian FC that first season at Tallaght, but they lost out towards the end of the season, when a 1–1 draw at Terryland Park against Galway United effectively ended their title hopes. It was the ten drawn matches over the course of that campaign that would prove so costly to Rovers. They defeated eventual champions Bohs twice and drew with them once, but still failed to overtake their north-side rivals in the championship race. They had, however, uncovered a very special talent in goalscorer Gary Twigg. His twenty-four league goals that season accounted for nearly half of Rovers' total and saw him finish as the league's top scorer. He also secured a place in the Rovers history books when he scored the first league goal at Tallaght against Sligo Rovers.

Rovers' 2009 efforts had them in good shape for the following season, when they battled it out again with Bohs all the way to the end. On the final Friday of league matches, the league table saw The Hoops two points ahead of Bohs and with a better goal difference of just two goals. It seemed that Bohs had thrown away their chance of three in a row the previous weekend when they had lost to Galway United. This result left The Hoops in the box seat.

Rovers had to travel to the seaside to take on Bray Wanderers, while Bohs welcomed Dundalk to Dalymount. Packed DARTs ferried expectant Hoops fans to the Carlisle Grounds as a sea of Rovers shirts and scarves took over the ground and brought with it Bray's best attendance in over twenty years. A sense of expectation and nervousness filled the air as Rovers took to the pitch wearing a garish purple strip for their date with destiny. An early goal for Bohs at Dalymount did little to calm the nerves. The Rovers fans certainly had the jitters when Jake Kelly gave Bray the lead after twenty minutes.

Kelly was put through on goal and lifted the ball delicately over the advancing Alan Mannus. It was nearly looking like curtains for The Hoops ten minutes later, when Kelly again had the ball in the net, only for the goal to be ruled out after a dubious off-side decision. However, The Hoops 'go-to' man, Gary Twigg, didn't disappoint on this important night and just before the break he brought the sides level. A defensive error found Twigg quickest to react and he rounded Bray goalkeeper, Matt Gregg. Still with work to do and from a tight angle, Twigg found the net, despite Adam Mitchell's best efforts to keep the ball out. It was 1–1 at the break and the championship was back on track.

It was looking all but decided just after half-time, when Dessie Baker and Gary Twigg linked up, with Twigg laying the ball off to Tommy Stewart, who scored past Gregg to put Rovers 2-1 up. Just after the hour mark at Dalymount, Dundalk's Fahrudin Kuduzovic scored an equaliser, which seemed to put any lingering doubts about the destiny of the title to bed. However, just seconds after Dundalk had equalised, Bray scored an equaliser themselves. Dessie Baker's brother Richie, who was with Bray Wanderers, came on as a substitute and his pass allowed Derek Doyle to cross for Gary Shaw to head past Mannus in the Rovers goal. Rovers would need to hold on for the remaining twenty minutes. Bohs needed help quickly at Dalymount as time and their title was slipping away. Two late goals from Aaron Greene and Jason Byrne gave Bohs three points, but despite three added minutes at Bray, which probably felt like three hours to The Hoops fans, there was no late goal from the Seagulls that could bail Bohs out. The title went to The Hoops for the sixteenth time amid scenes of unbridled joy on the pitch.

For Michael O'Neill, the overwhelming feeling at the whistle was one of relief: 'I'm sure I'll enjoy this an awful lot more tomorrow, but right now, if I'm 100 per cent honest, I'm mostly relieved'. Reflecting on the club's situation, O'Neill remarked that he hoped this title would mark a new chapter of success in the club's history. 'From a personal point of view, I'm delighted', he added. The sense of expectation after pushing Bohs close the previous season had heightened expectations amongst fans and O'Neill commented that he was happy that he and the team had been able to deliver on those expectations. Gary Twigg again finished as the league's leading goalscorer and had now been rewarded with a league title for his efforts.

Rovers were also in the FAI Cup final for the first time in eight seasons. Sligo Rovers were between them and a double. In front of a crowd of over 36,000, both teams failed to produce a goal in either normal or extra time. It was the dreaded penalty shoot-out and unfortunately for The Hoops, they failed to score any of the four penalties they took, with Twigg, Flynn, Turner and Kavanagh all missing. The cup went to Sligo, who scored two of their four spot kicks. The hunt for FAI Cup number twenty-five would continue for Rovers.

Rovers were back and brought home more silverware under O'Neill the following season. First up was the cross-border competition, the Setanta Cup. Rovers' opponents in the final were Dundalk, who had beaten the best the Irish League had to offer, seeing off the challenges of Linfield, Glentoran and Cliftonville en route to the final. Rovers meanwhile had received a bye in the first round as League Champions and had then disposed of Lisburn Distillery and Sligo Rovers.

The final itself was a one-off affair at Tallaght Stadium and goals from Gary O'Neill and Billy Dennehy were enough to see off The Lilywhites. However, the victory was clouded by the news the following day that RTÉ commentator and lifelong Hoops fan Philip Greene had passed away aged 90. It was fitting that Greene was around to see Rovers achieve their dream of a new home and to see them regain the championship. The Setanta Cup win the day before he passed away gave credence to what Philip Greene had probably always believed anyway, that Rovers were the best club in Ireland.

Rovers had a formidable side, with the likes of Alan Mannus, Ken Oman, Stephen O'Donnell, Ronan Finn, Garry Twigg and Billy Dennehy all regulars on the team. They would need all this experience as they set out on their amazing European adventure, beginning at home against Estonian side Flora Tallinn in July, in the second qualification round for the Champions League. A 1-0 win thanks to a Chris Turner goal was enough to give Rovers heart for the return leg. The Hoops had passed up a number of chances and they had a second goal disallowed for offside. It would be just the fourth time that Rovers would hold a lead going into an away leg of a European match. The second leg in Tallinn saw The Hoops turn in a determined display and secure a scoreless draw, which meant that they were through to face FC Copenhagen. Michael O'Neill was pleased with their progression to the next round: *'It's just amazing we didn't win the game, but the important thing is we won the tie and got two clean sheets'*.

FC Copenhagen had requested of both Rovers and Flora, prior to the second leg of their tie, that they consider playing the first leg of their prospective tie against the Danes at home. Rovers declined the request and put in a spirited performance in the first leg of the third qualification round at the Parken Stadium. The Hoops fell behind after an early goal, but rallied to keep Copenhagen at bay and created a chance or two of their own, thanks to Gary Twigg and Ronan Finn. Despite the defeat, there was optimism that the tie could be saved in the return at Tallaght. O Neill said, *'We're under no illusions about the scale of the task we face in the second leg, but I think the longer it stays as it is back in Dublin, then the better our chances of getting through become'.* The performances in the three European matches to date had raised fans' expectations of Rovers and had brought The Hoops back to national attention as the prospect of an historic Champions League place began to grow.

A crowd of 5,500 packed into Tallaght for the crunch return leg on 2 August to see if The Hoops could make history. But it was not to be and despite applying early pressure, Rovers just could not find the breakthrough goal needed to bring the tie to life. Their job was made significantly more difficult before the break when Copenhagen managed to get their noses in front on the night, following poor Rovers defence at a corner. That goal effectively killed off the tie and although Rovers tried to get back into the game, a second goal fifteen minutes from time saw the Danes comfortably through, 3–0 on aggregate. The real damage in the tie had not been done in Tallaght, but in the first leg, with good chances of an away goal too easily squandered.

The victory over Flora Tallinn had guaranteed The Hoops at least two more games in Europe. As they had failed to make it past Copenhagen, they now awaited their fate in the Europa League Group stage play-off match. If the football gods had given them a tough draw against Copenhagen, then those gods were certainly not smiling down on Rovers when Partizan Belgrade was pulled out of the hat. Partizan had won the last four Serbian titles and had also won three domestic Cups during that time. Although not unbeatable, they were another stern test for Rovers.

Meanwhile, The Hoops were fighting it out in the league and continued their title defence with a visit to Dalymount. The fixture was just what the team needed to re-focus the minds of all involved after their disappointment in Europe. Gary Twigg made sure that the points came back to Tallaght with the only goal of the game. The Saturday before the first leg against Partizan at Tallaght, Rovers took UCD to the cleaners with a six-goal demolition of The Students. It was good preparation, but the real key against Partizan would be preventing the goals going in at the other end and avoid allowing that dreaded away goal to slip into the net. Both Michael O'Neill and captain Dan Murray stressed the need to keep focused for ninety minutes. Murray warned, *'Concentration can be a little off in the league here and you can get away with it. In Europe, especially against the quality of teams we've played, you get punished'*.

Around 4,500 fans turned up at Tallaght for another night of adventure in Europe, in the hope that this evening would prove a little more favourable for The Hoops. Partizan showed Rovers the difficulty of their task by taking the lead after just fifteen minutes. All talk of keeping a clean sheet and how important that would be was suddenly redundant. Rovers looked a little startled and it took them a while to get into anything like a fluid, coherent groove. At half-time, O'Neill made changes, bringing on Chris Turner for Ronan Finn and, fifteen minutes later, going with two strikers up front, when Gary O'Neill replaced Billy Dennehy. These changes, coupled with Rovers' spirit and work ethic, began to pay off and gave heart to Hoops fans. Probably knowing that a goal was now imperative, O'Neill made his final change: Ciaran Kilduff came on for Stephen Rice. It was time for Rovers to step up to the mark, if their European adventure was to have any chance of continuing.

Rovers' goal when it came owed nothing to effort and commitment or any kind of luck. It was a wonderful piece of skill and composure. A clearance from a Partizan defender came to Gary McCabe in midfield. He dropped his shoulder and rounded a Partizan midfielder. As he continued to goal, a defender came out to meet him. McCabe shaped to shoot, but instead rolled the ball to Twigg's feet. Twigg laid the ball off into the path of McCabe, who had continued his run into the penalty area. As McCabe collected the ball, he rolled it through the legs of another defender before passing it into the net for the equaliser. The Hoops fans erupted with joy. A few moments later, Gary Twigg had a chance to give Rovers the victory, but it wasn't to be: 1–1 and everything was still to play for in the tie. At least Rovers knew they would have to score in Belgrade to progress.

Rovers were in good spirits before the second leg in Belgrade. A 3–2 win at Galway United in between the two legs had kept their league campaign on track, as Michael O'Neill refused to let Rovers become complacent about domestic issues. Their second-half performance against Partizan had given the Rovers players the belief they needed and McCabe's skilful goal had shown Partizan what Rovers could do. The club was now standing on the edge of a million euro payday if they could negotiate their way past Partizan and become the first Irish club to reach the group stages of a European competition.

The game started with a chance for The Hoops, but eventually Partizan took control and, roared on by the home support, they took the lead after thirty-five minutes. The goal mattered little to Rovers, as finding that away goal was still imperative. Once again, a half-time change in personnel and formation reaped rewards for Rovers. Karl Sheppard replaced Billy Dennehy and the change brought about a chance for Chris Turner, whose header just went the wrong side of the post. If Rovers fans had thought that McCabe's goal at Tallaght was one of Rovers' best in Europe, then they would soon witness a challenger to that title. Just before the hour mark, Pat Sullivan unleashed his unstoppable equaliser. The game was back up for grabs, but Rovers would have to work hard to get to extra time. Stephen O'Donnell's first contribution after coming on as a replacement for Gary McCabe was a goal-saving block on a Stefan Babovic effort. He also saved Rovers two minutes from time, with a great tackle on Lazar Markovic when a Partizan goal looked certain. O'Donnell would make one more significant contribution later on.

Extra time would be needed to decide the outcome. Could Rovers hang on for penalties? Could they survive another half hour in the heat? Did they believe in themselves enough to see the job through? These were questions those of us watching on television asked with a sense of giddy wonder. For those fans in the ground that had made the long journey, the sense of anticipation at the possibility of witnessing history was huge. Could anyone take the tension?

The goal frame came to Rovers' rescue after just two minutes of extra time and Ryan Thompson was in the right place to prevent Partizan taking the lead on two occasions. It was Enda Stevens' pass down the line that lead to Rovers' winner. A Partizan defender badly misjudged the flight of the ball and it came to Kilduff, who was making a run inside him. As the ball bounced, and with the angle narrowing at the corner of the six-yard box, Kilduff tried to lob the ball into the far corner of the goal. The keeper got a hand to the ball, but succeeded only in palming it straight to Karl Sheppard, who was unmarked on the penalty spot. Sheppard prepared to shoot, but the keeper caught his standing leg. A penalty was awarded to Rovers. Yet again, Stephen O'Donnell played a part, as he stepped up to take the penalty to send Rovers through. Amid a chorus of whistles, and after the referee had asked him to replace the ball, O'Donnell struck a calm penalty to the goalkeeper's left and killed of Partizan's chances.

The Serbian club's chances were further hampered in the remaining seven minutes as they were reduced to ten men. It was a night of glory for Shamrock Rovers and a huge moment in League of Ireland history. The group stage of a European competition had been achieved. On television a great shot of captain Dan Murray is captured as he falls to his knees with delight when O'Donnell's penalty hits the back of the net. The Rovers bench was equally ecstatic as the realisation of their achievement began to dawn on them. With qualification came the excitement of the draw held in Monaco the following day. As Emmet Malone pointed out in a piece for *The Irish Times*, it was a reflection of the differences in the financial situation of Rovers, who were delighted to be taking part in the Europa League, and other clubs, who seemed devastated at the thought of competing in anything other than the Champions League. Rovers, to their delight, drew Rubin Kazan, PAOK

A Fan For All Seasons

Salonika and Tottenham Hotspur. Rovers also succeeded in having the games held at their new ground in Tallaght and each European night was a special occasion for The Hoops faithful. Although the results didn't go their way, they did manage to score in four of the six matches, including when they took the lead at White Hart Lane against Spurs, thanks to a Stephen Rice deflection.

During their European adventure, Rovers kept their foot on the gas at home and succeeded in retaining their Premier Division title. It had been an amazing season for The Hoops and one that will live long in the fans' memory. After so many years in the wilderness and on the road, who could begrudge The Hoops a period of success and a spell back at the top of Irish football? For Michael O'Neill, it was time to move on to pastures new. During his short stay at the club, he had won the league twice and brought the club through many memorable nights. European fixtures against Juventus and Tottenham and the visit of Cristiano Ronaldo with Real Madrid for a friendly match were evenings to remember. O'Neill took up the post of Northern Ireland manager and would go on to lead his country to the European Championship finals for the first time in France in 2016.

For Rovers, the next man in the hot seat was Stephen Kenny. The side never really got the time to develop as Rovers failed to repeat their European success the following season and crashed out after just one tie, against Lithuanian side, Ekranas. Kenny was gone within the year and Rovers slipped back into the chasing pack as Dundalk and Cork City became the country's premier clubs.

Shamrock Rovers are now very much Tallaght's team and although Milltown will always remain special to the club, a new generation of supporters know only Tallaght as home. The club has made great strides, integrating itself into the community, with school projects and link-ups with schoolboy clubs in the area. All of these initiatives auger well for the club and for its continuation as an important focal point in Tallaght.

The only thing left for The Hoops to resolve is the long absence of the FAI Cup from their trophy cabinet. It has been nearly thirty years since the Rovers captain has lifted the big trophy, but with twenty-four wins to date in the competition the rest of the clubs will be playing catch up for many years to come.

Lilywhite Legends
Breakthrough at the Border

By 2012, Dundalk FC had been through its fair share of controversy and tribulations. The club had experienced spells in Division One and had fallen on hard times as the glory days of decades past seemed a distant memory. Oriel Park was a ground haunted by memories of yesterday. The air around the ground hung heavy with the fading applause for trophies won but now long since tarnished by age. It seemed that The Lilywhites had forgotten how to be successful. The 2012 season had seen The Lilywhites stave off another relegation to Division One, thanks to a play-off victory over Waterford United. The Blues had come away from Oriel with a 2-2 draw only to blow their chances at home in the RSC, when they crashed to a 2-0 defeat.

This play-off fixture came six years after the two sides had met in a notorious series of games to decide an ultimately futile overall league placing because of a restructuring of the domestic leagues. Dundalk had won that two-legged series of games 3-2, but had failed to gain a place in the restructured Premier Division the following season. The FAI and the League of Ireland had decided to merge and the new league placings were to be decided by the Independent Assessment Group. Dundalk fell short of the criteria laid down by the IAG and remained in Division One, much to the annoyance of Lilywhite fans.

One disgruntled fan decided to take his grievance with Dundalk's exclusion to the FAI directly, at their head office in Merrion Square, Dublin. His actions lead to the Gardaí being called after a tense stand-off, which allegedly involved the fan dousing himself in petrol and threatening to set himself alight. Thankfully, the situation was brought under control and there was no need for martyrdom to save Dundalk FC's honour. The escapade didn't alter Dundalk's position in Division One either.

Despite the poor showing in 2012, there was a ray of light shining through the gloom and that was the appointment of Stephen Kenny as manager. Kenny had been dismissed by Shamrock Rovers the previous season, but the Dundalk board were about to make a decision that would have far-reaching consequences for the club and would see Kenny guide The Lilywhites to unprecedented success at home and abroad.

Stephen Kenny's first league game as Dundalk manager was at home against Shamrock Rovers. Given Dundalk's financial constraints, Kenny did not have large sums of money to help in his task of restoring pride to the white shirt. However, it was Kenny's shrewd assessment of a player which would yield rewards. He signed two Galway men, Stephen O'Donnell from Rovers and Mark Rossiter from St Pats. Richie Towell came in from Celtic after a loan spell with Hibernian and had a tremendous impact, with the former Crumlin United player winning the PFAI Young Player of the Year award in his first season at Oriel Park. Another former Crumlin United player, Andy Boyle, joined the club to help improve the team's defence. Boyle had won a First Division title with UCD in 2009 and had played in the 2011 FAI Cup final with Shelbourne before Kenny brought him to County Louth. Kurtis Byrne also signed, bringing with him the experience of a number of seasons in Scottish football.

Kenny was used to starting during a low point for a club. In a preview of the league opener against Rovers, he commented that he had been in the same situation at three of his previous clubs: Longford Town, Bohemian FC and Derry City. *'We have signed a lot of players who are young and hungry and determined to do well and make a name for themselves',* he said, *'... I have great faith in the players and technically they are as good as anybody'.*

As for the game against Rovers, it ended in a goalless draw, largely thanks to Peter Cherrie's penalty save from Rovers' Gary McCabe. The Stephen Kenny era got underway quietly, but things were to get far more exciting at Oriel Park. Twenty-one league wins in that first season saw Dundalk chase St Patrick's Athletic all the way to the title. The Lilywhites came up just short and The Saints brought the title back to Inchicore thanks to a margin of three points. However, if the Dundalk fans had wanted a reasonable improvement on the previous season's poor form, they certainly got it and they got a return to European football.

Having been league runners-up the previous season, Dundalk still only found themselves fourth in the betting as the 2014 campaign opened. Pats, Sligo and Rovers were the bookies' top three favourites to win the title. Daryl Horgan had joined from Cork City, along with David McMillan from Sligo Rovers and Sean Gannon from Pats. Dundalk had the look of a quality side ready to backup the previous seasons form. Cork City and Dundalk would battle it out for the championship to confound the bookies, Pats, Sligo and Rovers all failed to rise to the occasion.

A first European home win in over thirty years against Jeunesse Esch of Luxembourg saw Dundalk negotiate the first UEFA Europa League qualifying round before bowing out to Hadjuk Split. Things were warming up in the league too and as the championship reached its penultimate round of games, there was just a point between Dundalk and Cork City. If City could at least match Dundalk's result in their next game, then it would be winner takes all as the two sides were due to meet in the last fixture at Oriel Park.

As it turned out, Dundalk's visit to Bray Wanderers proved to be more difficult than expected. The Seagulls took the lead in less than a minute, when David Cassidy scored after Peter Cherrie had initially saved a Dean Zambra shot. Bray were still looking for the point that would guarantee survival in the Premier Division and it seemed that it was that they were coping with the pressure of the situation better than Dundalk. Dundalk did manage to grab an equaliser thanks to Pat Hoban, but failed to really trouble Bray with any further attempts to find a winner. At the whistle, it was Bray who were happier with the point, as Dundalk found themselves back in second place in the table, following Cork City's 1-0 win over Bohemian FC at Turners Cross.

Cork just needed to avoid defeat at Oriel the following Friday night and the league title would be theirs. However, Oriel isn't known as the graveyard of champions for nothing. For Stephen Kenny, it was *déjà vu* as City once again stood between one of his teams and the title. Kenny had taken his Derry City side to Turners Cross on the last day of the season in 2005, in the hope that they would win and become champions, but City had won on the day by two goals to nil.

The build-up to the title showdown began on Wednesday as both managers went before the media to simultaneously talk up the opposition and talk down their side's chances of becoming champions. Stephen Kenny had seen his team lead the race for much of the season and was looking for a reaction to the side's slip to second place, behind City. John Caulfield pointed out that even though Dundalk had won the two previous league meetings between the sides that season, this would count for little as it came down how the teams played in those ninety minutes alone. Caulfield also noted that his side had overcome many challenges in recent weeks, with first wins of the season against Pats and Bohs, so a first win against Dundalk was well within the realm of possibility for the side.

While the difference between first and second was all about glory, as Kenny remarked, there was also a significant difference in prize money and potential earnings. This difference was estimated to be approximately €300,000, when the league winner's prize and European games were considered. This was not an insignificant amount for either club, but on match night it was all about the title and in front of a packed Oriel Park, The Lilywhites didn't disappoint.

It had been many years since Oriel had witnessed an occasion like this and the ground was packed to the rafters. Temporary seating had been installed behind one of the goals to accommodate the visiting fans, who travelled in their hundreds to County Louth. The first half was a tight affair and it was the hosts who could have found themselves behind after two great chances fell to City. Firstly, a counter-attack saw City move the ball out wide to John O'Flynn and his low cross to Mark O'Sullivan flew agonisingly wide for City. City's next chance came to Billy Dennehy, who cracked a free kick off the foot of the post for City. Nil all at half-time and a chance for everyone to take a break from the tension. As it stood, things were going well for City: they remained champions elect, with just forty-five minutes of the season left. For Dundalk, it was time to show what they were made of.

A little luck is usually needed in games of this kind and it can come in different guises. For Dundalk, it came as the referee failed to notice Richie Towell's handball in the lead-up to Dundalk's first goal. The handball was unintentional, but it was hugely influential in deciding the destination of the title. Ruaidhrí Higgins got onto a City clearance and played the ball to Richie Towell. Towell's first touch was okay, his second was with his arm and his third rolled the ball into the path of Stephen O'Donnell, whose low drive beat Mark McNulty at his near post in the City goal. O'Donnell was only recently back in the team, having been out due to injury since April. The cheer that greeted the goal nearly took the roof off the grandstand in Oriel. Again, O'Donnell was on hand to score another vital goal for his team.

The gauntlet had now been thrown down to City, who had one great chance when Rob Lehane's header flew just inches over the bar with under ten minutes left. An equaliser at that time may have been good enough to knock Dundalk's belief, but the chance had gone. The next moment of the game would secure the title for The Lilywhites. Dundalk won a free kick and clipped the ball into the box. After two scrambles to get the ball away by City defenders, the ball broke to Brian Gartland. The big defender showed quick feet as he took a touch with his left foot and then struck a low shot with his right past McNulty. It was 2-0 and game over. Pandemonium broke out in the ground as players, staff and fans celebrated what was surely the title-winning goal. There was also pandemonium in the press box as Dundalk FM commentators John Murphy and Ger Cunningham went apoplectic with delight: *'Goal! Goal! Its 2-0! Brian Gartland ... and this title is heading back to Oriel Park.'*

It was a remarkable achievement for the club and for Stephen Kenny, who had proven his capabilities once again. Kenny's effect on the players was emphasised by Brian Gartland after the game: *'The confidence and the belief that we could do it was always there and that's down to the gaffer'.*

This championship win was the making of the players and of the club. The side was admired for their style of play and the quality of their football was now on offer for all League of Ireland fans to see. Rogers, Gannon, Gartland, Boyle, Massey, O'Donnell, Finn, Mountney, McMillan, Towell and Sheilds were names as recognisable as any of those from Jim McLaughlin's cracking Dundalk team of the late seventies. Indeed, comparisons could be made with any of the greats from the Rovers and Waterford sides of the sixties. The club was riding high and created history by retaining their title the following season. It had been an unusual fact that no Dundalk team had managed this feat before. The team was now clearly ahead of the pack, as the eleven-point winning margin that separated them from Cork City in 2015 testified.

The true test of the side's quality would be how they compared in European games. In the wake of Rovers' Europa League adventure and the significant improvement in clubs' European results since the change to summer football, there was now a reasonable expectation of progression through the early rounds of European football. Of course, the luck of the draw always played a part in whether these expectations were realistic or flight of fancy.

A Fan For All Seasons

During their chase to retain the league title in 2015, Dundalk came up against BATE Borisov from Belarus in their Champions League qualifier. The match would prove to be a tough task for The Lilywhites, but one which would give a reasonable gauge of this side's ability. The first leg was away and the side travelled in a confident mood, despite BATE having an excellent record at home and despite the club having qualified for the Champions League group stages on four previous occasions.

Dundalk's confidence was well founded, despite a 2-1 defeat. Dundalk seemed to be capable of competing with BATE for long spells and a David McMillan equaliser after half an hour gave Dundalk a real chance of turning the tie around in the return leg at Oriel Park. McMillan had missed a golden opportunity to bring Dundalk level earlier in the game when he blasted the ball over the bar after his initial headed effort had been saved. However, the real difference between the two sides over both legs was their respective ability to create chances. Despite vociferous home support at Oriel, it was BATE who took the game to Dundalk and created at least five great unconverted chances before Dundalk got their only real opportunity of the game. BATE lost possession on the halfway line and the ball came to McMillan, with about thirty yards to the goal. He took off on a run and, after beating the centre back, was denied by a good save from the BATE keeper. The ball broke to the edge of the box, but Daryl Horgan was just beaten to an attempted follow-up volley by an excellent defensive challenge. The game finished 0-0 and it was perhaps at this point that Kenny learned more about his team then at any stage in the previous eighteen months. Dundalk needed to be more clinical and more focused when it came to European football . If the Holy Grail for Irish clubs was a spot in the Champions League group stages, then a lot more would be required to make the breakthrough. For now, it was back to the league race, but the next time Europe came around, they would be ready.

Before they could think of Europe again, there was the small matter of the 2015 FAI Cup final. The title had been secured and now there was an opportunity to add further glory to an already growing list of achievements. Dundalk and Cork City had developed something of a rivalry over the previous two seasons and both sides met in the final in November at the Aviva Stadium. Having been a distant second in the league, it was a chance for John Caulfield's side to bring some silverware back to Leeside.

The final was preceded by the Women's FAI Cup final between Shelbourne and Wexford Youths. The game finished level at 1-1 after ninety minutes, which necessitated extra time. A further goal apiece in extra time ensured that penalties would be needed to decide the winner. Alas, the organisers forgot to allow for this probability, which meant that the Cork City team ran out to warm up while the penalty shoot-out was taking place. In fairness to the Cork City team, they confined themselves to the other end of the ground, but the sight of them warming up while the girls were trying to prepare for penalties smacked of disrespect. For the record, Wexford Youths won the shoot-out to claim the cup, but the preparation and organisation proved disappointing for all involved.

When the men's final eventually got underway, it took until extra time to separate the sides. City gave their all in a first half full of effort and endeavour, but the second half proved to be Dundalk's. Despite a great deal of possession, The Lilywhites could not find a breakthrough and so it was on to extra time. Unsurprisingly, the winning goal came from Dundalk's goal machine Richie Towell, who scored his twenty-ninth of the season to seal the double for Dundalk. Daryl Horgan deserved the lion's share of the credit for the goal as it was his run from midfield which set City back on their heels. As Horgan made it into the penalty box, he pulled the ball back across the six-yard box, where Towell had time and space to take a touch before shooting low into the net. City had a late chance to force yet another penalty shoot-out, but Darren Dennehy's headed effort clipped the top of the crossbar, much to Gary Rogers' relief.

While history was made with a third league and cup double for the club in 2015, Dundalk would write themselves into the history books the following season with a European adventure that would capture the imagination of the Irish football public. Dundalk's reward for their 2015 league title was an opening Champions League qualifying tie against Icelandic side FH Hafnarfjörður. It was hardly a tie to set pulses racing, but over 3,000 turned out at Oriel Park to see David McMillan give The Lilywhites the lead. Within ten minutes of that goal, disaster struck as former Dundalk player Steven Lennon scored for FH, giving them a priceless away goal and leaving Dundalk with work to do in the second leg a week later.

Things didn't seem to be going a whole lot better during the return leg in Iceland, as a Sam Hewson goal gave the home side the lead after just twenty minutes. Steven Lennon was out to torture his old club and it was some neat play between himself and Hewson that led to the opening goal for FH. It was time for Dundalk to fulfil their potential and perform in Europe in much the same way as they had dominated at home. Just after the interval, Dundalk were given a lifeline when

A Fan For All Seasons

McMillan was fouled in the penalty area. A great chance for the Lilywhtes to erase FH's away goal was missed when Ronan Finn saw his penalty saved.

However, there was one man who was destined to make a name for himself in the Dundalk line-up. David McMillan, who had scored the Dundalk goal at Oriel Park the week before, now grabbed two goals in ten minutes, drastically altering the tie. His first came from almost thirty yards out, but the quality of the goalkeeping was suspect, as a low-struck shot seemed to beat Gunnar Nielsen with ease. His second came after some good work by Horgan, who got free on the left and had the presence of mind to pick out the incoming McMillan, who steered the ball home from ten yards out. Despite a late Finnbogason goal, which set up a grandstand finish, Dundalk managed to hold on and book their place in the third round of qualification. The result and manner of progression highlighted a determination within the team, which complemented their obvious ability. Perhaps it was a result like this that proved to be the catalyst for the bigger things yet to come.

In the third-round draw, Dundalk faced a familiar foe in BATE Borisov. The first leg was once again in the Ukraine, with BATE winning by a goal to nil. It was all to play for in the return leg, which was held at Tallaght Stadium, as Oriel Park did not meet the minimum UEFA ground regulations.

In much the same way as Shels had gathered support from all corners for their game against Hadjuk Split over ten years earlier, huge numbers of fans sporting various clubs' shirts travelled to Tallaght to augment The Lilywhites' support. Not that the Lilywhite supporters were small in number; thousands made their way down the M1 from the Wee County to roar on their team. Revenge was in the air, along with a staggering number of inflatable bananas, which had been given out by Dundalk's main sponsor. There was a carnival atmosphere at the ground and a sense of expectation amongst fans. Dundalk were a fine team but could they deliver on their potential and seize a place in Irish football history? A crowd of nearly 5,000 packed in to see if it could be done.

The game started off with the visitors having the better of the exchanges and it took a while for Dundalk to get into their stride. Tallaght has been a happy hunting ground for Dundalk and tonight was to be no different. With the clock ticking ever closer to half-time, Patrick McEleney picked up the ball after sloppy play from BATE had ceded possession to Dundalk. McEleney played the ball out left to Horgan, who beat two BATE defenders before clipping a ball into the far post. McMillan managed to get himself a half-yard between two statuesque defenders and headed the ball into the net for a wonderfully worked goal. The timing couldn't have been better and Dundalk were roared off the pitch at half-time by the ecstatic Lilywhite supporters.

If the noise that greeted the half-time whistle was loud, it was noting compared to that which accompanied McMillan's second goal just before the hour mark. Chris Shields determination to prevent a throw-in resulted in his clearance being headed out of play by BATE in a promising position near the BATE corner flag. Gannon took the throw-in and again McEleney was involved as he took on and beat two defenders. As he drove into the penalty area, he beat another BATE defender, but the chance appeared to have gone as his cross was too high for those in the six-yard box to attack. The ball broke out to the left, where Dane Massey came onto it like an express train. He fizzed a cross back into the danger area and David McMillan was on hand to head the ball into the net. It was 2–0 and there was jubilant scenes in the stands and a giddy sense of disbelief amongst fans. McMillan was mobbed by his teammates as he ran off to celebrate. The striker had scored all five of Dundalk's goals in Europe that season and would become known as the man who scored the million-euro goal for The Lilywhites.

BATE were still in this tie and a single goal for them would change the complexion of the game completely. They had two chances, but spurned both and as the rain began to fall, Kenny made a change by bringing off goal hero McMillan and replacing him with Robbie Benson. Benson would go on to make an impact when, with the game in injury time, he wrapped up the tie with a third goal for Dundalk. A bad mistake from BATE in midfield left Benson in possession thirty-five yards out. As he neared the goal, he kept his nerve to calmly beat the goalkeeper and seal a memorable evening in Europe for Dundalk.

The Lilywhites had learned their lesson from the previous season's encounter and were clinical when the chances presented themselves. They had ridden their luck on occasion, but their second-half display and the overall maturity of their performance led to their deserved win and progression to the play-off round against Legia Warsaw. The victory ensured that Dundalk would play in the Europa League group stages at the very least, but the prospect of an Irish club side in the Champions League group stage was now a real possibility. There was also good news on the financial front for the club as progression to this stage was estimated to be worth around €7 million.

A Fan For All Seasons

Champions League fever gripped the League of Ireland public, and Dundalk fans in particular. Over 30,000 turned up at Aviva Stadium to see if Dundalk could keep their run going. In a game during which Dundalk gave their best and remained competitive, the cruel hand of fate intervened again in the story of League of Ireland clubs in Europe. This time it was in the form of a penalty, harshly awarded by the German referee Herr Aytekin, for a handball offence. That the ball struck Andy Boyle's arm is certain, but to claim that it was intentional was ludicrous. The decision seemed to leave Dundalk deflated and they conceded another goal in injury time that left them with a mountain to climb in the return leg. Manager Stephen Kenny was disappointed after the game: *'I'm angry'*, he said. *'It was an appalling decision … You can't give big decisions with such huge ramifications on a whim like that'*.

Despite Kenny's obvious anger, he once again had his side well prepared for the task at the Polish Army Stadium in Warsaw a week later. Promising that his side would go all out to retrieve the tie, Robbie Benson gave Dundalk hope as he volleyed The Lilywhites into the lead on the night after twenty minutes. Good work by Gannon and McMillan had given Benson the chance and he took it with aplomb, shooting into the left-hand corner of the net. It seemed like that mountain could be climbed after all. Benson had another chance when McEleney, Horgan and McMillan combined, but Benson's bicycle kick was just over. Legia had their chances too, but the fact that the tie was alive into injury time was testament to the Dundalk players' and management's endurance and ability. The final curtain on the Champions League came down for Dundalk when in injury time Legia grabbed an equaliser on the night. A tired Dundalk team had been picked off while trying to press for a second goal, which would have brought the tie to extra time. The Europa League Group stage was to be the Lilywhite's reward.

Although the run came to an end, the club had done a tremendous amount of good in creating publicity for themselves and in capturing public attention both at home and abroad. Dundalk had shown that they could play an attractive brand of football, based on attacking qualities and collective adherence to a set game plan. It was remarkable to see a League of Ireland team in such unison when they played and it didn't seem to matter if the game was at home or away or who the opposition was. Dundalk believed in their ability and in each other. For a period of time during the European games and their subsequent league title challenge, which secured three in a row for the club, they were arguably the best League of Ireland team ever seen. Other sides had more success, but this Dundalk team played football with purpose and style and as one collective unit.

The Europa League games ensured that Dundalk were playing European football until December, at least. They were grouped with AZ Alkmaar, Zenit St Petersburg and Maccabi Tel Aviv. Their opening game was in The Netherlands against AZ and it seemed that the adventure would go on that bit longer as a very late Ciaran Kilduff header resulted in a 1-1 draw. This draw also secured the very first group points earned by a League of Ireland side in Europe.

A fortnight later, Kilduff was at it again as his goal saw off Maccabi and gave Dundalk the first ever group win. It was history-making stuff for The Lilywhites and the crowds continued to come out in their thousands. The only minor disappointment was that Oriel Park was not the host ground on these great nights. Dundalk played their three Europa League games at Tallaght Stadium. Back-to-back games against Zenit would see 2-1 defeats on both occasions and a 1-0 defeat by AZ in their last home game left Dundalk needing results to go their way in the last round of games to achieve progression. Another defeat to Maccabi in Israel ended Dundalk's interest in Europe for that season, but it was a season the likes of which no other club has ever experienced.

Dundalk had played twelve games in Europe and scored twelve goals. David McMillan had scored five, Robbie Benson three, Ciaran Kilduff two with Daryl Horgan grabbing one along with one own goal. In between this run, they had successfully defended their league title, despite a backlog of games and had brought a lot of positive public attention to the league. They were just denied a double double, on top of this, when they lost out to a last-minute goal in the 2016 FAI Cup final, which was against Cork City again. John Caulfield's side had finally managed to get one over on Dundalk.

On a recent visit to Oriel, I raised the question of which side was better, the current side or Jim McLaughlin's team of the late seventies, with some fans. After some debate, it was agreed that the current side was particularly special because of their style of play. While McLaughlin's team had been one of the best seen at Oriel, it was the added extras of retaining the league title and a slightly greater achievement in Europe which seemed to swing it for Stephen Kenny's team. It is a reflection of the stature of the club that it has produced two such exceptional sides and leaves the fans with a real sense that this is a club that believes in itself and that strives to bring the best to its fans.

At the Whistle
Where to Next?

As 100 years of League of Ireland football approaches it is time for all those who have the best interest of the league at heart to take stock. It is time to reflect on where the league stands and ask where we want to go. The history of the game at home has given us some great memories which will always be treasured and recalled whenever the League of Ireland is discussed. As fans we can look back at the unique FAI Cup achievements of Shamrock Rovers, League domination by Cork United and Waterford and exciting European games since the 1950's. However, there have also been days when it seemed that the lights were fading fast on the league. Financial folly, court actions and administrative incompetence, contributed to tarnishing the image of the league when it most need help.

The League of Ireland will probably never have the public appeal of the internationally star studded leagues elsewhere in Europe, but for the majority of fans who pay homage at League of Ireland grounds each week, this doesn't really matter. It is the league's local nature that draws fans and this should be celebrated. It is also time to recognise that the vast majority of football fans in Ireland support teams abroad with terrific dedication. On any given weekend, fans travelling from Ireland to any number of destinations in Britain can be seen sporting their club shirts in airports and ports around the country. This is as much a ritual to them as heading to Dalymount, Oriel, or Turners Cross is to fans of the League of Ireland. Instead of some clubs and fans bemoaning a perceived lack of patriotism from this section of the Irish football public, their right to choose should be acknowledged and league and club administrators should take on the challenge to win fans over to our home product. The real secret here is to encourage football fans to come to League of Ireland matches in addition to those games they attend elsewhere. Preaching that attendance at League of Ireland matches should replace trips to Celtic Park, Anfield and Old Trafford is both ludicrous and self-defeating.

There is real talent in our league and this has been reflected in the number of senior Ireland internationals who have begun their careers in the league. Who can forget that great photograph of the eight former League of Ireland players wearing their former club shirts when on duty for the national team at the 2016 European Championships in France. The picture of Wes Hoolahan, Seamus Coleman, James McClean, Daryl Murphy, Stephen Ward, Stephen Quinn, Shane Long and David Meyler brought a great sense of pride to all League of Ireland fans. In addition, the improvement in European results offers support to the theory that our players are competitive and skilful when facing challenges from abroad.

 All sports and leagues have their failings and ours in no different. In spite of these, I think that fans hold their own magic moments and memories near to their hearts and think of these more than the shortcomings of the league. Generations of fans will always remember the things which made the League of Ireland dear to them. Perhaps it was being brought to the packed terraces at Kilcohan Park or Flower Lodge for the first time, or seeing the sea of bicycles outside Glenmalure Park while walking up Milltown Road with family and friends. Maybe it was seeing the great players in action, like Frank O'Neill, Peter Thomas & Tommy McConville all of whom were so much a part of the league's seasonal storyline. The great rivalries of Shels and Bohs, Drums and Rovers and Dundalk and Cork City will not be forgotten by those who witnessed and enjoyed them, relishing their importance at the time. Who can forget Drums' floodlit friendly matches at Tolka, Derry City's treble of trophies in 1989 or Jimmy O'Connor's hat trick for Shels in 1967, the fastest hat trick in top level league football in Europe.

For all football fans, once the whistle is blown and the game is on we are totally absorbed by what unfolds before us on the pitch. It makes no difference whether you are a fan seating in the San Siro or The Showgrounds, the passion and emotion invested is exactly the same. I hope this look back at some of the highlights of the League of Ireland will rekindle memories of excitement, fun and enjoyment and leave us wondering what players and clubs will next write themselves into League of Ireland folklore and what glory and achievements they will reach.

References

The Irish Times online archive
Irish Independent
Irish Examiner
RTÉ Archives
Derry Journal
Munster Express
Dundalk Democrat
Dundalk FM
Plunkett Carter *'Cork Past & Present'* – Cork City Council
'We Are Rovers' by Eoghan Rice – The History Press ISBN: 978-1845885106
Gerard Farrell – bohemianfc.com
fai.ie
shamrockrovers.ie
shelbournefc.ie
sligorovers.com
drumcondrafc.com
dundalkfc.com

Acknowledgments

I would like to thank my wife Ethel and our daughter Lucy who have supported and encouraged me during this project. They have kept me smiling and focused throughout and have turned a blind eye to the additional number of games I have attended over the last two seasons. Thanks to my father Gerard, who started and encouraged my interest in football, and my mother, Bernadette who had to console me when one of my teams lost, which used be fairly regularly. Thanks to my sister Gemma who has always been available for advice and guidance and who has been happy to read numerous drafts of this book. Further thanks are due to my uncle Pat who firstly brought me to Dalymount thirty years ago and provided encouragement and support from the beginning. Also, thanks to my pal Cillian for listening to me going on about games from the 1940s and 50s while he was trying to watch Spurs.

I would like to acknowledge all the help, guidance and advice provided by Ronan Colgan at Carrowmore Publishing Consultancy, without which this book would never have made it off my PC. Many thanks to Michael Garvey for his work on editing the text and for his suggestions and guidance.